D1715476

THE
CONQUEST
OF
CANAAN

AMS PRESS
NEW YORK

THE
CONQUEST
OF
CANÄAN;

A POEM, in ELEVEN BOOKS.

By TIMOTHY DWIGHT.

Fired, at firſt ſight, with what the Muſe imparts,
In fearleſs youth we tempt the height of arts.

POPE.

HARTFORD:
PRINTED BY ELISHA BABCOCK,
M,DCC,LXXXV.

Reprinted from the edition of 1785, Hartford
First AMS EDITION published 1971
Manufactured in the United States of America

International Standard Book Number: 0-404-02226-X

Library of Congress Catalog Number: 78-129380

AMS PRESS INC.
NEW YORK, N.Y. 10003

To his EXCELLENCY,

GEORGE WASHINGTON, ESQUIRE,

Commander in chief of the American Armies,

The Saviour of his Country,

The Supporter of Freedom,

And the Benefactor of Mankind;

This Poem is inscribed,

with the highest respect for his character, the
most ardent wishes for his happiness, and the
most grateful sense of the blessings, secured,
by his generous efforts, to the United States
of North America,

by his most humble,

and most obedient servant,

TIMOTHY DWIGHT.

Greenfield, in Connecticut,
    March 1, 1785.

A S this poem is the first of the kind, which has been published in this country, the writer begs leave to introduce it with several observations, which that circumstance alone may perhaps render necessary.

He has taken to himself the liberty of altering the real order of the two last battles, because he imagined the illustrious events, which attended the battle of Gibeon, would make it appear to be the catastrophe of the poem, whereever inserted.

He has varied the story of the embassy from Gibeon, for reasons, which he thinks will be obvious to every reader, and which he hopes will be esteemed his sufficient justification.

To give entire Unity to the Action, he has made Jabin the Canäanitish hero through the whole poem ; and has transferred the scene of the battle, between Hazor and Israel, from the shores of the lake Merom to the neighbourhood of Ai.

In the Manners, he has studied a medium between absolute barbarism and modern refinement. In the best characters, he has endeavoured to represent such manners, as are removed from the peculiarities of any age, or country, and might belong to the amiable and virtuous, of every age : such as are elevated without design, refined without ceremony, elegant without fashion, and agreeable, because they are ornamented with sincerity, dignity, and religion, not because they are polished by art and education. Of such manners, he hopes he may observe, without impropriety, that they possess the highest advantages for universal application.

He has made use of Rhyme, because he believed it would be more generally relished than blank verse, even amongst those who are esteemed persons of taste.

It may perhaps be thought the result of inattention or ignorance, that he chose a subject, in which his countrymen had no national interest. But he remarked that the Iliad and Eneid were as agreeable to modern nations, as to the Greeks and Romans. The reason he supposed to be obvious,-the subjects of those poems furnish the fairest opportunities of exhibiting the agreeable, the novel, the moral, the pathetic, and the sublime. If he is not deceived, the subject he has chosen possesses, in a degree, the same advantages.

It will be observed that he has introduced some new words, and annexed to some old ones, a new signification. This liberty, allowed to others, he hopes will not be refused to him : especially as from this source the copiousness and refinement of language have been principally derived.

That he wishes to please he frankly confesses. If he fails in the design, it will be a satisfaction that he shall have injured no person but himself. As the poem is uniformly friendly to delicacy, and virtue, he hopes his countrymen will so far regard him with candour, as not to impute it to him as a fault, that he has endeavoured to please them, and has thrown in his mite, for the advancement of the refined arts, on this side of the Atlantic.

THE

CONQUEST of CANÄAN:

BOOK I.

ARGUMENT.

*Subject proposed. Invocation. After the battle, mentioned
in the beginning of the seventh chapter of Joshua, the
Israelites, in correspondence with the sacred history are
represented in circumstances of extreme distress. With this
event the poem opens, in the evening. Morning. Scene
of war. Story of Zimri, and Aram. Zimri returns
to the assembly of Israel, and brings an account of the
death of Aram, and of an army, sent by Jabin, king of
Hazor, to assist Ai. Distress of the Israelites. Char-
acter and oration of Hanniel. After a pathetic address,
and rehearsal of their miseries, he attempts to prove the
impossibility of succeeding in their present design, because
of the strength, skill, and numerous allies of their enemies;
foretels their approaching ruin, asserts that GOD is op-
posed to them, that they were led out of Egypt to silence their
murmurs, and, the end being accomplished, ought to re-
turn. Panegyric on that country; obviates objections to
a return, and informs them that, if they should conquer
Canaan, they will be ruined, during the war, by the
necessary neglect of arts and agriculture, difficulty of di-
viding the land, of settling a form of government, and of
avoiding tyranny; and concludes with a new exhortation
to return to Egypt. Applause. Joshua replies, and be-
ginning to explain the dispensations of Providence, is
interrupted by Hanniel, who first obliquely, and then open-
ly accuses him of aiming at the usurpation of kingly autho-
rity; and asserts the return to be easy. Joshua vindicates
his innocence with severity upon Hanniel; and allowing
they can return, paints to them the miseries, they will ex-
perience from the Egyptian king, lords, people, and man-
ners; and from providential dispensations terminating in
their ruin. He appeals to them to judge of the falsehood
of Hanniel's ideas of the purposes of Heaven, in leading
them out of Egypt; and declares the certainty of their
success from their union, with a few exceptions, their
previous prosperity, and the favour and revealed designs
of Heaven, and exults in their future glory. Applause.
Preparation for war. Caleb opposes immediate war,
and advises a fast of two days. Joshua approves of it.*

THE CONQUEST OF CANAAN.

BOOK I.

THE Chief, whose arm to Israel's chosen band
   Gave the fair empire of the promis'd land,
   Ordain'd by Heaven to hold the sacred sway,
Demands my voice and animates the lay,
  O thou, whose Love, high thron'd above all height,   5
Illumes th' immense, and sunns the world of light;
Whose distant beam the human mind inspires,
With wisdom brightens, and with virtue fires;
Unfold how pious realms to glory rise,
And impious nations find avenging skies: 10
May thy own deeds exalt the humble line,
And not a stain obscure the theme divine.
  When now from western hills the sun was driven,
And night expanding fill'd the bounds of heaven,
O'er Israel's camp ten thousand fires appear'd   15
And solemn cries from distant guards were heard,
Her tribes, escap'd from Ai's unhappy plain,
With shame and anguish mourn'd their heroes slain,

   Line 1.) Wherever *Chief*, *Hero*, *Leader*, &c. with a capital, re-
spect the Israelitish army, Joshua is intended; when they respect the
Canäanitish army, Jabin is intended. The *Youth*, with a capital,
denotes Irad.

B

Pierc'd with deep wounds the groaning warriors stood;
Their bosoms heav'd, their tears incessant flow'd;   20
Their sons unburied on the hostile plain,
Their brothers captiv'd, and their parents slain.
The tender father clasp'd his lovely child,
That thoughtless-sporting innocently smil'd,
To his fond arms with soft endearments leapt,   25
Gaz'd on his tears, and wonder'd why he wept.
Her woes with his the trembling mother join'd,
Edg'd all his fears, and sunk his drooping mind,
Array'd in tenfold gloom th' approaching light,
And gather'd foes unnumber'd to the fight.   30
Thus trembling, sad, of every hope forlorn,
The hapless thousands watch'd the coming morn.

In Joshua's ear their sad complaints resound,
As slow, unseen, he trac'd the camp around.
Where'er shrill cries, or groans distinguish'd flow'd   35
Propp'd on his lance, the Hero listening stood:
For oft the secret hour of night he chose,
To hush their tumults, and to learn their woes;
Each tear, each cry his feeling mind oppress'd,
And schemes of pity fill'd his labouring breast.   40

And now bright Phosphor wak'd the dawning day,
The tents all whitening in th' expanded ray;
The sun's broad beam the scene of war display'd,
A wide extent, with distant groves o'erspread;
A tall, dark forest gloom'd the northern round,'   45
And eastern hills o'er hills th' horizon bound:
Far south, a plain in vivid green withdrew,
And one unvaried level fill'd the view;
Beyond, Ai's grandeur proudly rose on high,
And azure mountains pierc'd the western sky.   50

Around their Leader's tent, th' unnumber'd train
Throng'd from the camp, and gather'd on the plain.
When Zimri slow approach'd; of Asher's race
The first in merit, as the first in place.

Him, not a chief, that dar'd the battling field,   55
In swiftness equall'd, or in strength excell'd ;
Save *Joshua's* arm, that still unconquer'd shone ;
From every rival every prize he won.

In night's last gloom (so Joshua's will ordain'd)
To find what hopes the cautious foe remain'd,   60
Or what new strength, allied, increas'd their force,
To Ai's high walls the hero bent his course.
Aram, his friend, unknowing vile dismay,
With willing footsteps shar'd the dangerous way.
In virtue join'd, one soul to both was given ;   65
Each steer'd his path, and led his friend to heaven.

O'er earth's dim verge as dawn'd the cheerful day,
Near slumbering Ai they cours'd their fearless way ;
Unseen, in twining shrubs, a heathen sate,
Mark'd their still path, and boded Aram's fate ;   70
Swift hurl'd, his javelin sought the hero's side,
Pierc'd to the heart, he groan'd, and gasp'd, and died.
The heathen flew, fierce Zimri clave his breast,
But Aram's eyes were clos'd in endless rest.

Thus, while fond Virtue wish'd in vain to save,   75
Hale, bright and generous, found a hapless grave.
With genius' living flame his bosom glow'd,
And science charm'd him to her sweet abode :
In worth's fair path his feet adventur'd far ;
The pride of peace, the rising grace of war ;   80
In duty firm, in danger calm as even,
To friends unchanging, and sincere to heaven.

75.) *While*, *amid*, and *among*, are used throughout this poem,
euph. grat. instead of *whilst*, *amidst*, and *amongst*.

76. *Hale bright)* The comparisons of this kind were all writ
ten in the early stages of the late war, and annexed to the poem to
indulge the Author's own emotions of regard to the persons named
in them. As it was impossible to pay this little tribute of respect to
all the deserving characters, who have fallen in defence of American
Liberty, the Author determined to desist, after the first attempt. The
lines on Major Andre are an exception to the above remark, as are
those on General Mercer.

How ſhort his courſe, the prize how early won !
While weeping friendſhip mourns her favourite gone.
With ſoul too noble for ſo baſe a cauſe,   85
Thus Andre bow'd to war's barbarian laws.
In morn's fair light the opening bloſſom warm'd,
Its beauty ſmil'd, its growing fragrance charm'd;
Fierce roar'd th' untimely blaſt around its head ;
The beauty vaniſh'd, and the fragrance fled ;   90
Soon ſunk his graces in the wintry tomb,
And ſad Columbia wept his hapleſs doom.

    As now o'er eaſtern hills the morning burn'd,
Alone brave Zimri to the camp return'd ;
Pale in his front deſpair and anguiſh ſate,   95
And each kind boſom fear'd for Aram's fate,
When thus, the Leader---Say, exalted chief,
What dire misfortune clouds thy mind with grief?
O beſt of men, he cried, my tears deplore
The hero's fate, brave Aram is no more.   100
Weep, weep, my friends : his worthy life demands
This laſt, poor tribute from your grateful hands,
Nor weep for him alone : dread ſcenes of grief
Surround our ſteps, and Heaven denies relief.
Th' inſulting wretch, that ſeal'd the hero's fate,   105
In death proclaim'd what terrors round you wait.
I die, he cried, but know, thou culprit, know,
To the dark tomb thy harbinger I go.
O'er Iſrael's race aſcend, from realms afar,
The clouds of ruin, and the ſtorms of war.   110
The hoſts, that bow to Jabin's great controul
From Hazor's rocky hills, in thunder roll ;
Hoſts, that ne'er knew the tender tear to ſhed,
Born in the field, beneath the ſtandard bred ;
That raptur'd fly, where ſhrilling trumpets call,   115
Plunge on the pointed ſpear, and climb the kindled wall.
Theſe dauntleſs bands (to Ai the meſſage came)
Shall ſink in night thy nation's hated name ;

Even now brave Oran, Jabin's martial boaft,
Speeds his glad courfe and moves a countlefs hoft :   120
Raptur'd I fee thy camp in flames arife,
And Ifrael's afhes cloud the angry fkies.
He fpoke. Aftonifh'd at th' impending doom,
Round the pale thoufands breath'd a folemn gloom ;
Rent were their martial veftments, torne their hair,   125
And every eye fpoke pangs of keen defpair.
   Mid the fad throng, in mournful robes array'd
Vile duft befprinkled o'er his down-caft head,
Pale Hanniel rofe, and with diffembled woe,
Clouded his front, and urg'd the tear to flow.   130
Of princely blood, his haughty fire, of yore
Proud Pharaoh's favourite on th' Egyptian fhore,
O'er Ifrael's race was fcepter'd to prefide,
To rule their tributes and their toils to guide.
   In the fon's mind again the parent liv'd,   135
His pride rekindled, and his art reviv'd.
Where'er pride call'd, his changing foul would turn ;
Grieve with the fad, and with the envious burn ;
Vaunt with the brave, be ferious with the wife,
And cheat the pious with uplifted eyes ;   140
In Youth's fond fports with feeming zeal engage,
Or lift, delighted, to the tales of Age.
   When Joſhua's hand the facred rule adorn'd,
With pangs he faw, but ftill in fecret mourn'd :
His clofe revenge the Hero's fate decreed,   145
And fmooth, fure flander taught his name to bleed.
With friendly grafp he fqueez'd each warrior's hand ;
With jefts familiar pleas'd the vulgar band ;
In fly, fhrewd hints the Leader's faults difclos'd ;
Prais'd his whole fway, but fingle acts oppos'd ;   150
Admir'd how law fo ftern a face could wear ;
Stil'd combat rafhnefs, and nam'd caution fear :
With angels then his fame and virtue join'd,
To tempt coarfe fcandal from each envious mind :

Bleſt his own peaceful lot, and ſmil'd, that Heaven, 155
To minds, that priz'd them, empire's toils had given.
Yet baſe-born fear his vigorous ſoul diſdain'd;
Each danger ſhar'd and every toil ſuſtain'd;
Joy'd, in terrific fields, the ſoe to dare,
And claim'd the honours of the fierceſt war. 160

Now the bleſt period, long in vain deſir'd,
His fond hope flatter'd, and his boſom fir'd;
To end his rival's ſway, his own ſecure,
Reſolv'd, his fancy deem'd the triumph ſure.

In ſeeming anguiſh oſt his hands he wrung, 165
And words imperfect murmur'd on his tongue;
At length, with feeble voice, he thus began,
While round the tribes a mute attention ran.

Friends! brethren! ſires! or by what tenderer name
Shall I addreſs the heirs of Jacob's fame? 170
Dear to my ſoul, as thoſe red drops, that flow,
Thro' my warm veins, and bid my boſom glow,
If chill'd by grief's cold hand, the vital flood
Still pours its warmth, nor yet forſakes the road!
Long has this heart with deep compaſſion view'd 175
Your generous tribes, by countleſs ills ſubdu'd;
Ills, theſe pain'd eyes foreboding, long beheld,
And this ſad warning voice in vain reveal'd.
Thoſe counſels, now by ſure experience prov'd,
That voice, alone by Iſrael's welfare mov'd, 180
Once more attend. Ye guardian powers, be near,
Enlarge their minds and give them hearts to hear!
Let baſe-born prejudice no more controul
The native candour of each generous ſoul;
Aſſert yourſelves; your future conduct ſcan; 185
Reaſon's the nobleſt privilege of man.

Long have our feet with reſtleſs error rov'd,
And the ſad waſte with all its miſeries prov'd;
That waſte, by Heaven's unerring ſentence curs'd
With ceaſeleſs hunger, and eternal thirſt, 195

The tyger's rage, the lion's fearful path,
Beftrew'd with bones, and red with recent death,
The fun's keen fury, midnight's gloomy dread,
And all the horrors of th' impoifon'd fhade.

   How oft thefe eyes the haplefs child have view'd, 195
By hunger famifh'd and by pain fubdu'd,
While the fond parent o'er his beauties hung,
And look'd diftrefs, that froze his faltering tongue,
Diftrefs, to hear the young, the piercing cry,
'That claim'd relief, when no relief was nigh ;   200
To fee the babe, its face with death o'erfpread,
Stretch forth its little hands, and fue for bread :
While friends, all impotent, roll'd down the tear,
Rocks learn'd to feel, and forefts bent to hear.

   When pale Difeafe affum'd her fatal reign,   205
Chas'd the warm glow, and rack'd the joints with pain,
Oft have thefe failing eyes the chief beheld,
In counfel fam'd, and glorious in the field,
Condemn'd the pangs of ficknefs to endure,
Far from relief, and hopelefs of a cure ;   210
No downy couch to reft his drooping head,
The fkies his covering, and the earth his bed ;
No foftening plant his ftiffen'd wounds to heal,
Soothe his rack'd nerves, and learn them not to feel ;
Nor fweet, embowering fhade to drive away   215
Night's baleful damps, and fummer's fcorching ray.
But who the various ills can number o'er,
Or tell the fands that form the fea-beat fhore ?
Even now by flow degrees our thoufands fall,
Till one wide, common grave involve us all.   220

   For fee what woes furround our daring courfe,
That tempts the terrors of unmeafur'd force ;
Safe in high walls, infulting foes deride,
Our boaftful impotence, and banner'd pride ;
On boundlefs wealth, with carelefs eafe, rely,   225
And hofts unnumber'd never taught to fly ;

Proud of the dreadful steed, the wasting car,
And all the strength, and all the art, of war.
  These foes to aid, what countless throngs will join !
What peopled realms against our arms combine !   230
From Gibeon's walls, and where tremendous powers
Surround imperial Hazor's hundred towers,
Or where proud shores the western main behold,
Or orient Gihon's haughty tides are roll'd,
I see to fearful combat millions rise,   235
Chiefs mount the car, and point the fated prize ;
See in the van-guard haughty Conquest ride
Lo, murder'd thousands pour the ruddy tide !
O'er Israel's camp the clouds of vengeance lower,
Fear wings our flight, and flames our race devour.   240
  At that dread season, chain'd in bonds forlorn,
Of men the proverb, and of Heaven the scorn,
Hiss'd by vile slaves, our tribes the rack shall feel,
Or gasp, far happier, on the griding steel :
Slow round the form the fires of Molock burn ;   245
Chiefs mount the pile, and babes to ashes turn :
Impal'd with anguish, bleeding fires behold,
Their wives polluted and their virgins sold ;
Their sons, sweet solace of declining age,
In sport transfix'd, or cleft in causeless rage ;   250
While threats, while insults rend with sore dismay,
And hungry hounds stand gaping for their prey.
But cease my faltering tongue ; ere these befal,
Oh Heaven, let Hanniel's blood bedew yon impious wall.
  And will no happier hand direct the road,   255
And tell, where Quiet builds her sweet abode ?
Where is the sage, on whose angelic tongue
Bright wisdom dwelt, and soft persuasion hung ?
Does no kind breast with patriot virtue glow,
And claim an interest in his country's woe ?   260
Here then, ye heirs of Jacob's name, behold
A friend, whose bosom terror ne'er controul'd ;

Whose voice, though envious thousands dare oppose,
Shall pour the balm, and heal his country's woes.

How long, brave heroes, shall your feet pursue   265
Such keen distress, as nations never knew ?
How long your host the chains of slavery own,
And millions die, to swell the pride of one ?
'Gainst Heaven's decree let folly cease to rise,
And tempt no more the vengeance of the skies.   270
To other lords that firm decree ordains
Th' expected mountains, and the promis'd plains.
Our every path unnumber'd woes surround ;
Our blood in streams bedews polluted ground ;
No glad success arrays our steps in light,   275
And smiling Victory triumphs in our flight.

Search ancient years ; thro' time's long course return,
When earth first wanton'd in the beams of morn ;
Success unchang'd attends, when GOD approves,
And Peace propitious smooths the path he loves.   280
Base flight, and dire amaze, and creeping shame,
Man lost in guilt, and alien'd skies, proclaim.
If still your fetter'd minds, by folly sway'd,
Doubts wavering toss, and leaden fears invade,
To yon bright dome your eyes convicted turn ;   285
Say why forgets the guiding flame to burn ?
Why round its point forgets the cloud to roll,
Sublime pavilion of th' all-moving soul ?
The dreaded truth must Hanniel singly own ?
Fled is the smile of Heaven, the Guardian gone.   290
But Virtue asks, Why, led by GOD's command,
Rov'd this brave host thro' many a weary land ?
Each hour, with pains replete, each field replies,
And with dread language, loud as clarions, cries,
In Egypt's realms, where every pleasure smil'd,   295
And, far from famine, labourers lightly toil'd,
Wanton with feasts, our thankless hearts repin'd,
And tainted prayers provok'd th' all-ruling Mind ;

C

Tir'd by long scenes of woe, th' ungrateful host,   299
Learn'd humbler thoughts, and priz'd the good they lost:
Reclaim'd, each spotless mind adores his ways,
And every blessing wakes the voice of praise.
The end thus gain'd, his terrors lifted high
Bid his warn'd sons the unbless'd purpose fly.
See, swiftly borne, the storm of vengeance rise !   305
Cloud after cloud invades the angry skies ;
Even now o'er earth, fierce peals commencing roar,
And round the concave flames vindictive pour ;
Hark, with what din the distant whirlwinds roll !
How the floods threaten from the thundering pole !   310
Rise, nimbly rise, burst every dead delay,
And fly, ere fury sweep our race away.

But where, oh where shall hapless Israel fly ?
Where find a covert, when the ruin's nigh ?
Will no kind land the wish'd recess disclose !   315
No friendly refuge soothe our long, long woes ?
Yes, the fair, fruitful land, with rapture crown'd,
Where once our sires a sweet retirement found,
That land, our refuge Heaven's high will ordains,
Pleas'd with our prayers, and piteous of our pains.   320

Hail favour'd realms, where no rude tempest blows !
Serene retreats, and shades of kind repose !
Ordain'd, the union'd bliss of life to prove,
The wreaths of glory, and the bowers of love !
There the great prince, with awful splendor crown'd,   325
From foes shall guard us, and with peace surround,
In no rude combat fated to engage,
Nor fir'd by clarions to vindictive rage.
There cates divine shall yield the sweet repast,
Charm the pall'd eye, and lure the loathing taste ;   330
With die refulgent crimson vestures glow,
And robes of kings succeed this garb of woe :
Our tribes, in spicy groves, at ease recline,
Press the swell'd fig, and pluck the cluster'd vine;   334

Her floods of boundless wealth the river roll,   [the pole.
And spring, with autumn join'd, beam temperate round
  For these bless'd joys, what mind, so left to shame,
Can grudge the tribute, regal glories claim ?
Return, how due ! Devoid of decent show,
How soon would Power to trampled weakness grow ? 340
How soon base minds the feeble judge deride,
And beggar'd rulers quake at wealthy pride ?
Nor the just doom can Avarice' self deny,
Who share the blessing must the tax supply.
No danger now even timid minds can fear,   345
Lest stern Oppression lift her rod severe :
Unlike our sires, who rais'd impatient cries,
A fairer doom awaits us from the skies.
Taught by our hated flight, the nation knows
How, join'd with ours, their vast dominion grows ; 350
Disjoin'd, how swift the weaken'd tribes decay,
To foes a triumph, and to schisms a prey.

  Even now with friendly joy their bosoms burn,
And with fond prescience hail our wish'd return ;
Bid our own hands the grateful covenant frame,   355
Prepar'd to give, what avarice scarce can claim ;
Our sons invite their boundless wealth to share,
Garlands of fame, and sweet repose of care.

  Here, warriors, here the dreaded miseries flow,
Scenes of dire scorn, and seats of thickening woe.   360
For bless'd as hope can paint, o'er all our toil
Let conquest flourish, and let glory smile ;
Still in long train, what ceaseless ills await !
The waste of war, and frowns of adverse fate !   364
  While sheath'd in arms, the conquer'd realms we guard,
End of long pains, and patience' wish'd reward,
Those realms what culturing hand shall teach to bloom ?
Or bid bright vesture purple o'er the loom ?
Unfed, uncloath'd, our tribes shall waste away,
Our lands grow wild, and every art decay.   370

Whose wisdom then shall equal lots divine,
And round each province lead the bordering line?
Will none, for fancied wrongs, the falchion draw,
His arm the umpire, and his will the law,
O'er his friend's prize with rude irruption pour,   375
Burst nature's bonds, and bathe in kindred gore?

Whose chosen hand the sceptre then shall sway?
What system'd rule the union'd tribes obey?
To my pain'd eyes what hideous prospects spread,
When impious Faction rears her snaky head!   380
Array'd in savage pomp, Destruction reigns
O'er flaming cities, and o'er crimson plains;
Friends, against friends, that knew but one fond heart,
Aim the dark knife, and lift the secret dart;
In brother's blood unfeeling brothers wade,   385
And parent's bosoms sheath the filial blade.
Let Pity round the scene extend her veil,
And thrilling virtue shun the dreadful tale!

Or shall one arm the state forever sway?
And, sunk to stocks, our torpid race obey?   390
One voice, thro' ages, Jacob's pride controul,
Ourselves the clay, and he th' all-moving soul?
Perish the thought! t' oppose a tyrant's reign,
One patriot life shall flow from every vein;
In Israel's cause shall burst this fearless voice,   395
And this bold arm avenge the free-born choice.

Rise, warriors, rise! desert this dreary plain,
These fields of slaughter, and these haunts of pain!
To scenes of brighter name, to happier skies,
To other Edens lift your raptur'd eyes!   400
The world's fair Empress chides our dull delay,
Spreads her fond arms, and bids us haste away,
To bliss, to glory; seize th' auspicious road,
And claim your interest in the bless'd abode!

The hero spoke. As when, in distant skies,   405
Slow-roll'd, the darkening storm begins to rise,

Thro' the deep grove, and thro' the founding vale,
Roar the long murmurs of the sweeping gale :
So round the throng a hoarse applause was heard,
And growing joy in every face appear'd.   410

  On a tall rock, whose top o'erlook'd the plain,
The Leader rose, and hush'd the reverent train.
By Hanniel warm'd, with airy visions fir'd,
He saw gay hope their glowing minds inspir'd,
In prospect bright, at hand fair Egypt lay,   415
Divine the pleasure, and secure the way ;
With calm, frank aspect, that serenely smil'd,
His port all-winning, and his accent mild ;
Too wise, to thwart at once the general choice,
Or hope to sway alone by reason's voice,   420
He thus began.   Ye heirs of Jacob's name,
Let Joshua's voice your generous candor claim.
In Israel's sacred cause my toils ye know,
My midnight watchings, and my morning woe.
Your long, lone path my wakeful eye survey'd,   425
Charm'd the sad wild, and cheer'd the languid head ;
Sooth'd drooping sickness, banish'd fear's alarms
And clasp'd the orphan with delighted arms :
'Gainst fierce invasions rais'd a guardian shield,
The first to seek, the last to leave, the field ;   430
For all your tribes a parent's fondness prov'd,
Fulfill'd each wish, and even your wanderings lov'd.

  In those sad scenes, when pity owns applause,
Not Hanniel's tears adorn a fairer cause.
For Israel's woe does Hanniel singly feel ?   435
Are these eyes blind ? or is this bosom steel ?
When ceas'd these hands from toil ? or what strange sun
Saw Joshua's feet the haunts of danger shun ?
Your eyes have seen, these honest scars proclaim
How oft this breast has pour'd the vital stream :   440
Still be it pour'd.   A nation's cause to save,
Life's a poor price ; the field an envied grave.

Whatever voice your welfare fhall divine,
My heart fhall welcome and my hand fhall join :
But, calmly weigh'd, let Truth our counfels guide.   445
And Reafon's choice the deftin'd courfe decide.
So prone the mind in error's path to rove,
T' explore is wifdom, and 'tis blifs to prove.
Charm'd, at firft fight, when pleafures rife to view,
Each painted fcene our ventrous thoughts purfue ;   450
In airy vifions far-feen Edens rife,
And ifles of pleafure tempt enamour'd eyes.
On the calm tide, to aromatic gales,
Our fearlefs hands exalt impatient fails ;
Thro' fapphire floods the bark forefees its way,   455
While wanton billows fmoothly round it play,
Nor heeds the angry ftorm, that with dread power,
Climbs dark behind the hill, and hopes th' avenging hour,
Warn'd by my voice, fuch hidden dangers fly,
And each gay profpect fcan with fearching eye.   460

In realms far diftant fpreads th' expected fhore,
Hills rife between, and boiling oceans roar :
Two tirefome ways invite our wearied bands,
Thro' tracklefs deferts, or through hoftile lands.

Say, fhall our fteps again the wafte pervade,   465
Dare the fierce heat, and tempt th' impoifon'd fhade ?
Confult yon chief; his voice again fhall tell
Thofe dreary fcenes, he painted now fo well.

Or fhall our feet, its dangers hid from view,
Thro' peopled realms, a nearer path purfue ?   470
I blufh, when falfehood leads the chofen tribes,
Where folly dictates, and where fear prefcribes.
One foe to fhun, fhall fiercer foes be tried ?
Death their delight, and war their earlieft pride.   474

Lo the fierce wrath, at Taberah's plain that burn'd,
And Korah's hoft to inftant corfes turn'd,
Rous'd to more dreadful flames, our guilt to fpy,
And fee our feet to hated Egypt fly,

Shall wing Philiftia's hoft to death and war,
And bid fierce Midian whirl the thundering car;   480
Full on her prey avenging Amalek fall,
And guilt and terror every heart appall;
Our wives, our fons, to favage wrath be given,
Feaft famifh'd wolves, and glut the hawks of heaven.

   No fancied doom my boding words declare: 485
Truth, fix'd as mountains, fills your ftartled ear.
To every beaft the lamb prefents a prey,
And coward bands invite the world to flay.

   But will ye tremble for one fhameful fall?
Shall one loft combat Abraham's race appall?   490
Is Aram dead! to rapid vengeance fly;
By me his orphan babes for vengeance cry;
Fir'd by his fate, your nerves let ardour ftring,
Exalt the ftandard, and to combat fpring.

   Even Zimri fears, by ftrong affections led,   495
While his fond bofom mourns his Aram dead.
Of all the fympathy, that woes impart
To the foft texture of the good man's heart,
Departed friendfhip claims the largeft fhare,
And forrow in excefs is virtue there.   500
But, timid paffion! Grief, with ftartled eye
Spies fancied ills, and quakes, ere danger's nigh.

   Yon chief demands, why fled the guardian fire?
What unknown folly bade the cloud retire?
That bafe diftruft, which glorious fight delays,   505
That fmooth, clofe fraud which tempts to dangerous ways,
Thefe claim the fcourge of Heaven: be thefe aton'd,
Each fear fhall vanifh, and each hope be crown'd.

   While thus the Chief their bofoms warm'd anew,
And every ear, and heart, to virtue drew;   510
Their kindling zeal impatient Hanniel eyed,
Shook for his caufe, and frown'd with ftartled pride:
When thofe, he cried, whofe choice our warriors loft,
Of truth expatiate, and of wifdom boaft,

With juft difdain my rifing fpirits burn,   515
And my pain'd heart, at times, forgets to mourn ;
To fhame, to flight, does facred Wifdom lead ?
Does facred Truth command our fons to bleed ?
Roufe then to arms ; lo Aï impatient ftands,
And yields the doom, our eager wifh demands ;   520
In wifdom's caufe with active zeal engage,
And fall, a fplendid triumph to their rage.
Far happier lot, to meet the falchion's fway !
Than, one by one, thus lingering, wafte away.

    Far other end yon Chief ambitious eyes ;   525
Conceal'd by virtue's mafk the danger lies.
Unbrib'd, unaw'd, the honeft tafk I claim,
To burft the veil, and ward.th' impending fhame.
Long vers'd in wiles, the luft of power his guide,
He lulls our caution, and inflates our pride;   530
With fenfe, that darts through man a fearching view,
With pride, that reft, or limits never knew,
To deep defigns miftruftlefs hearts he draws,
With freedom foothes, and cheats with flatter'd laws ;
A crown to feize, the patriot's fire can claim,   535
And mock with feeming zeal the fearful Name.
Full well he knows that, worne by flow delay,
Our generous tribes fhall fall an eafy prey ;
That long-felt influence, great by habit grown,
Climbs to firm fway, and fwells into a throne.   540

    Be warn'd, be warn'd ; the threatening evils fly,
And feek repofe beneath a kinder fky.
Short is the toil, the well-known path fecure,
The pleafure endlefs, and the triumph fure.
Rejoic'd, each land will ope the deftin'd road,   545
And fmiling guide us to the wifh'd abode.
Freed from the fearful ftorm that round them fpread,
Their hearts fhall hail us, and their hands fhall aid. ·
No giant chief in terror there fhall rife ;
No dreadful Jabin fpring to feize the prize :   550

From Madon's hills, to fierce vindictive war
No frowning Jobab roll his iron car :
From death's alarms the potent king shall guard,
And bowers of transport yield the bright reward.

   He spoke. Like Angels dress'd in glory's prime, 555
With conscious worth, and dignity sublime,
While the still thousands gaz'd with glad surprize,
His great soul living in his piercing eyes,
The Chief return'd. By wild ambition toss'd,
To shame impervious, and to virtue lost,   560
Here bend thine eye, thy front unblushing rear;
Let frozen Conscience point no sting severe ;
Then tell, if falsehood lends thee power to tell,
Thy mind believes one scene, thy lips reveal ;
One black aspersion, form'd to blot my name ;   565
Or one vain prospect, rais'd for Israel's shame.
Disclose what dreaded toil this arm has fled ;
On what dire plain this bosom fail'd to bleed :
Tell, if thou canst, when, lur'd by interest's call,
One nerve, one wish forgot the bliss of all.   570

   In virtue arm'd, while Conscience gayly smiles,
I mock thy fraud, and triumph o'er thy wiles :
Thy darts impoison'd peace and glory bring ;
'Tis guilt alone gives slander strength to sting.
Blush, Hanniel, blush ; to yonder tent depart; 575
Let humbler wishes rule thy envious heart ;
Calm the wide lust of power ; contract thy pride ;
Repent those black designs, thou canst not hide ;
Once more to Heaven thy long-lost prayers revive,
And know, the mind that counsels can forgive. 580

   Can I, as God, unfailing bliss assure,
Foil with a wish, and peace at choice secure ?
What nature can, this arm unbroke shall bear,
Whate'er man dar'd, this breast unshaken dare
Canäan's host, those eyes with pain shall view 585
My falchion vanquish, and my feet pursue ;

D

On Ifrael's faithful fons this hand beftow
The blifs of quiet, and the balm of woe.

Should then thefe thoughts, to bafe ambition grown,
With impious madnefs build the envied throne,   590
To wing my doom let rapid lightnings fly,
And pamper'd hounds the peaceful grave deny.
Mine be the blifs, the blifs fupreme to fee
My long-lov'd nation blefs'd, and blefs'd by me:
Let others rule; compar'd with this pure joy,   595
A throne's a bubble, and the world a toy.

In reafon's face let all thy wifhes fpeed;
Let foes befriend thee, and let Heaven fucceed:
Then count thy gains; the mighty prize furvey;
And ftraws, and bubbles, fhall thofe gains outweigh.   600
Wrought in gay looms, thy golden robes fhall glare;
Rich banquets tempt, and lufcious wines enfnare:
But to vile fhow fhall Men their blifs confine?
Or fink to brutes, and only live to dine?

On thefe poor joys what dreadful ills attend?   605
Fears ever rifing! miferies ne'er to end!
Tho' whelm'd in floods one impious tyrant lies,
In the thron'd fon fhall all the father rife;
The fame black heart; the fame beclouded mind;
To pity marbled, and to reafon blind.   610
Search ancient times: the annal'd page run o'er;
With curious eye the fun's long courfe explore;
Scarce can each age a fingle king confefs,
Who knew to govern, or who wifh'd to blefs:
The reft, of earth the terror, or the fcorn,   615
By knaves exalted, and by cowards borne.
To lords like thefe fhall Ifrael's millions bow?
Bend the falfe knee, and force the perjur'd vow?
A few fhort years, our wealth content to fhare,
The reft their greedy hands to toil may fpare: 620
But foon, full foon, their envious minds fhall know
Our growth their ruin, and our peace their woe.

Then all the plagues, from jealous power that spring,
And death, the tender mercy of a king,   624
Your breasts shall feel ; and, rack'd with anguish, mourn
The day, when madness counsell'd to return.

Can I forget, how, from the dunghill rais'd,
Villains who bow'd, and sycophants who prais'd,
O'er Jacob's heirs were scepter'd to preside,
Their tributes gather, and their labors guide ?   630
From them, each cruel pang your heart shall rive,
That coward minds, or offic'd slaves, can give :
Their daring hands prophane the spotless charms,
That yield soft transport to your melting arms ;
Each generous thought the brandish'd scourge controul
And Insult rend the agonizing soul.   636

Then too shall Egypt, fir'd with wrath, recal
The plagues they felt, their king's, their nation's fall ;
Against your race, while Vengeance spreads the wing,
With fury arm them, and to torture spring ;   640
Your sacred dome shall burn ; your altars rend ;
Your priests destroy ; your hated worship end.

In that dread period, what auspicious shore
Shall banish'd Virtue's lifted wings explore ?
In what new realm, when, crush'd, her votaries fail, 645
Build the bright dome, and spread the hallow'd veil ;
Her priests inspire ; her altars teach to rise,
And waft her morning incense to the skies ?
Her final flight your hearts in vain shall mourn ;
In vain, with anguish, call her wish'd return ;   650
In vain the hour extatic sigh to find,
And the sweet sabbath of a guiltless mind.

To Egypt's crimes our sons shall fall a prey,
And learn her manners, while they own her sway :
From many a bower obscene the poison glide,   655
Taint the young soul, and freeze the vital tide ;
The sacred Law our rising hope forsake,
And lisp out curses, ere they know to speak :

Sad Conscience bow beneath an iron rod,
And torpid Reason own a reptile God.   660
    Then, rous'd to wrath, shall Heaven refuse to hear;
Mock all your pangs, and hiss your bitter prayer:
In poison'd gales, its wasting curses rise;
The plague empurpled taint the sickly skies:
The fields all wither, famine rend the breast,   665
And babes, sad victims! yield the dire repast.
    Then from Sabean climes, with hideous sound,
Swift cars shall roll, and savage war resound;
To blood, to vengeance, chiefs their hosts inspire,
Spread boundless death, and wrap the world in fire: 670
Our sons, bless'd refuge of the waning year!
Charm of sad toil, and sweet repose of care!
'Gainst their own hapless sires with foes combine,
And with new anguish point the dart divine.
    Thus o'er our race shall matchless misery roll,   675
And death, and bondage blast the rising soul;
Till the last dregs of vengeance Heaven expend,
Blot out our race, and Israel's glory end;
In final darkness set our sun's pale beam,
And black oblivion shroud our hapless name.   680
    For this dire end, were such bright scenes bestow'd?
For this, th' eternal covenant seal'd by God?
For this did ocean's trembling waves divide,
And o'er pale Egypt roll their whelming tide?
For this, the seraph lead our sacred bands?   685
For this loud thunder speak the dread commands?
From the hard rock refreshing waters rise?
The food of angels shower from balmy skies?
The sun-bright waste its flaming heats allay,
And Jordan's parting billows yield our way?   690
    But Hanniel cries, These wondrous signs were given,
To scourge our guilt, and bend our hearts to Heaven.
Were this the end, fierce famine had annoy'd;
The plague had wasted, or the sword destroy'd.

To fairer bliss he led the chosen train 695
Thro' the dark wave, and o'er the howling plain,
Ordain'd, when yon proud towers in dust are hurl'd,
To found an empire, and to rule a world;
O'er earth's far realms bid truth and virtue shine,
And spread to nature's bounds the Name divine. 700
    What tho' a few base minds the course oppose,
Slaves of poor pride, and Israel's bitter foes;
For pomp, for banquets would their race destroy,
And smile, to sell a nation for a toy;
What tho' of lifeless mold, a feeble race 705
With souls of maids the shape of men disgrace;
Think life no life, unbless'd with torpid ease,
Shrink from a shield, and shiver at a breeze:
'Gainst those let Justice' angry falchion flame,
And hissing Vengeance blast their impious name: 710
These dress th' inglorious loom; in sleep decay,
And to their kindred nothing fleet away,
    Far other mind our true-born race inspires;
Keen bravery prompts, and Abraham's virtue fires:
I see to combat ardent heroes rise; 715
I see bright glory flash from sparkling eyes;
Hark a glad cry! that every danger braves,
" Perish the day, ere Israel's sons be slaves;"
Swift pour new transports thro' my thrilling veins;
Heaven's voice in thunder calls to hostile plains: 720
Mark, mark the sound divine! cease every care;
Gird on your arms, and wake to manly war:
To bright possessions glory points the way,
And calls her sons, her heroes, to the prey.
    By friendship's ties, religion's bands combin'd, 725
By birth united, and by interest join'd,
In the same view our every wish conspires,
One spirit actuates, and one genius fires;
Plain, generous manners vigorous limbs confess,
And vigorous minds to freedom ardent press; 730

In danger's path our eyes serenely smile,
And well-strung sinews hail accustom'd toil.

'Gainst hosts like these what foe with hope can arm?
What numbers daunt them? or what fears alarm?
To reeds before them deadly spears shall turn,　　　735
Swords blunt their edge, and flames forget to burn;
To the slight mound descend the heaven-topp'd wall,
The floods grow dry, and hills and mountains fall.

Rise then to war; awake to bright alarms;
Hail the glad trump, and seize your eager arms!　　　740
Behold, my sons, behold with raptur'd eyes,
How slight the toil, how vast the glorious prize!
These golden robes the fate of Sihon tell,
How Midian yielded, and how Amalek fell;
How sunk proud Jericho's invaded wall,　　　745
And wide Canäan trembled at her fall;
How through each region rings the dreadful cry,
And their wild eye-balls see destruction nigh.
That faith, that arm of steel, that dauntless soul
That bade o'er Bashan's walls destruction roll,　　　750
O'er fields, o'er towers, shall Israel's standard bear,
Turn realms to flight, and wrest the prize of war;
Fill life with glory; Heaven's complacence gain,
And call fair Peace to cheer the crimson plain.

Then o'er wide lands, as blissful Eden bright,　　　755
Type of the skies, and seats of pure delight,
Our sons, with prosperous course, shall stretch their sway,
And claim an empire, spread from sea to sea:
In one great whole th' harmonious tribes combine;
'Trace Justice' path, and choose their chiefs divine;　　　760
On Freedom's base erect the heavenly plan;
Teach laws to reign, aud save the rights of man.
Then smiling Art shall wrap the fields in bloom,
Fine the rich ore, and guide the useful loom;
Then lofty towers in golden pomp arise;　　　765
Then spiry cities meet auspicious skies:

The soul on Wisdom's wing sublimely soar,
New virtues cherish, and new truths explore:
Thro' time's long tract our name celestial run,
Climb in the east, and circle with the sun;   770
And smiling Glory stretch triumphant wings
O'er hosts of heroes, and o'er tribes of kings.

   The Leader spoke; and deep in every breast
A thrilling joy his cheerful voice impress'd.
Round the wide train, late drown'd in sad dismay,   775
His eyes refulgent cast a living ray:
Soul caught from soul the quick, enlivening charm;
Each parent's visage bade his children arm;
In every heart th' undaunted wish began;
O'er the glad field a pleasing murmur ran;   780
On Ai's high walls they cast a longing eye,
Resolv'd to conquer, or prepar'd to die.
So, when the northeast pours a deepening storm,
Night shades the world, and clouds the heaven deform,
Loud on some ship descends the driving rain,   785
And winds imperious toss the surging main;
Dissolv'd in terror, sailors eye the wave,
Lift ardent prayers, and wait the gaping grave:
If chance in beauty's bloom the morn arise,
Still the rough roar, and charm the troubled skies,   790
Serenely opening, far the billows o'er,
The blue-seen mountains, and the native shore;
Raptur'd the new-born day with shouts they hail,.
And stretch their canvas to the joyous gale.

   When sickening Hanniel saw their bosoms glow,   795
Their fierce eyes burn, and tears of transport flow,
The lov'd, the fond design, his changeful mind,
With secret pangs, to happier hours consign'd.
High o'er the rest his shouts distinguish'd rose;
With well feign'd smiles his artful visage glows,   800
And thus his voice---When pierc'd with Israel's **grief**
I strove in vain to lend the wish'd relief,

Perhaps this heart, by nature prone to know
The good man's interest in his country's woe,
Of peace, and prosperous arms too soon despair'd,   805
Unreal ills foresaw, and fancied dangers fear'd.
Yet still those views a kind indulgence claim,
Your fame their glory, and your bliss their aim.
Should this bold course be doom'd to woe severe,
Pure is my warning voice, my conscience clear ;   810
On destin'd fight should friendly Conquest smile,
With joy, my soul shall welcome every toil ;
In Israel's cause, to scenes of danger driven,
To war is transport, and to die is heaven.

The hero ceas'd : a faint applause was heard,   815
And half-form'd smiles around the plain appear'd,
With startling sound the trump's deep voice began ;
To seize their arms the raptur'd thousands ran ;
When Caleb, reverend chief, all white with age,
Serenely rose, and hush'd the tumult's rage.   820
Deep thought sate musing on his furrow'd face ;
Calm wisdom round him cast an awful grace ;
With smiles just Heaven survey'd his constant truth,
Innerv'd his limbs, and lengthen'd out his youth :
Even now his arm rejoic'd the sword to wield,   825
To lead the contest, and to sweep the field.
Near the great Chief, in purple robes he stood ;
Sense, from his tongue, and sweet persuasion flow'd ;
Round the wide plain attentive silence hung,
And thus sage counsels sway'd the listening throng.   830
My voice impels to arms ; but let the sky
Lead on our host, and bid the heathen fly.
Were Israel spotless in the ETERNAL's sight,
Ai had not boasted a victorious fight.
When Virtue dress'd us in divine array,   835
Joy cheer'd each hour, and smooth'd the rugged way :
To scenes of fame each warrior ardent ran,
And claim'd the glories of the dreadful van.

But when black Vice our breafts with poifon ftain'd,
We fhook for dangers timorous Fancy feign'd ;   840
Each fhameful field beheld our fquadrons fly,
And heroes arm'd for battle but to die.

And now fome fin, fome folly, not bemoan'd,
Rebellion bold, or injury unaton'd,
Pours on our heads their flood of grief and care,   845
Bids Ai exult, and all our fons defpair.
Elfe round the heavenly dome the cloud had fpread,
And facred fires illum'd the nightly fhade.

Let the whole race to GOD fubmiffive bend :
Let ceafelefs prayer to Mercy's throne afcend ;   850
'Till the third morn, the pious faft endure ;
Each deed be holy, and each bofom pure ;
Then o'er our path with joy fhall HEAVEN prefide,
Our guilt difcover, and our counfels guide.
Then, nor 'till then, to war let trumpets call ;   855
Lead forth thefe bands, and mount the yielding wall.
But fhould our courfe, this day, to fight be driven,
Should arms be brandifh'd in the face of HEAVEN,
Look round your fteps ; furvey the dreadful road ;
Think if the fword and fhield can war with GOD.   860

Thus fpoke the fage. Bleft man ! the Chief replied,
The war's firft honour, and the council's pride !
Thine is the voice of GOD : th' infpiring ray
Shines thro' thy breaft, and gives the brighteft day.
Two days fhall combat ceafe. The camp around,   865
Let the fad faft in every tent be found :
Two days to HEAVEN be rais'd by pious fear
The grateful tribute of a humble prayer.
So fhall we wipe away the crimfon ftain,
And Ifrael's glory gild the conquering plain.   870

He fpoke. Each warrior with delight obey'd ;
Each cheerful face th' obfequious mind difplay'd.
The hoft difpers'd ; and prayers, and reverent fighs
Rofe in foft incenfe to th' approving fkies.   *

THE

CONQUEST of CANAAN.

BOOK II.

ARGUMENT.

Morning. Gibeonites assemble for the worship of the Sun. Mina refuses to join them in this worship; the king enquires the reason. She mentions her adoration of the true GOD. *The king being anxious to know more of the matter, after an apology for speaking in such an assembly, she gives a general account of the Deity, and his dispensations. As he is still further inquisitive, she gives him a more minute account of the Divine works, in a history of the creation---our first parents---the fall---general succeeding apostacy---deluge---second apostacy---calling of Abraham ---Israelites journeying into Egypt---oppression and plagues of Egypt---Israelites' deliverance---journey through the wilderness---promulgation of the divine law --destruction of Sihon, and Og---last prophecy, death, and burial of Moses, and the commission of Joshua. The Gibeonites being much afflicted at the prospect of their destruction, Mina proposes an embassy to Joshua, to solicit peace. The king approves the proposal. Conclusion.*

The CONQUEST of CANÄAN.

BOOK II.

BEYOND those western hills, whose haughty brow,
To heaven exalted, scorn'd the world below,
A plain outspread, with growing verdure bright,
And stole, extensive, from the aching sight.
Here, in proud pomp, adorn'd with countless spires,   5
That mock'd the glories of the solar fires,
Gibeon's imperial towers sublimely rose,
And spurn'd the terrors of surrounding foes.

   Now o'er the hills red streams began to burn,
And bursting splendors usher'd in the morn ;   10
With living dies the flowers all-beauteous glow'd ;
O'er the glad fields etherial odours flow'd ;
The forest echoed with a boundless song,
And rising breezes pour'd the strains along.

   Adorn'd with green, before the palace lay   15
A spacious square, and smil'd upon the day.
Here, ere the dawn the kindling skies illum'd,
Or opening flowers the fragrant gales perfum'd,
Of every age, a vast, assembled train
Pour'd from the lofty domes, and fill'd the plain.   20
   High in the midst two sacred altars shone,
Adorn'd with honours to their God, the Sun.
This, deck'd with art, and bright in royal pride,
With sable gore the quivering victim died :

On that gay flowers in rich profusion lay,   25
And gales of Eden bore their sweets away.

   Here, white with age, in snowy vesture dress'd,
Aradon stood, their monarch, and their priest;
Red in his hand a torch refulgent shone,
And his fix'd countenance watch'd the rising sun.   30

   When first the flaming Orb, with glorious rays,
Roll'd o'er the hills, and pour'd a boundless blaze;
Charm'd at the sight, the monarch stretch'd his hand,
And touch'd the tributes with the sacred brand;
Through freshen'd air perfumes began to rise,   35
And curling volumes mounted to the skies.
Thrice to the earth the raptur'd suppliants bow'd,
Then struck the lyre, and hymn'd the rising God.

   O thou, whose bursting beams in glory rise,
And sail, and brighten, thro' unbounded skies!   40
The world's great Parent! heaven's exalted King?
Sole Source of good! and life's eternal Spring!
All hail, while cloath'd in beauty's endless ray,
Thy face unclouded gives the new-born day!

   Above all scenes is plac'd thy heavenly throne;   45
Ere time began, thy spotless splendor shone:
Sublime from east to west thy chariot rolls,
Chears the wide earth, and warms the distant poles;
Commands the vegetable race to grow,
The fruit to redden, and the flower to blow.   50
This world was born to change: the hand of Time
Makes, and unmakes the scenes of every clime.
The insect millions scarce the morn survive;
One transient day the flowery nations live:
A few short years complete the human doom;   55
Then pale Death summons to the narrow tomb.

Line 28. *Aradon stood, their monarch,*) Gibeon is generally sup-
posed to have been a commonwealth. But as most nations, in that
early age, had a chief magistrate, vested with more or less civil and
religious powers, I have supposed such a magistrate, and given him
the usual epithets.

Lash'd by the flood, the hard rocks wear away ;
Worne by the storm, the lessening hills decay ;
Unchang'd alone is thine exalted flame,
From endless years to endless years the same ;   60
Thy splendors with immortal beauty shine,
Roll round th' eternal heavens, and speak thy name divine.

When thy bright throne, beyond old ocean's bound,
Thro' nether skies pursues its destin'd round,
Lost in th' ascending darkness, beauty fades ;   65
Thro' the blank field, and thro' the woodland, spreads
A melancholy silence.   O'er the plain
Dread lions roam, and savage terrors reign.

And when sad Autumn sees thy face retire,
And happier regions hail thy orient fire,   70
High in the storm imperious Winter flies,
And desolation saddens all the skies.
But when once more thy beam the north ascends,
Thy light invigorates, and thy warmth extends ;
The fields rejoice, the groves with transport ring,   75
And boundless nature hails the sky-born spring.

Nor even in winter's gloom, or night's sad reign,
Darts the warm influence of thy beams in vain.

Beyond the main some fairer region lies,
Some brighter isles beneath the southern skies,   80
Where crimson War ne'er bade the clarion roar,
Nor sanguine billows died the vernal shore :
No thundering storm the day's bright face conceals,
No summer scorches, and no frost congeals ;
No sickness wastes, no grief provokes the tear,   85
Nor tainted vapours blast the clement year.
Round the glad day-star endless beauties burn,
And crown'd with rainbows, opes th' imperial morn ;
A clear unbounded light the skies display,
And purple lustre leads the changing day.   90
O'er conscious shades, and bowers of soft repose,
Young breezes spring, and balmy fragrance blows ;

The fields all wanton in fereneſt beams,
Wake fairer flowers, and roll diviner ſtreams ;
Thro' the long vales aerial muſic roves,   95
And nobler fruitage dies the bending groves.

Thro' ſpotleſs nations as the realm refin'd,
Thine influence there ſublimes th' immortal mind ;
Its active pinions ſwift thro' nature roam,
Loſe the low world, and claim a nobler home.   100
Their limbs, of endleſs life, with glory crown'd,
New youth improves, and growing charms ſurround :
On the bleſs'd ſhore thy ſplendors love to ſhine,
And raiſe thy ſons each hour, to raptures more divine.

Thus ceas'd the ſound : the harp's melodious ſtrain 105
Join'd the glad hymn, and charm'd the liſtening train ;
A ſparkling joy each ſpeaking face diſplay'd,
While light expanding leſſen'd every ſhade.

Fair as the lucid ſtar, that up the ſky
Leads the gay morn, and bids the darkneſs ſly,   110
Beſide the king a lovely Virgin ſtood,
Nor join'd the ſong, nor with th' aſſembly bow'd.
A ſweet diſpleaſure ting'd her melting eye,
And her ſad boſom heav'd th' oppreſſive ſigh.
Her ſoft diſtreſs the watchful king ſurvey'd,   115
And thus, with friendly ſmile, addreſs'd the maid.

Say, lovelieſt fair one, whence the meaning gloom,
That damps our joys, and clouds thy roſy bloom !
Why does thy ſoul the reverence due deny
To yon bright orb, that gilds the orient ſky ?   120
Far other God, replied the fair, demands
My vocal tranſports, and my ſuppliant hands ;
A GOD, whoſe power rais'd high yon azure round,
Form'd the wide earth, and fix'd the ocean's bound ;
Who more the ſun tranſcends, than his gay glare   125
The tranſient glimmerings of ſome half-ſeen ſtar.

Strange ſcenes, the monarch cries, thy voice declares,
And breathes ſweet muſic thro' our raptur'd ears.

But canft thou, unconvinc'd, yon orb behold,
O'er earth, o'er heaven, in endlefs triumph roll'd?   130
What boundlefs joy his gladfome courfe attends!
What glory brightens! and what good defcends!
Round the blue void his beams unchanging fhine,
And fpeak his nature, and his name, divine.
Yet ftill my curious thoughts the tale demand,   135
And afk improvement at thy lovely hand.
Say then, O fair, what all-exalted Power
Thy wifhes reverence, and thy hands adore.

    With down-caft eye, and cheek of crimfon bright
That fweetly mingled with the fpotlefs white,   140
Replied the virtuous maid: To bolder tongues
Of man's bold fex, the arduous tafk belongs.
But thy fond cares, that fav'd my life, demand
Toils far fuperior from my grateful hand.
Thy blifs, thy endlefs blifs, my voice fhall bribe   145
To pafs the bounds, the maiden's laws prefcribe.

    Far, very far beyond this lower fky,
Beyond the fun, beyond the flames on high,
Dwells in pure light, in heaven's ferene abode,
The Source of life, the Spring of endlefs good;   150
All fcenes, all heights above, fublimely reigns;
All worlds created, and all worlds fuftains.

    Yon orb, whofe brightnefs wakes thy raptur'd praife,
Is but a beam of his unbounded blaze.
His breath illum'd, his hand exalted high,   155
And roll'd him flaming thro' th' expanded fky.

    His bounteous influence, thro' all nature driven,
Warms the wide earth, and cheers the wider heaven.
All fcenes, all beings his pure fight furveys,
Where morn begins, and where pale eve decays;   160
Where hell's dark fhores the glooms of night difplay;
Or heaven's broad palace glows in lafting day;
Thro' worlds of endlefs youth, where angels fhine,
And unknown nations rove in light divine.

'F

He moves, informs, directs, and rules the whole ; 165
Their cause, their end, their guardian, and their soul.

He wakes the beauties of the vernal morn ;
He bids the flames of sultry summer burn ;
He showers th' autumnal wealth ; and his dread power
Sounds in the wintry storm, and bids the wild waves roar.

In these vast regions countless beings move, 171
Live in his smiles, and wanton in his love :
In all, his power, and boundless wisdom, shine,
The works, the glories of a hand divine.

Thron'd in high heaven, in starry mansions reign, 175
Of purest intellect, th' angelic train
All sense, all soul, all love, eternal power
Their thoughts contemplate, and their songs adore.

Thro' earth's wide realms unnumber'd tribes we find,
Of different ranks, for different ends design'd. 180
On every leaf the insect millions swarm,
Hum round the flower, or in the sun-beam warm ;
The birds, on painted pinions, gayly fly
Thro' the wide regions of the sapphire sky ;
Beasts climb the cliff, or walk the savage wood ; 185
And fishes sport around the foamy flood.
These, with the reptile race, to time a prey,
Of dust were fashion'd, and to dust decay.

To man of nobler rank, two parts were given,
This form'd of earth, and that inspir'd by heaven. 190
Such as the texture, such th' allotted doom ;
His body moulders in the narrow tomb :
But the wing'd soul, when earth in dust is hurl'd,
Shall spring, immortal, from the sinking world ;
Ordain'd, if crimes its earthly course distain, 195
To bathe in fire, and waste with endless pain ;
If cleans'd from guilt, with active joy to rise
To the pure transports of angelic skies ;
But man, unmindful of his nobler birth,
In vain seeks pleasure from surrounding earth. 200

Far different, far, the scenes by Heaven defign'd
To fill the wifhes of the active mind.
This bounded point is but our being's morn;
To endlefs life th' etherial Soul was born.
Upward with nimble flight her thoughts fhould foar,   205
And, wing'd by virtue, brighter worlds explore;
Earth's groveling joys difdain with confcious pride,
Like angels fafhion'd, and to heaven allied.

For this fair train our nature to prepare,
And the pure fragrance of immortal air,   210
To raife the downward heart from earthly toys,
And mould our wifhes to fublimer joys,
Thro' earth's wide realms, afflictions firft began,
The nobleft bleffings HEAVEN beftows on man.
Toil, difappointment, hunger, thirft, and pain,   215
A long, long, difmal, melancholy train,
Cleanfe the dim eye, diffolve the powerful luft,
And loofe the chains, that bind our hearts to duft.
From forrow's fire, like filver well refin'd,
Freed from vile earth, fhall rife th' undroffy mind,   220
Each hour, with beams of clearer beauty fhine,
And ceafelefs claim an image more divine.
At length, when ficknefs brings th' expected doom,
Its powers fhall rife triumphant o'er the tomb,
Forward to nobler fcenes with rapture fpring,   225
And hail the meffage of th' undreaded king;
While life's long ftream its fartheft fhore fhall lave,
And feek the bofom of th' eternal wave.
Then fhall we fee diviner winds arife,
The main grow calm, and fmiles inveft the fkies: 230
Then fhall our happy hands exalt the fail,
Launch on the deep, and call th' etherial gale;
With joy, our fpirits leave the fading fhore,
And hear the leffening ftorms at diftance roar.
Inwrapp'd in beams of uncreated light,   235
All heaven, difclos'd, fhall burft upon the fight;

Streams of immortal blifs in vifion roll,
And hofts of angels hail the kindred foul,

   With rofy fmiles, thus fpoke the lovely maid,
While o'er the plain a boundlefs filence fpread.   240
Like the tun'd lyre, the mufic of her tongue
Pour'd foft perfuafion on the truths fhe fung :
Pleas'd, her fweet grace, and fparkling eye, they view,
And the frank mein, that Falfehood never knew.

   To all, Aradon bent a yielding ear ;   245
For Heaven infpir'd his honeft heart to hear,
Mid favage realms, fair Gibeon's fons inclin'd
To manners gentler, worfhip more refin'd :
Each focial art adorn'd the generous door ;
The ftranger welcom'd, and reliev'd the poor ;   250
And hence they liv'd.   From nature's bounteous Lord,
Even virtue's femblance finds a fure reward.

   A calm delight exulting in his eyes,
With gentleft voice, the monarch thus replies.

   O brighteft of thy fex, an angel's tongue   255
Alone can boaft the fweetnefs of thy fong.
Led by thy voice, my raptur'd mind would know
The mighty Power, from whom all bleffings flow ;
Would learn what holy feers his will explain,
What prayers delight him, and what offerings gain ;   260
Safe in his fmiles, beyond the grave refpire ;
Exult o'er death, and flee from endlefs fire ;
To thofe immortal regions fpeed my flight,
And prove fome humble feat, amid the fons of light.

   But fay, O fair, when form'd the Power divine   265
The lamps that round yon fky forever fhine ?
Know'ft thou the day when earth's wide realms were made,
The hills exalted, and the ocean fpread ?
Whofe hand thine infant mind to reafon wrought,
In virtue nurs'd thee, and in wifdom taught ?   270
Tho' age my trembling brow has whiten'd o'er,
Strange unknown fcenes thy curious thoughts explore.

Return'd the lovely maid, Thy glad requeſt
Wakes my fond hope, and warms my grateful breaſt---
Know, mighty prince, when Elam's deathful ſpear   275
Pierc'd the fell foe, and looſ'd my ſoul from fear,
From Iſraël's camp, thro' unknown paths, I ſtray'd,
My lone ſteps wandering round the woodland ſhade.
'Twas there, the ſacred truths the prophet ſung,
And thus ſweet muſic tun'd his heavenly tongue.   280

From realms divine high-rais'd beyond all height,
Th' almighty Parent caſt his piercing ſight;
With boundleſs view, he ſaw the etherial vaſt
A clouded gloom, an undelightſome waſte:
Around the extended wild, no ſun's broad ray   285
Mark'd the clear ſplendor of immortal day;
No varying moon, ordain'd at eve to riſe,
Led the full pomp of conſtellated ſkies;
No day in circling beauty learn'd to roll;
No fair ſpring ſmil'd, nor froſt congeal'd the pole;   290
Subſtantial darkneſs ſpace unmeaſur'd fill'd,
And nature's realms lay deſolate and wild.

He ſpoke: at once, o'er earth's far diſtant bounds
The heavens wide-arching ſtretch'd their ſapphire rounds
With hoary cliffs the far-ſeen hills aſcend;   295
Down ſink the vales, and wide the plains extend;
Headlong from ſteep to ſteep the billows roar,
Fill the broad main, and toſs againſt the ſhore.

He ſpoke; and beauty thro' all nature flow'd;
With ſpringing verdure earth's wide regions glow'd;300
Forth ruſh the flowery tribes, and trees on high
Shroud their tall ſummits in the ambient ſky.

He ſpoke the heavens with ſudden glory ſhone;
In godlike pomp burſt forth the golden ſun;
Far thro' immenſity his kindling ray   305
Shot life and joy, and pour'd the new-born day;
With milder luſtre roſe the charms of even,
The moon's broad beam, and all the pride of heaven.

He spoke; and fishes fill'd the watry rounds,
Swarm'd in the streams, and swam the Ocean's bounds;
The green sea sparkled with unnumber'd dies,   311
And varying beauty wav'd upon the skies;
Whales through the foaming billows proudly rode,
And unknown monsters gambol'd o'er the flood.
From the deep wave, adorn'd with nobler grace,   315
In countless millions sprang the feather'd race;
Thro' the far clouds the eagle cleft his way,
And soar'd and wanton'd in the flames of day;
Full on the morn the peacock op'd his beams,
And swans majestic row'd th' expanded streams.   320

He spoke; and, wondering, from disparted plains
In throngs unnumber'd rose the bestial trains:
Their snowy robes the harmless flocks reveal'd;
Gay steeds exulting pranc'd the vernal field;
The lion glar'd, and mid the gazing throng   325
Shook his rough main, and grimly stalk'd along.

The wide earth finish'd, from his western throne,
In splendid beauty look'd the gladsome sun;
Calm were the skies, the fields with lustre crown'd,
And nature's incense fill'd th' etherial round.   330
Enshrin'd in sacred light, the Maker stood,
Complacent smil'd, and own'd the work was good.
Then from his hand in silent glory came
A nobler form, and Man his destin'd name;
Erect, and tall, in solemn pomp he stood,   335
And living virtue in his visage glow'd.
Then too a fairer being shew'd her charms;
Young Beauty wanton'd in her snowy arms;
The heavens around her bade their graces fly,
And Love sate blooming in her gentle eye.   340
O pair divine! superior to your kind;
To virtue fashion'd, and for bliss design'd!

He, born to rule, with calm, uplifted brow,
Look'd down majestic on the world below;

To heaven, his manfion, turn'd his thought fublime ; 345
Or rov'd far onward thro' the fcenes of time ;
O'er nature's kingdom caft a fearching eye,
And dar'd to trace the fecrets of the fky ;
On fancy's pinions fcann'd the bright abode,
And claim'd his friend, an Angel, or a GOD. 350
   Her he indu'd with nature more refin'd,
A lovelier image, and a fofter mind.
To her he gave to kindle fweet defire,
To roufe great thoughts, and fan th' heroic fire :
At pity's gentle call to bend his ear ; 355
To prompt for woe the unaffected tear ;
In fcenes refin'd his foftening foul improve,
And tune his wifhes with the hand of love.
To her he gave with fweetnefs to obey,
Infpire the friend, and charm the lord away ; 360
Each bleeding grief with balmy hand to heal,
And learn his rending finews not to feel ;
Each joy t' improve, the pious wifh to raife,
And add new raptures to his languid praife.
   To this lov'd pair a blefs'd retreat was given, 365
A feat for angels, and a humbler heaven ;
Fair Eden nam'd : in fwift fucceffion, there
Glad fcenes of rapture led the vernal year ;
Round the green garden living beauty play'd ;
In gay profufion earth her treafures fpread ; 370
The air breath'd fragrance ; ftreams harmonious rung,
And love, and tranfport, tun'd th' aerial fong.
   With tranquil beams the feventh bright morn appear'd
And thus, from firey clouds, a voice was heard.
This day, O Man, to facred tranfports rife, 375
And pafs the hours in converfe with the fkies :
To prayer, to praife, be all thy wifhes given ;
Soar from the world, and here begin thy heaven !
So fhall thy fons purfue the virtuous road,
And, each returning fabbath, wake to GOD. 380

The fovereign voice the reverent pair obey'd ;
A folemn beauty earth and heaven array'd :
With joy the pinion'd tribes, in every grove,
Hymn'd the bleft influence of immortal love :
Man join'd the concert, and his raptur'd lays   385
Charm'd the gay fields, when angels ceas'd to praife.

   Mid Eden's groves the tree of glory ftood,
That taught the unalter'd bounds of ill, and good :
Its fruit, all beauteous to the ravifh'd eye,
Denied to man, and facred to the fky :   390
Denied alone ; a boundlefs ftore was given,
Food for bright angels, tranfcript fair of heaven.
And thus the law---If vain defire to tafte
Prompt thee, rebellious, to the dire repaft ;
Hear, hear, O man ! on that tremendous day,   395
Thy life, thy blifs, thy virtue, pafs away ;
No more the heir of endlefs joys refin'd,
But guilty, wretched, to the duft confign'd ;
Toil here thy lot, thine end the dreary tomb,
And hopelefs anguifh thine eternal doom.   400
The fovereign voice the pair obfequious heard,
Th' injunction reverenc'd, and the danger fear'd :
'Till urg'd by impious luft, by hell infnar'd,
They pluck'd the fruit ; the guilt, and fentence fhar'd,
For one poor banquet, one unreal joy,   405
Rebell'd, and yielded blifs without alloy ;
To howling deferts were from angels driven,
And loft the fweet fociety of heaven.

   Then ills on ills unnumber'd rofe forlorn ;
No more the orient beam'd th' angelic morn ;   410
Fragrance and Beauty clos'd their blifsful reign
Nor Spring perennial danc'd along the plain.
Cold Night her fearful clouds around them fpread,
And gave new terrors to the howling fhade.
Loft in the bofom of th' afcending ftorm,   415
The fun's faint beam in winter ceas'd to warm ;

O'er plains, and hills, the chilling froft congeal'd;
The fnow tempeftuous fadden'd all the field;
On the wide wave the headlong whirlwind pour'd,
And all the thunders of the ocean roar'd.   420
Where late gay bloom'd the harveft's waving pride,
And purpled fruits the bending branches died,
Imperv'ous thorns, and clinging brambles fpread,
And unblefs'd famine gloom'd th' autumnal fhade:
For blood, the raging wolf began to arm;   425
Fierce, hungry tygers rung the dread alarm;
The lion's fovereign voice, with thrilling found,
Clear'd the wide grove, and fhook the hills around.

The facred ftamp the mind forever loft,
The fkies' perfection and the angel's boaft: 430
Elfe had our life roll'd on, from forrow clear,
A femblance bright of heaven's eternal year.
Now ftain'd with guilt, the foul to hatred turn'd;
With pride was lifted, and with envy burn'd.
Fierce bickerings rofe; with conqueft noife was crown'd,
And Reafon's ftill, fmall voice in curfes drown'd: 436
In vain fweet Friendfhip charm'd the ftubborn ear;
She fung, and wondering found no heart to hear.

By hands, not wifdom, next the caufe was tried,
And blows obtain'd what argument denied.   440
Revenge foon taught to point the murdering knife,
And fecret ambufh hedg'd the hated life.
The villain's gloomy path black night conceal'd,
And virtuous blood bedew'd the lonely field.
Then roufing banners War with tranfport rais'd;   445
Forth flafh'd the fteel; the far-feen fignal blaz'd:
O'er the fcar'd hills the warning clarion rang,
And fwift to combat ftartled nations fprang;
In floods of ftreaming gore the fields were drown'd,
And flaughter'd thoufands heap'd th' embattled ground.
The regal dome, the turret's golden gleam   451
Grac'd the fad triumphs of th' imperious flame;

G

From wall to wall insulting engines frown'd,
And all the pride of art fell crumbling to the ground.

   To earth's wide realms, from scenes above the sky, 455
Th' Almighty Ruler turn'd his searching eye:
Deep sunk in boundless guilt the regions lay,
And vice exulting claim'd a single sway.
Her countless millions, lur'd by Pleasure's charms,
Bask'd in her smiles, and sported in her arms;   460
The song, the feast, inspir'd the jocund hours,
And Lewdness wanton'd in luxurious bowers.
In vain from door to door the beggar stray'd;
His portion hunger, and the frost his bed:
In vain sad Sickness rais'd her feeble cry;   465
No friendly hand appear'd, nor melting eye:
Virtue, fair pilgrim, cast a wishful view,
And spread her wings, and sigh'd a last adieu.

   He saw, while terror veil'd his awful face,
And bade fierce ruin wrap the guilty race,   470
Borne by the vengeance of his lifted arm,
Far roll'd the black immensity of storm;
From east to west were pour'd the glooms on high,
And cloudy curtains hung th' unmeasur'd sky.
Shook by the voice that rends th' immortal plain,   475
In one broad deluge sunk th' etherial main;
Huge floods, imprison'd in the vaulted ground,
With wild commotion burst the crumbling bound;
O'er earth's broad climes the surging billows driven
Climb'd the tall mountains, and invaded heaven: 480
The pride of man, the pomp-embosom'd tower,
Towns wrapp'd in gold, and realms of mighty power,
All plung'd at once beneath th' unfathom'd wave,
And nature perish'd in the boundless grave.

   From realms, where suns with milder glory shine, 485
His voice awak'd the western wind divine.
At once the balmy wind obedient blew,
And springing beauty cloth'd the world anew;

In rosy youth her climes emergent smil'd,
And flowery visitants rejoic'd the wild.   490

How, doom'd to pass beyond the liquid grave,
The ark's rich treasure triumph'd o'er the wave;
How the bless'd favorite, rising from the main,
Rul'd orient lands, and peopled earth again,
Thou know'st.   The wonderous tale, thro' every clime,
Tradition wafts along the stream of time.   496
With circling splendor, and etherial die,
The covenant bow spread sudden round the sky,
From those gay heavens, that arch'd with pomp divine,
Fair o'er the angelic world forever shine,   500
To earth remov'd, and fix'd by God's decree,
An endless barrier 'gainst th' ambitious sea.

Safe in the sacred sign, ungrateful man
New scenes of guilt with eager zeal began.
Again black Vice o'er nature stretch'd her sway, 505
And magic Pleasure charm'd the foot astray.
No sacred anthems climb'd the bright abode;
Nor Reason blush'd to hail a golden god:
With rage, and conflict, earth was cover'd o'er;
Towns sunk in flames, and fields were drench'd in gore.
With impious jests they mock'd a future doom;   511
Sung o'er the shroud, and danc'd into the tomb.
From land to land the clouds of death unfurl'd,
And one wide lethargy benumb'd th' oblivious world.

Then too, proud Ashur, queen of realms, began   515
To forge her chains, and bind inglorious man.
Hence, tyrants sprang, and dar'd with impious claim,
Demand the honours of the sacred Name;
Hence stern Oppression rais'd his iron rod,
Hence crimson Slaughter wrapp'd the world in blood:
Thro' every clime the night of slavery spread,   521
And Heaven repenting griev'd that man was made.

From this black mass, this mingled host of foes,
One sainted friend th' Almighty Ruler chose;

For him, blefs'd champion of his yielding caufe !   529
He chang'd the ftable courfe of nature's laws ;
(An hundred fummers faw the circling morn,
Ere his firft hope, the promis'd heir was born)
To him, to his he gave Canäan's fhore,
'Till the bright evening gild the weft no more.   530
To Idol guilt the world befide was given,
Their name, their memory blotted out of heaven.

When the dire famine o'er all nations fpread,
His hand the favorite race to Egypt led.
As fome fair tree, where fruitful ftreams are roll'd,   535
Lifts fpiry fhoots, and bids its leaves unfold ;
O'er the green bank ambitious branches rife,
Enjoy the winds, and gain upon the fkies ;
While opening flowers around it gayly fpring,
And birds with tranfport clap the painted wing :   540
So each fond fun, and each fucceffive fhade
Beheld with fmiles the infant nation fpread ;
From field to field the rifing boughs expand,
Share the glad fmiles of heaven, and fill the jealous land.

Their fudden growth the envious tyrant view'd,   545
And impious hands in infant gore imbru'd,
With bold oppreffion bath'd the ftreaming eye,
Rack'd the fad foul, and rous'd the fuppliant cry.

Their bleeding wrongs the omnifcient Mind furvey'd,
And bade fierce Vengeance bare her flaming blade.   550
No more the limpid wave ferenely flow'd ;
But thro' fad fhores the river roll'd in blood ;
Unnumber'd reptiles climb'd the ftately dome,
Croak'd o'er the feaft, and crawl'd the pillar'd room ;
Infects in countlefs millions earth o'erfpread ;   555
The fickening murrain gloom'd the paftur'd fhade ;
From darken'd fkies the ftorm's red bolts were hurl'd,
And hail, and lightening fwept the wafted world ;
Like cloudy curtains, locufts hung the day ;
Pale death, and famine mark'd their baleful way :   560

Three days blank midnight wrapp'd the realm in gloom,
And all her firft-born funk in one broad tomb.

Then, high in air his lucid banner fpread,
To the bright fign collected Ifrael fled,
With tranfport trac'd the finger of the fky, 565
Wing'd their glad path, and hail'd redemption nigh.
In vain its countlefs ills the wafte difclos'd ;
In vain the fea their facred path oppos'd ;
Back roll'd th' inftinctive main ; and round their fide
In cryftal fplendor ftood the confcious tide. 570
In the bright front, a cloud his dark abode,
Thron'd on the rufhing winds, an angel rode,
The fpreading volumes mark'd their path by day,
And guiding flames illum'd their nightly way.
Behind, the tyrant, urg'd by Heaven's decree, 575
Drove his pale hoft, and trembled thro' the fea.
On the tall fhore fublime the Prophet ftood,
And ftretch'd his hand above the eager flood ;
Wide-circling all, far clos'd the billow'd womb,
And Egypt's glories found a watery tomb. 580
Thro' fpacious climes of fierce and fcorching day,
The cloud expanded led their lonely way,
'Till, white with cliffs, and crown'd with many a fhade,
In cloudy pride fam'd Sinai rear'd its head.
On this lone mount, the all-difcerning Mind 585
To teach his name, t' unfold his law, defign'd ;
On earth to witnefs truth and power divine,
And bid o'er Jacob's fons his fplendors fhine :
Beneath its haughty brow the thoufands lay,
And hop'd the wonders of th' expected day. 590

Fair rofe the dawn : from heaven's fublime abode,
Th' almighty Power in boundlefs glory rode ;
Long dufky folds a cloud around him fpread,
His throne furrounding with impervious fhade,
Its flame-bright fkirts with light exceffive fhone, 595
A noon-tide morn, that dimm'd the rifing fun.

Forth from its womb unusual lightnings fly,
And thunders, hurl'd on thunders, rock the sky:
To Sinai's top the wonderous scene descends;
Down plunge his cliffs; his tottering summit rends; 600
O'er all the mountain burn devouring fires,
Wreath'd in dread smoke, and crown'd with lofty spires.
Loud as hoarse whirlwinds earth and heaven deform,
Loud as the thousand thunders of the storm,
With clear, dread voice, in pomp tremendous, roll 605
The trump's long-sounding terrors thro' the pole.
The Seer majestic climbs the towering height,
And, bosom'd deep in glory, leaves the sight.

There, while the world was hush'd in silent awe,
The Sovereign Mind disclos'd th' eternal Law; 610
And thus the dread commands. O Israel, know,
I am the LORD, who snatch'd thy sons from woe,
From Egypt's bondage trac'd thy various ways;
Nor shall base Idols share my sacred praise.
Let no vain words my fearful Name prophane; 615
Nor toil, nor sports my holy sabbaths stain.
Thy parent's voice with reverent mind obey:
Thy hand from dire revenge, and murther stay:
Let not a thought thy neighbour's couch ascend;
And not a wish to others wealth extend: 620
Let truth thy converse, truth thy oaths confine:
And every passion to thy lot resign.

Unnumber'd statutes then his voice ordain'd,
The poor protected, and the rich restrain'd;
And taught, what manners prosperous rule assure, 625
Their foes to vanquish, and their peace secure.

Then thro' long, weary climes their course was turn'd,
Still mov'd the cloud, and still the glory burn'd.
With ceaseless care he fill'd their hearts with good;
The skies dissolving shower'd immortal food: 630
With wondering joy they saw the streamy rain
Pour from the rock, and spread along the plain;

And clouds of quails, from every region driven,
Blacken'd the fields, and fill'd the bounds of heaven.
* 'Twas then, near Edom's realms the thousands lay, 635
And her proud prince denied th' expected way.
Whate'er their state, whate'er their God concern'd,
From their great Seer my curious parent learn'd ;
Charm'd with the scene, he left his native soil,
Shar'd all their wants, and barter'd ease for toil.   640

Thro' long, lone paths we bent our circling course,
Untir'd by winter's rage, or summer's force ;
Bright angels led the van ; and round the road
Dread scenes of terror mark'd the present God.

Even now I see fierce Sihon's hostile train,   645
Sheath'd in dire arms, and frowning o'er the plain.
In childhood then, around my sire I clung,
Danc'd in his arms, and in his bosom hung.
With nimble steps the sacred warriors sped,
Blew the shrill trump, and fill'd the field with dead. 650
Like drifts of rushing dust, that sweep the skies,
On fear's light pinions swift the remnant flies ;
From town to town we wing our rapid way,
And the wide region sinks an easy prey.

Then giant Og his heroes drove to arms,   655
Whirl'd his proud car, and thunder'd hoarse alarms :
In distant fields I saw the storm ascend,
Its shades all darken, and its clouds extend ;
Down the grim hills I heard the volumes roll,
And bursting terrors rend the shuddering pole.   660
As snows, slight fabric, in warm suns decay,
The impious squadrons sudden melt away.

Now o'er the Seer had six-score summers run,
And hoary locks around his temples shone,
When sounds melodious, opening from the sky,   665
To the sad train declar'd his end was nigh.

* See Book IV, Line 239.

His mind infpir'd with more than mortal fight,
Saw future fcenes and ages rufh to light;
And thus his voice.   On Ifrael's chofen train,
Like vernal fhowers let endlefs bleffings rain: 670
Each rifing age, afcend thy glory higher,
With time roll on, and with the fkies expire!
But oh, my fons, this voice attentive hear;
Let thefe laft ftrains command the liftening ear!   675

    To unborn years I ftretch my raptur'd eyes;
I fee the promis'd feed in glory rife!
The etherial ftar triumphant mounts on high,
And fairer beams adorn the unmeasur'd fky:
All heaven impatient waits the facred morn;   680
Jefus defcends; the filial GOD is born:
Hofts of bright angels round the favorite fhine,
And earth is ravifh'd with their hymns divine.
'Tis he, whofe offering guilt fhall wafh away,
And raife Mankind to climes of ceafelefs day;   685
The blifs of truth, and virtue, fhall infpire,
And warm the bofom with feraphic fire.
Hafte, hafte, ye days of heaven! with rapid wing,
To this fad world the hope of nations bring!
Defcend, O Prince of peace! thy love beftow;   690
Cleanfe the dark foul from feeds of endlefs woe;
With all earth's myriads Jacob's fons unite,
And bid immortal glory fpring to light.
No more the gentile realms in duft fhall mourn;
Nor evening altars to th' infernals burn;   695
But wak'd, reviv'd, by thy celeftial name,
One cloud of incenfe, one unbounded flame,
To heaven afcend: the fun fhall brighter rife,
And peace, and light, and glory gild the fkies.

    Thus the great Seer; and warm'd with heavenly grace,
Befought all bleffings for his darling race;   700
Then up fam'd Pifgah's fide ferenely drew,
Where all Canäan met his rapturous view;

Thence his glad soul explor'd her native day,
And left, for bliss, the tenemental clay:
His soul, scarce lower than the angels made,   705
With glory mitred, and with truth array'd.
As the bold eagle, borne from humble vales,
Lifts his strong wings, and up th' expansion sails;
O'er groves, o'er hills, o'er mountains, wins his way,
And climbs exulting in the noon-tide ray;   710
Now far beneath him sees each birdling fly;
Now clouds light-floating skim the lower sky;
In prospect wide, with piercing ken, descries
Far, lessening towns, and spacious empires rise;
Here rivers wind, the lakes their borders spread;   715
And there the blue-seen ocean smooths his bed;
In pride sublime, he holds his upward way,
And basks, and triumphs, in the flame of day.
So, borne with angel-flight, his mighty mind,
Ascending, left the common wing behind;   720
Full on the sun's great Source superior drew,
'Till truth's wide regions stretch'd in glorious view:
There fair Creation spread her boundless plan;
There op'd, mysterious, all the world of man:
With every splendor bright Redemption shone;   725
And, one immense of beauty, God the Son.
Still up the heavens he wing'd his solar flight,
And soar'd, and mingled with unborrow'd light.
    Far in a wild vale's solitary gloom,
Jehovah form'd his favourite's lonely tomb;
For life distinguish'd, there his limbs refine,   730
'Till morn's last beams in purple glory shine;
Then, rob'd in beauty, shall the Prophet rise,
And sail, the peer of angels, thro' the skies.
    But, ere his spirit sought celestial day,
To Joshua's hand he gave the destin'd sway,   735
A Chief divine! with every virtue crown'd,
In combat glorious, and in peace renown'd,

To him the Almighty voice---Thy chosen hand
Shall guide my sons, and rule the promis'd land.   740
That land, where peace, and every pleasure reigns,
O'er heaven-topp'd hills, and fair, extended plains;
Where countless nations build the lofty dome,
Nurse purpling vines, and teach the vales to bloom;
That land is thine.   Where'er thy foot shall tread,   745
From the parch'd climes where Midian's thousands spread,
To realms, where Hazor, arm'd with potent sway,
Bids kingdoms bow, and conquer'd chiefs obey:
Or where Euphrates winds his gentle flight;
Or the broad ocean rolls in evening light;   750
All, all is thine.   Who dare thy course withstand,
Shall feel the fury of th' Eternal hand.
Lost in black crimes the torpid nations lie,
And claim fierce vengeance from an injur'd sky.
Rise, rise to arms! o'er Jordan's yielding flood   755
My guardian hand shall point the destin'd road.

     Thus spoke the fair: and while th' etherial strain
Breath'd a soft music o'er the wondering train,
With anxious look th' impatient monarch cried---
O best of maids, thy sex's noblest pride!   760
Far round the neighbouring realms by fame is rung
The wonderous race, thy lovely voice has sung.
Oft have I heard, how, arm'd with dreadful rod,
Before his votaries march'd their mighty God;
How kings in vain their rapid course oppos'd,   765
Their hosts all vanquish'd, and their empire clos'd.
But still, misled by Rumour's dubious tongue,
In sad suspense my mind all-anxious hung.
Now with clear truth the scenes tremendous shine;
Of force convinc'd, I own the Power divine.   770
And must our race with one wide doom expire?
These turrets sink? these walls be wrapt in fire?
Must yon bright maid, whose soft and lovely smile
Could murderers charm, and wolves of rage beguile;

These beauteous infants, scarce to reason born,   775
Sweeter than flowers perfume the vernal morn,
To war's unpitying fury yield their breath,
And helpless close their little eyes in death?
O thou great GOD, whose sway o'er heaven presides,
Whose searching eye the world's vast empire guides : 780
Stay, stay thine hand ; this guilty nation spare ;
Let these sweet babes thy boundless pity share !
Unform'd our infant prayer—but cries sincere
And honest hearts will find a bounteous ear.

    He spoke ; around, the melting voice of woe   785
Breath'd sad complaints, and tears began to flow ;
When thus the Prince again--O loveliest maid !
Where, where shall Gibeon find the needed aid ?
Can no kind hand the friendly refuge give ?
No pitying saviour bid my children live ?   790
Say, loveliest fair, canst thou no succour lend ?
Our teacher thou--be thou our guardian friend.
Perchance thy bounteous Ruler, form'd to bless,
O'er suppliant realms may lift the branch of peace.

    The maid return'd--perhaps a virgin's mind,   795
Though wisdom fail, the wish'd retreat may find.
To Israel's camp two trusty heroes send ;
Let me, restor'd, their peaceful steps attend.
The maid, thou seest by blest adoption shares
Their mighty Leader's fond, parental cares.   800
Pleas'd with the offering, Joshua's hand may give
The palm of peace, and bid thy nation live.

    Charm'd with the thought, joy sparkling in his eyes,
With voice exulting, strait the king replies.
O fair divine ! thy mind, with wisdom bright,   805
Even age out-soars, and climbs an angel's flight.
Let peace thy life surround.   The task be mine
Soon to prepare, and end the blest design.
Thy lovely voice must find a generous ear ;
So sweet a strain even oaks would bow to hear.   810

The Monarch spoke ; and o'er the circling throng
Bright smiles broke forth, and pleas'd applauses rung ;
A beauteous semblance of the fields around,
Starr'd with young flowers, and with gay verdure crown'd,
Where airy songs, soft proof of raptur'd love,   815
Wav'd on the gale, and echo'd thro' the grove ;
While the clear sun, rejoicing still to rise,
In pomp roll'd round immeasurable skies.

THE

CONQUEST OF CANÄAN:

BOOK III.

ARGUMENT.

Characters of Hexron, Irad, and Selima. Morning. Irad
and Selima walk out on the plain, northward of the camp,
and hold a conversation on the justice of the War. As
they are returning to the camp, they overhear two Israel-
ites conversing on a design of returning into Egypt. Irad
communicates the discovery to Joshua. The alarm is gi-
ven, and an army perceived, coming from Ai to attack
the camp. Joshua goes out to the place of rendezvous,
marshals a body of troops, and sends them, under the com-
mand of Zimri, to meet the army of Ai. In the mean
time the camp is in a general uproar, and a large body of
the Israelites assembled, westward of the camp, for the
purpose of returning into Egypt. After the confusion is in
a degree allayed, Tadmor harangues the insurgents, with
a list of grievances, and stimulates them to perseverance.
Caleb who, with Hexron, had been sent by Joshua, upon
Irad's information, to watch the motions of the camp, re-
plies to him. Ardan answers him, with impudence, and
Hexron him, with severity. Insurgents march. As they are
quitting the plain, Joshua comes out, with a body of troops
to attack them. The chieftains set their forces in array.
Joshua orders them to disperse. Ardan affronts him, and
is killed. The insurgents disperse, and the chiefs return
to the camp. Irad goes out to view the battle. Armies
engage with violence, and equal success ; until the chiefs
of Ai, influenced by superstitious fears, excited by the ap-
pearance of a thunder storm, order a retreat. Zimri also
retires. Scene of the beauties of an evening after the
storm concludes the book.

THE CONQUEST OF CANÄAN.

BOOK III.

OF Judah's thousands Hezron held the sway;
    And love, and reverence, bade them all obey.
The chief, of simple manners, knew no art;
Truth was his language; honesty his heart:
To bless mankind his life's unvaried end;   5
His guest the stranger, and the poor his friend.
    So fair his strong, and stubborn virtue shone,
Heaven crown'd his wishes with a lovely son.
To mould young Irad was his darling care;
To form for peace, to animate for war;   10
His limbs t' innerve; his vices to controul,
And lead to wisdom's fount his thirsty soul.
    In earliest years, the favourite Youth began
To shew those charms, which rarely grace the man.
To rashness brave, his bosom burn'd for fame;   15
Yet knew a milder, and a nobler flame:
Love's gentle fire his passions could controul,
And pure Religion warm'd his manly soul.
Not that, which broods upon the surly brow,
Or walks on frozen joints, demure, and slow;   20
At truth, and virtue, points the fatal wound,
Swells on the tongue, and vanishes in sound:
But that, whose influence fires th' angelic band;
Smooths the rough bosom; opes the narrow hand;

Serenely brightens in the cheerful face ;   25
Casts round each act unutterable grace ;
With rising morning, bows the secret knee,
And wafts, great God! the humble soul to thee.

His raptur'd father wish'd no second son ;
But found both parents' charms combin'd in one ;   30
His own strong sense, and daring thought, refin'd
By the soft graces of a mother's mind.
His lively duty cheer'd the waning year ;
With hand all gentle wip'd the aged tear ;
Explor'd each wish, prevented each request,   35
And thought it heaven to make a parent blest.
Nature's politeness, unaffected ease,
Mov'd in his limbs, and fram'd his soul to please ;
To worth complacent gave the just reward,
And notic'd humble life, with kind regard.   40

Nature can form the soul, or rough, or fine ;
But all her clouded beauties faintly shine :
Religion bids a new creation rise,
Fragrant as spring, and fair as spangled skies.
Thus, on the canvas, West, with raptur'd view,   45
Sees new-born worlds his magic hand pursue ;
Th' impassion'd forms dissolve in soft desire,
Or glow, and tremble, with seraphic fire ;
They breathe, they speak, they move, the field around,
And the ear listens for th' expected sound :   50
But these must fade : while Virtue's strokes shall live,
Transcend earth's sky-built tomb, and with the heavens
[revive.

Beyond his peers, by nature, Irad shone ;
By virtue, ripen'd to the duteous son ;
By virtue, aim'd at life's sublimest end,   55
Rose to the saint, and soften'd to the friend :
Pleas'd his fond nation saw his glories rise,
And a new Joshua charm'd their raptur'd eyes.

The virgins view'd, how could they not approve ?
Esteem's the silent harbinger of love.   60

The kind eye, gliftening with a frequent tear,
The confcious blufh, that faw difcovery near,
Th' unbidden figh, that fwell'd the beating breaft,
And the fix'd gaze, that fcarce could be reprefs'd,
The foft emotions to his eye reveal'd,   65
And new, ftrange tremors through his bofom thrill'd.

  But far o'er all Selima's charms prevail'd,
When his pleas'd heart her piercing eyes affail'd.
His youngeft birth, blefs'd Caleb own'd the fair,
His life's chief folace, and his favorite care.
Not nature's hand her beauty could improve ;   70
Her voice was melody ; her mind was love ;
Her ftature tall ; her air intrancing eafe ;
Her fkin the lilly, opening to the breeze ;
Her cheek was health's inimitable die,
And the bright foul fate fparkling in her eye.   75

  No vile cofmetic ftain'd her lovely face ;
No affectation murder'd real grace :
Her robes all neatnefs, told the world how fine,
How pure, th' angelic habitant within.
Sweetnefs etherial majefty controul'd,   80
And form'd an Irad of a fofter mould.
Such was her foul, as when, of darknefs born,
O'er young creation rofe beginning morn,
Fair, in her front, a blufhing Virtue ftood,
Juft fprung to life, and ey'd the forming God ;   85
From grace to grace with glowing wifdom grew,
And fmil'd, and triumph'd, in the rapturous view.

  Now twice nine years had o'er the fair-one roll'd,
Illum'd her eyes, and bade her charms unfold ;
When her quick fancy, felf-infpir'd to rove,   90
Attun'd her feelings to romantic love.
Oft on the youth fhe fix'd a fecret gaze,
And oft, with tranfport, liften'd to his praife.
The charms of face, the beauty of defert,
Stole foft, and filent, through her yielding heart.   95

I

Esteem, which hermits scarce could disapprove,
Bloom'd in his smiles; and open'd into love.

Nor shone her glances on his breast in vain;
The gaze, that gave, return'd the pleasing pain.   100
Judgment, in both, the spotless flame improv'd;
They lik'd from fancy, but from reason lov'd.

Oft would each sire his tender wish declare,
To see one band unite the lovely pair.
Oft sigh'd the youth t' unfold his anxious mind;   105
But still a modest fear his lips confin'd:
In pleas'd attention on her charms he hung,
And half-heard wishes trembled o'er his tongue.
At length, kind Heaven, propitious to the pair,
Led his fond steps, where love had led the fair.   110
In a lone walk, far-distant on the plain,
Surpriz'd, his tongue unbidden told his pain.
The beauteous maid, of frank and gentle mind,
Smil'd in his hopes, and bless'd with love refin'd,
In truth's mild beam the spotless union grew,   115
And gave such joy, as youthful angels knew.

Now wak'd the dim-seen dawn. O'er hills afar
Rose in gay triumph morn's refulgent star;
Up the gay skies fore-running beauty spread;
The grey mist sail'd along the mountain's head;   120
In clouds th' embosom'd lark her matin sings,
And from his couch impatient Irad springs,
To morn's unnumber'd sweets invites the fair,
Gay prospects, magic songs, and fragrant air.

Rapt with the charms, which nature gives to view   125
The great, the high, the beauteous, and the new,
To her soft power they bow'd the yielding mind,
Warm'd as they heard, and as they gaz'd refin'd;
In flowery tribes, where thousand splendors play;
When magic prospect holds the lingering day;   130
When brighten'd Evening spreads her gayest train,
And hails young Hesper to his native main;

In cloudy wilds, where gloomy thunder lies,
The pale moon mourns, and mountains prop the skies.

O'er northern plains serene the lovers stray,   135
And various converse charms their easy way---
How sweet, O fair---the Youth with rapture cries---
Earth's beauteous scenes, and wonders of the skies!
The folding clouds! the gates of morn unbarr'd!
The dewy plains, with flowery gems instarr'd!   140
The cliff-topp'd mountain! the deep-waving grove?
The air all odour! and the world all love!

Thrice fair are nature's works---the maid replied,
And her face bloom'd in beauty's living pride---
When round her fields my thoughts untroubled roll,   145
An easy joy steals softly on my soul:
Fir'd as I gaze, my breast with rapture warms,
Her glories ravish, and her music charms.
But oh the fate of Ai's unhappy field,
That every joy, and every hope, dispell'd!   150
Fled are the charms, that nature once attir'd
And lost the sweets, that ether once inspir'd.
As now through well-known paths, retir'd I stray,
And seek accustom'd beauties round my way;
At every turn, the seeming trump alarms,   155
Pale corses rise, and groans, and clashing arms;
From my pain'd bosom heaves th' unbidden sigh;
The still tear trembles in my labouring eye;
Lost, but to grief, my feet bewilder'd rove,
And my heart deadens to thyself, and love.   160
O fatal hapless combat! cause unjust!
That blends the noblest heroes with the dust;
From sad Canäan's sons their wealth demands,
The flocks they tended, and their cultur'd lands;
Bids o'er their peaceful domes destruction flame,   165
And blots with deep dishonour Israel's name.

The Prince rejoin'd, By all-creating Heaven,
To Abraham's sons these fruitful fields were given

Whate'er he made, the Maker claims his own ;
Gives, and refumes, advis'd and rul'd by none.   170
By him beftow'd, a righteous fword demands
Thefe flocks, thefe cities, and thefe promis'd lands,
Yet not 'till crimes, beyond long-fuffering great,
Had fill'd their cup, and fix'd their changelefs ftate,
Would Heaven permit our race its gift to claim,   175
Or feal the glory of th' almighty Name.
In vain mild Mercy hop'd their hearts to gain,
And Patience look'd for Penitence, in vain.
As rolling ftreams one courfe eternal keep,
All rufh impetuous down the guilty fteep.   180

The maid return'd, The nations' foul difgrace,
Stain'd with black guilt, I grant Canäan's race.
But not alike are all from virtue driven ;
Some, more than others, claim the fword of Heaven :
Yet undiftinguifh'd falls the general doom,   185
The beft, the worft, we deftine to the tomb.

Where Hazor's hundred towers majeftic rife,
Frown o'er her plains, and dare avenging fkies ;
In all that elegance of artlefs charms,
Which prompts mild love, and rival hate alarms ;   190
In that fweet union of ferene defires,
Which blows with fragrant breath unmingled fires ;
Young, beauteous fair-ones, through her regions known,
Outvie the maid, thou lov'ft to call thy own.
To thefe bright virgins chofen Irads bow ;   195
Lefs wife, lefs virtuous, and lefs fair than thou ;
But crown'd with many a grace ; of thoughts refin'd,
Of pleafing perfon, and of dauntlefs mind.
Shall this blefs'd train, fo young, fo fair, fo brave,
Fall, with black wretches, in a firey grave ?   200
Or round wild regions muft they haplefs roam,
Exil'd from joy, and forc'd from cheerful home ?
To hunger, thirft, and forrow, fink and pray,
And breathe, with lingering death, their lives away,

Should'ft thou, when war to Salem drives her courfe,
Seize the keen fteel, and join the conquering force,   206
While thy bold breaft with glory's warmth beats high,
And wreaths well-twin'd approach thy ravifh'd eye,
To fome lone hamlet loofely wandering come,
Where fimple fwains had built their peaceful home,   210
Where care in filence fmoothly pafs'd away,
And home-bred happinefs deceiv'd the day;
Should there fweet, helplefs children meet thy view,
Fair as young rofebuds look thro' early dew,
With infant wonder, on thine armour gaze,   215
And point, with artlefs hands, the fteely blaze :
Say could thy heart one angry purpofe know,
Or doom fuch cherubs to a fingle woe ?
Charm'd by foft fmiles, I fee thy heart retire,
And mild compaffion breathe a gentler fire ;   220
Thy love parental o'er them kindly yearn,
Prompt pleafing hope, and all their wifhes learn ;
Thy bounteous hand each needed blifs beftow,
And in the angel lofe th' intended foe.

   Yet fhould dread war o'er thefe fair regions fly, 225
Unnumber'd virgins, bright as thofe muft die ;
To flames unnumber'd babes refign their breath,
And ere life bloffoms, meet untimely death.

   To thee, O prince ! without a blufh, I own
Such woes tremendous freeze my heart to ftone.   230
Ere Irad's arm fuch precious lives deftroy,
Let me, far guiltier, ceafe from every joy ;
Quick to the dreary grave my form defcend,
Our love all vanifh, and our union end.

   The Prince replied, Blefs'd gentlenefs of mind !   235
The grace, the glory of a heart refin'd !
When new-born, helplefs beings meet our eyes,
In noble minds, fuch thoughts refiftlefs rife :
Even brutes, when young, our tender wifhes try,
And love forbids the infant whelp to die   240

Yet oft this kindest impulse of the soul
Bids wild desire in murmuring tumults roll,
And blames the Power, whose love alone, to earth,
And all earth's drear and dark events, gave birth.

In thy pure bosom, angels must approve.   245
For sad Canäan's youth, this generous love.
But once as fair, as young, as soft as they,
As white with innocence, with smiles as gay,
Were those black throngs, whose crimes as mountains rise,
And wipe out pity from th' all bounteous skies.   250
As eggs innoxious, oft in meadows strew'd,
Break into asps, and pour the viper's brood ;
Nurs'd in rank soils, to strength the reptiles grow,
Resound the hiss, the sting of vengeance throw,
Uprear the crest, inroll the snaky spire,   255
Light the keen eye-ball with terrific fire ;
From fields, and forests, death, and poison gain,
And scatter wide destruction round the plain :
So, harmless once, by vile affections lur'd,
In guilt, and years, those babes alike matur'd ;   260
Athirst for sin, all patterns left behind,
The form all putrid, poison'd all the mind,
To every crime, to every madness, driven,
Curs'd the sad world, and hiss'd the name of Heaven.
There the sot reels, the murderer prowls for blood ;   265
There the starv'd orphan sues in vain for food ;
For man man burns, with Sodom's tainted flame,
And the world sickens with incestuous shame.
Even nature's ties their bosoms bind no more,
Wives wade in nuptial, sires in filial gore ;   270
To howling Molock blooming babes expire,
And mothers round them dance, and light the funeral fire,
     Should then these infants to dread manhood rise,
What unheard crimes would smoke thro' earth and skies !
What hosts of demons sin's dark realm would gain !   275
How hell gape hideous round Canäan's plain !

This sea of guilt unmeasur'd to prevent,
Our chosen race eternal Justice sent,
At once the bright possession to reclaim,
And 'gainst its victims point the vengeful flame,   280
Thus crimes their due and dire reward shall know;
Thus God be witness'd sin's unchanging foe;
From land to land Jehovah's glory shine,
And fear, and homage, wait the Name divine.

But, O unrivall'd maid! the kindest doom   285
These babes may destine to an early tomb.
To manhood risen their guilt, beyond controul,
Would blot their names from life's celestial roll.
Now, in fair climes, their souls, forever bless'd,
May bloom in youth, and share immortal rest;   290
And hail the boundless grace, that snatch'd its foes
From sins unnumber'd, and from lasting woes.

And, O bright maid! whate'er high Heaven design'd
Is just, is glorious to th' omniscient Mind.
When Heaven commands, the virtuous ask no more: 295
His will is justice, as his arm is power:
Led by his voice, our cause divine we know;
We tempt no evil, and we fear no foe.

All gentle Youth! Selima soft replied---
How well thy words from falsehood truth divide!   300
With what sweet tenderness, thy voice displays
The truth, the lustre, of th' Eternal ways.
But say, bless'd Prince! will Heaven our race succeed?
Shall we victorious gain the darling meed?
So oft our host rebellion blackens o'er,   305
I fear, lest triumph crown our arms no more.
When will the friendly cloud again return?
When o'er yon dome the nightly glory burn?

Rejoin'd the smiling Prince; too anxious maid,
Let faithless terror ne'er thy heart invade,   310
To Abraham seal'd, the sacred covenant stands---
Thy countless sons shall rule Canaan's lands.---

Guilt's impious frain thefe tumults fhall deftroy ;
Too vile, too bafe, to fhare the promis'd joy.
And he, whofe foul, a plant for earth too fair,   315
Has grown, and ripen'd for a kinder air,
Full foon may feel the hand of blafting time,
By Heaven tranfplanted to a nobler clime,
Pafs the cold winter of the frozen tomb,
And rife, and flourifh in eternal bloom.   320

    But to glad fields, beyond thofe hills that lie,
'And drink mild influence from the weftern fky,
The reft triumphant foon fhall wing their way,
Seize their vaft towns, and reign from fea to fea.

    Then join'd in love, in bands connubial join'd,   325
Each paffion calm'd, and every tafte refin'd,
Our fears fhall end, unclouded hope begin,
Peace' gentle morning o'er Canaan fhine ;
In foft beatitude the feafons roll,
And growing union mix the kindred foul.   330

    The maid return'd---O day fupremely fair !
Not blooming Eden own'd a happier pair.
But, Youth belov'd ! my bofom, rack'd with pain,
Tells me, fad tale ! the darling wifh is vain.
Tells me that chofen morn will never come,   335
Nor blifs be finifh'd, but beyond the tomb.
For earth too bright were thefe love-lighted fires !
Too blefs'd th' indulgence of fuch pure defires !
Here unallay'd, no lot, no joy appears ;
Grief poifons hope, and pleafures mix with tears.   340

    Ah faireft, wifeft, lovelieft of thy kind !
Of form all finifh'd' and of matchlefs mind !
Sweet-fmiling vifitant from yonder fky !
Too bright to live, and O too dear to die !
Why, haplefs Mina ! why from friends, and home,   345
Didft thou, unguided, in the wild wood roam ?
Perhaps the hungry wolf around thy way
Lurk'd with grim rage, and feiz'd his helplefs prey.

Perhaps, O lot of anguish ! brutal men
Thy path unguarded, with fell eyes, have seen. 350
Or dost thou pale, unseen, unburied, lie,
Sad sorrow's victim, in th' inclement sky ?
How soon is thy fair course of glory run !
Thy hopes all ended ! all thy duties done !
Sleep, lovely maid ! in hollow'd silence rest, 355
Let fragrant gales thy form with leaves invest ;
There with new sweets, the lovely wild-rose bloom,
And pitying strangers raise thy verdant tomb.

   Ah hapless maid ! the tender prince rejoin'd---
How thy rich graces charm'd each generous mind ! 360
Even Joshua's love how nobly didst thou claim,
Thy wishes virtue, and thy actions fame !
When his toils rose, when dangers dire opprefs'd,
And Israel's griefs hung heavy on his breast,
Thy gentle mind, a soul-supporting stay, 365
Seren'd those toils, and charm'd those griefs away ;
A calm retreat from fear, and doubt, and strife,
And all the hidden pangs of scepter'd life.
Rest in mild slumbers, lovely maiden ! rest ;
Thy life be copied, and thy memory blefs'd ! 370
Each soft-eyed virgin bid thy fame revive,
Attune her lyre, and in her actions live ;
So, join'd with thee, in beauty's distant clime,
Her praise shall triumph o'er the death of time.

   As thus the converse pafs'd, with many a tear, 375
To the still camp approach'd the sadden'd pair.
In th' utmost skirt, a tent at distance stood ;
Whence mingling voices, scarce-distinguish'd, flow'd.
Heard'st thou--a warrior low his zeal exprefs'd--
When generous Hanniel Jacob's sons addrefs'd ? 380
How on his words the thousands listening hung !
How sweet persuasion charm'd us from his tongue !
From pride, from pomp, from love of titles free,
He loves the poor ; he feels for thee and me.

Oh, could our tribes by sad experience learn   385
What children tell, and what the blind discern,
Him for their leader would they raptur'd claim,
And fly from endless toil, and endless shame.
From hideous war my wearied soul recoils ;
I ask no treasures rais'd from battle's spoils.   390
To painful arms let sons of slaughter run ;
By them be glory's painted bubble won :
To peace, of aims far different, would I fly,
In peace inglorious live, inglorious die :
While peace, while plenty, much-lov'd Egypt knows,
Hears no shrill trump, and dreads no banded foes,   395
These boasted flocks, and towns, and promis'd fields,
To them my first, last wish delighted yields.

    With earnest voice, his fellow pleas'd replies---
Since toil and pain have taught thee to be wise,   400
Know, my brave friend, a secret, faithful band
Soon point their course to Egypt's darling land.
When first to combat Joshua bends his way,
To guard the camp these bold associates stay';
With one firm heart, our path we then begin,   405
And noble Hanniel leads the bless'd design.
But hush'd in silence must these counsels rest,
Scarce even to tried, and faithful friends confess'd ;
Lest the dread Chief's all-watchful, piercing eye,
With sun-like ken, the hated plot descry.   410
Thou know'st what ills a plot disclos'd attend ;
Our names must perish, and our lives must end.

    His friend return'd---The lov'd, the bold design
My glad soul welcomes, and my hand shall join.
Hail happy tidings ! hail auspicious fields !   415
Where genial nature every pleasure yields---
Too bless'd, to that sweet native land I fly,
That cot, that heritage, that friendly sky---
Dear scenes of youth ! where peace and pleasure mild,
With cheerful health, and ceaseless plenty smil'd---   420

Might these, O envied lot! again be given,
'Twere bliss too great : I claim no higher heaven.

This heard, Selima to her tent withdrew ;
While strait to Joshua ardent Irad flew,
To him, apart, the dangerous plot disclos'd,   425
And what the tribe, and where the tent, expos'd.
As some fond parent eyes his darling child,
Pleas'd, the great Hero on the favourite smil'd,
His zeal, his prudence prais'd, and on his head
Besought the Heavens their choicest bliss to shed.   430

Mean time from distant guards a cry ascends,
And round the camp the dinning voice extends ;
Th' alarming trump resounds ; the martial train
Pour from the tents, and crowd th' accustom'd plain.
In mazy wanderings, thickening, darkening, roll,   435
Fill all the field, and shade the boundless pole.
As where proud Erie winds her narrowing shores,
And o'er huge hills a boiling ocean pours,
The long white-sheeted foam, with fury hurl'd,
Down the cliffs thundering, shakes the stable world, 440
In solemn grandeur clouds of mist arise,
Top the tall pines, and heavy, seek the skies :
So spread the volumes of the dust afar ;
So roar the clamors of commencing war.

Anxious, and active, there the Leader strode,   445
Nerv'd every heart, and steel'd for death and blood ;
From rank to rank, he hush'd the tumult's sound,
And spread deep silence o'er th' attentive ground :
Then while the chiefs combin'd the dread array,
Tow'rd a high rock he bent his rapid way ;   450
From the tall height, to Ai he cast his eyes,
And saw, in southern fields, her squadrons rise ;
A cloud, far-spreading, o'er the plain impell'd,
Roll'd up th' expanse, and wrapp'd the gloomy field ;
Approaching, widening, slow the darkness came,   455
Emblaz'd with gleams of intermitted flame.

So, long and black, like fkirts of rifing even,
Thick clouds, now gathering, fill'd the northern heaven ;
Borne on flow winds, that ceafelefs chang'd its form,
O'er the dark mountains fail'd th' expanding ftorm ; 460
In rifing grandeur far-off thunders roll,
Dim lightnings flafh, and gild the clouded pole ;
More wide, more vaft, the folemn gloom afcends,
And frowning, deepening, round th' horizon bends.

At once the Hero gave the loud command ;   465
In awful filence mov'd the chofen band ;
Compact, to Ai they cours'd their dreadful way,
And generous Zimri rul'd the long array,

Mean time new fcenes around the camp began,
The tribes all motion, man confus'd with man ;   470
From tent to tent fwift-haftening feet appear'd ;
Low-murmuring voices, mingling founds were heard ;
Loud, and more loud, the earneft clamors grow,
Hum through the tents, and all the camp o'erflow.
To Egypt's realms---refounds the general cry---   475
From thefe fad fcenes, with profperous feet, we fly,
Thefe hofts of foes, thefe fields of ceafelefs fight,
This fway of bondage, and this war of flight.
Hafte, freedom's fons, and feize her happy fhores,
For all her peace, and wealth, and joy, are yours.   480
Thus round the hoft the mingled clamor flew,
And loud, and fierce, debates tumultuous grew ;
They urg'd, perfuaded, threaten'd, flatter'd, cried,
With love conjur'd, with ftubborn breaft denied ;
Friends left their friends, with anfwering look fevere, 285
Sigh'd fad departure, dropp'd th' expreffive tear ;
From parents children headlong burft away,
While groans recall'd them from the dire affray ;
To brothers brothers gave the parting hand,
And Virtue eyed, with tears, the fwerving band.   490
All drefs'd in arms, and cloth'd in rich array,
Forth from the camp the warriors bent their way :

Their hands their gold, and favourite treasures bore,
And each fond bosom hail'd th' Egyptian shore.
O'er the broad circuit of the western plain,   495
From all sides gathering, mov'd the numerous train,
This way, and that, in thousand paths impell'd,
Immingling, rushing, darkening, hid the field,
To one great central phalanx swiftly driven,
Gloom'd the sad ground, and cast a shade on heaven, 500
Frowning, and fierce, expanded o'er the plain,
And, proud of numbers, deem'd resistance vain.

Of name obscure, before th' increasing throng
Two haughty chieftains proudly stalk'd along ;
Felt all the joys, which little minds o'errun,   505
From sway first tried, and influence scarce begun ;
Look'd wise, inportant hurried o'er the field ;
Commanded, question'd, with loud threats compell'd ;
Spoke with stern voice ; advising, wavering stood,
And scarce the ground was printed, where they trode. 510

Far round the plain the mingled tumult ran,
Chief answer'd chief, and man rehears'd to man.
Thro' each small circle loud the murmur spread,
Of spoils ungiven, virtues unrepaid,
Woes unextinguish'd, labours ne'er to end,   515
The starving houshold, and the naked friend---
Where now's the heart, that bless'd the prophet's sway,
That sooth'd the tribes, and bade the soul obey,
Swept Bashan's fields, o'erthrew proud Sihon's throne,
And to poor warriors left the spoils they won ?   520
But now new chiefs, in wiles and learning train'd,
Wield a dread sceptre, with an iron hand ;
All, all but Hanniel ; Hanniel singly glows
With Israel's good, and weeps for Israel's woes.
Hail then, oh hail the bless'd, auspicious day,   525
That opes to brighter realms our happy way !
The chiefs, we chose, the glorious path shall guide,
Uncurs'd with learning, and unstain'd with pride.

Thus round the plain the tumult shrill resounds ;
Of different note, immix unnumber'd sounds ;   530
High toss'd in ether helms confus'dly fly,
And clashing shields to clashing shields reply :
Loud, hoarse, and rough, wide jars discordant noise,
And raging passions swell the clamorous voice.
So, where on ocean's brim the long beach winds,   535
Breaks his proud waves, and all his fury binds,
Unnumber'd fowls, of various wing, arise,
And toss in wild gyrations to the skies ;
From each harsh throat hard strains of discord roar,
Break with dire din, and grate along the shore ;   540
Loud, and more loud, the nations heaven deform,
Or gloom the strand, and croak the coming storm.

    As round the plain the mingled tumult ran,
Tadmor, the elder chieftain, thus began---
Hail, sons of freedom ! Jacob's fairest boast !   545
Heirs of the sky, and virtue's genuine host !
Well did brave Hanniel teach, in words divine,
How fast our tribes, with toils, and griefs, decline ;
Full well he mark'd what deep designs are laid
By chiefs, of man, nor truth, nor Heaven, afraid ;   550
That, swell'd with pride, and train'd in artful lore,
O'erleap all right, and crush the hapless poor.
To us no leader tells the deep design,
What hosts oppose us, and what lands combine ;
What towns are next besieg'd ; what dangers tried ;   555
What spoils are won, and who those spoils divide.
In Egypt's realm the long-wish'd rule to gain,
They found each art, and each bold effort, vain :
Thence thro' the waste they urg'd our fatal way,
And hop'd, in this dire land, untroubled sway ;   560
Yet there the poor a lot far happier found,
With fasts unburden'd, and with rites unbound :
Our tributes paid, at plenteous feasts we sate,
Stretch'd in soft ease, and every dainty ate.

Oh, why from thofe fair regions did we come ?   565
Why, blind and headlong, leave our darling home ?
Here our own leaders Egypt's kings outdo,
And change of lords is all the good we know.

Hafte then, from thefe dread fields of mifery fly ;
With chiefs you chofe again to Egypt hie ;   570
Where eafe, and wines, and feafts, and foft delight,
Earth ever fruitful, fkies forever bright,
Awake fweet pleafure, raptur'd love revive,
And teach poor mortals what it is to live :
Now feize the hour, by Jofhua's folly given,   575
Or op'd for Ifrael by a pitying Heaven.
Ai's gallant fons will fweep his hoft away,
Worne by long labours, and to fafts a prey ;
Or, fcap'd the field, their weary feet muft fail ;
Or, join'd in fight, our arms will foon prevail ;   580
This day beyond purfuit our courfe removes,
And leaves the tyrant to the flaves he loves.

He fpoke ; at once, from all th' impatient train,
A buft of triumph fhook the founding plain ;
Thence rofe the fhout ; as oft the heavens replied ; 585
And, borne thro' fields, and woods, the far-off murmur died.
Thus, when the vernal ftorm forbears to rave,
And the wild river fwells his torrent wave,
Huge ifles of ice, along the clifted fhore.
Float flow, and cumbrous ; folemn thunders roar,   590
In deep gradations, rife, and burft, and roll,
Wave o'er the founding hills, and leffen to the pole.

When firft from Jofhua faithful Irad went,
He fummon'd Judah's heroes to his tent,
Bade them the tribes with prudent caution eye,   595
Purfue their motions, and their views defcry,
Their tumults hufh, or fhould their efforts fail,
With fpeed to him convey th' unpleafing tale.
When round the camp diforder'd fcenes began,
Strait to the found th' attentive heroes ran ;   600

Watch'd all the murmurs of the gathering train,
And follow'd anxious to the troubled plain ;
But firſt the tidings to the Leader ſped,
What bands aſſembled, and what chieftains led,
Urg'd him with haſte to arm a numerous force,   605
And 'gainſt th' inſurgents bend his rapid courſe.

And now, when Tadmor ceas'd, the ſhouts decay'd,
With ſweet, mild accent, thus grave Caleb ſaid---
How ſlight the toil, miſtaking chief, to prove
'Tis wiſdom's voice directs the path, we love !   610
Though thorns, though ſerpents hedge the fatal way,
The fond heart bids, and anſwering feet obey.
Each truth, each argument, thy voice runs o'er,
Forbids our hoſt to ſeek th' Egyptian ſhore.
The waſte's dire ills thy plaintive words reſound,   615
Yet through that waſte the darling realm is found ;
Again thoſe countleſs woes our race muſt try ;
Again with toil, and thirſt, and famine, die.
Or ſhall we flee, by Hazor's bands compell'd,
To meet fierce Amalek, in the hoſtile field.   620
Wili hoſts that tremble, where Ai's ſons appear,
Abide the conflict, when Philiſtia's near.

But to what end, againſt unnumber'd foes,
Shall Iſrael war to gain Egyptian woes ;
Shame, vice, idolatry, and bondage, join'd,   625
The wrath of Heaven, and hiſſing of mankind ?
If war is deſtin'd Iſrael's fearful doom,
With war, let freedom, wealth, and glory come :
Let peace, let realms, let empire crown the toil ;
The world applaud us, and th' Eternal ſmile   630
In this fair land, ſhall each poor warrior reign
Lord of himſelf, and monarch of the plain.
His houſe, his herd, his harveſt all his own,
And changeleſs law tranſmit them to his ſon.
But Egypt's wealth her king alone commands,   635
Her ſons, her gold, her products, and her lands.

For him our hands, in flavifh woe, muſt toil,
And pamper fplendor on the beggar's fpoil,
Poor beyond thought, fufpended on a breath,
Our life a fufferance, and a nod our death.   640
    But Ifrael's chiefs are train'd in dangerous lore,
And hence regardlefs of the humble poor.
Say, Tadmor, fay, the wiles of art to fhun,
To Egypt's realms impatient doft thou run?
To courts, to lords, with fmooth deceit o'erhung,   645
Where art firſt budded, and where learning fprung?
Truth, confcience, Heaven, thine idle dreams deny;
Repent, return; nor, fnar'd by treafons, die.
    The hero fpoke.   From all the angry train
A rifing murmur wav'd along the plain: 650
As 'twixt tall hills, where rufhing torrents roll,
A flow, and lingering groan afcends the pole;
Thro' gloomy caverns hums the folemn found,
Fills all the hollow realm, and fhakes the fhady ground.
    Ardan, the younger chieftain, quick return'd,   655
And from his eye-balls kindling fury burn'd---
Imperious prince, I know thy heart of ſteel
Ne'er lov'd the poor, and never knew to feel.
But that proud voice, which aw'd my breaſt before,
Now fails to rule, and guides the hoſt no more.   660
I mock thy threats, thy utmoſt power defy,
Thy reafons trample, and thy words deny.
Chang'd is the fcene.   Thy pride muſt now obey
In worth thy betters, and thy lords in fway.
Go tell yon flaves, that bafe, and beſtial train, 665
Thy arts, thy arguments, and threats are vain;
Bid them their friends, their gallant brethren fee,
A hoſt of heroes, daring to be free,
Of numbers countlefs, bravery never aw'd,
Dup'd by no laws, and blinded by no God,   670
Their courfe now bending to the bliisful fhore,
Where peace and plenty bid the cup run o'er:

While they, poor reptiles ! in dread bondage lie,
Drag life in mifery, and unburied die.
Hafte, hafte, ere vengeance on thy helmet light,   675
And plunge thee fwift to everlafting night.

Bafe, reptile mifcreant !---Hezron fierce replied---
Go dream of Egypt ; fwell thine infect pride ;
Thy wings expand ; around thy dunghill fly ;
Buzz thy fmall moment, and forgotten die.   680
For know, vain wretch ! the voice of peace is o'er ;
The hand of Mercy lifts her branch no more ;
To fpeed thy doom impatient Juftice flies,
And wings the vengeance of affronted fkies.

The hero fpoke.   A rifing hifs began,   685
And round the plain contemptuous murmurs ran :
Quick tow'rd the camp the princes bent their courfe,
And, turn'd to Egypt, mov'd the rebel force.
Their ftandard rofe : a fhout to heaven afcends,
And wide, and deep, the gloomy hoft extends.   690
Far round the files each cafts exulting eyes ;
Each feels the prowefs of his arm arife :
By pride their force, their numbers doubled o'er,
All foes defpis'd, and Jofhua fear'd, no more ;
From voice to voice the haughty tale rebounds,   695
And air re-echoes with the mingling founds.

As near the diftant groves the warriors drew,
And homeward caft a lingering, parting view ;
Behold ! in eaftern fields, a numerous train
Pour'd from the camp, and haften'd o'er the plain.   700
There trembled Ephraim's enfign in the fkies ;
There the bull's vengeance blaz'd from wrathful eyes ;
In act to wound, with threatening horns, he ftood,
Felt his vaft ftrength, and fnuff'd his rival's blood.
Behind the mighty Chief, in pomp, impell'd,   705
The darkening phalanx widen'd o'er the field ;
Sublime, the Hero wing'd his dreadful way,
And round the rebels fhed a dire difmay.

Amaz'd, the chieftains saw his haftening courfe,
And rang'd, with active fpeed, their numerous force ; 710
In wild, diforder'd ranks, confus'd they flood,
Spoke founding boafts, and thirfted loud for blood.

As near the noify fquadrons Jofhua drew,
Round the rude files he caft a fearching view ;
For Hanniel's fteps he gaz'd ; but gaz'd in vain,   715
Nor found the hero on the troubled plain.
For well his mind, by fad experience, knew
What fearful ills defeated plots purfue,
How fway accuftom'd, faction wild o'erthrows,
And fudden tumults end in certain woes.   720
Thence, to his tent by cautious thoughts confin'd,
Disjointed counfels throng'd his reftlefs mind ;
He view'd, he wifh'd ; but knew the wifh was vain,
And boded ruin to his favorite train.

Too wife the Chief, too fix'd the hoft, he faw ;   725
Too firm th' obedience to the facred law ;
In fullen filence mourn'd his lot fevere,
And wail'd devoted treafon, with a tear.

High in the van, the Leader rais'd his voice,
The hofts all trembling at the dreadful noife---   730
Hafte to your tents, with fwift obedience hafte,
That Mercy's veil may hide the follies paft ;
Hafte, ere this hand, by injur'd juftice driven,
Plunge in your breafts, th' avenging fword of Heaven :
Your Maker's voice, with confcious fpeed, obey,   735
And let deep forrow wafh your guilt away.

Thus he.   Bold Ardan with fhrill voice replied---
Let no vain hope inflate thy fwelling pride---
Know, proud, mif-deeming leader ! Heaven defign'd
Jacob's brave fons to bow with willing mind ;   740
The chiefs, we freely chofe, our hearts obey,
And crouch no more, obfequious to thy fway.
To happier realms, with profperous feet, we go,
And leave thy bondmen here to every woe ;

Leave them to toil, to groan, to mourn their doom,   745
Languish out life, and die without a tomb :
While we, fair freedom's sons, superior fly
To peace, and transport, in a kinder sky.

   The Chief disdain'd return.   With wrathful look,
His eyes stream'd terror, as the culprit spoke ;   750
Forth from the van, with awful port, he strode ;
O'er his bright arms reflected lightnings glow'd ;
With lifted hand, he drove th' avenging blade,
And plung'd proud Ardan swift to endless shade.
Th' astonish'd train, like hunted harts impell'd,   755
Scatter'd in headlong terror, o'er the field.

So, on heaven's plain when war and tumult sprung,
By Britain's pride, and earth's bright Phœnix, sung,
When Satan, madden'd with Tartarean rage,
Dar'd Michael's sword, and Michael's might engage ;
In pomp divine the great Archangel stood ;   761
A sun's broad splendors round his forehead glow'd ;
Down his long wings thick, branching lightnings fell ;
Dire as ten thunders, rush'd his flaming steel ;
Th' Apostate sunk ; fear wing'd the rebel train,   765
Swift as the rapid whirlwind, o'er th' empyreal plain.

   Pleas'd, the great chief, and Judah's heroes view'd
The flying train, by guilt and fear subdued ;
While to high heaven their grateful praises rose,
Whose guardian hand had sav'd from countless woes. 770
Then loud the cries proclaim---to Egypt's land
Whatever wretch shall lure a guilty land,
By stones oppress'd, his life shall fall a prey,
And dread oblivion sweep his name away.

   While thus the rod of vengeance Joshua sway'd, 775
And the dread tumults of the plain decay'd,
Th' approaching hosts, at distance, Irad view'd,
And Zimri's thousands, with glad feet pursued,
Trac'd all the pomp of war, with wild delight,
And wish'd, unarm'd, to share th' impending fight. 780

Like ocean's waves, the sons of Ai were driven,
And lowering Israel cast a gloom on heaven ;
Proud chiefs, in golden splendor, trod the plain,
And tower'd majestic o'er the vulgar train.
So, straight and tall, beyond the forest fair,   785
The pine, ambitious, stands without a peer ;
O'er every grove beholds his boughs ascend,
Oaks climb beneath, and humble cedars bend ;
Shares the mild winds, the sullen storm defies,
And towers, and waves, and wantons, in the skies ;   790
In pride sublime, demands the sylvan reign,
And glows, and triumphs, in immortal green.

   As now the tempest hid the orb of day,
The threatening fronts approach'd, in dark array ;
Swift through th' expansion clouds of arrows fly ;   795
Stones shower on stones, and whizz along the sky ;
Sing the shrill strings ; the hissing darts resound ;
From clanging bucklers rattling pebbles bound ;
Now here, now there, the warriors fall ; amain
Groans murmur ; armour sounds ; and shouts convulse the
   With deep amaze, the sons of Ai beheld   [plain. 800
Their foes, with ardour, tempt the deathful field.
For now, elate, they fought the early fight,
To certain victory march'd with fierce delight ;
And fondly hop'd, ere Oran's hosts should come,   805
To seal devoted Israel's hapless doom.
But vain their hopes ; for with firm duty strong,
Undaunted Zimri fir'd the martial throng---
Now, warriors, now--the glowing leader cried---
Shall Israel's arms regain their ravish'd pride ;   810
Ai now shall learn, untaught our force to slight,
What virtue warms us to the generous fight :
That one lost field shall ne'er our race dismay,
Nor shame, nor terror, stain the glorious day.

   While thus untroubled thoughts his words confess'd, 815
All-anxious fears disturb'd his boding breast.

The hoft he knew diftruftful of the fky,
Propenfe to terror, and prepar'd to fly ;
He faw them fad move lingering o'er the plain,
New arm their foes, and double all their train :   820
And the great Chief a ftrong injunction gave,
Each poft with care to guard, each band to fave,
Each opening fair for wife retreat t' imbrace
To tempt no lofs, and hazard no difgrace.
But far beyond his thoughts, the found of war,   825
The clafh of arms, the fhouts that rend the air,
Th' infpiring tumults of the dreadful plain,
New ftrung their nerves, and rous'd their hopes again.
In quick oblivion, flight and fear were loft;
Increafing ardours every bofom tofs'd ;   830
Firm-wedg'd, unfhaken, rufh'd the darkening train ;
Spears flew ; air murmur'd ; corfes heap'd the plain ;
One flight of twinkling arms, all ether fhone ;
Earth roar'd one fhout confus'd, one mingled groan ;
Each hoft prefs'd eager; each difdain'd to fly ;   835
And wide confufion blended earth and fky.

   Mean time the ftorm, along dark mountains driven,
Hung o'er the plain, and wrapp'd the mid-day heaven ;
More frequent lightnings blaz'd the fkies around,
And peals more dreadful fhook the folid ground.   840
From the black clouds the whirlwinds burft amain,
Scour'd all the groves, and rag'd along the plain ;
Beneath, huge fhouts the murmuring concave rend,
And drifts of duft in gloomy pomp afcend.

   With boding hearts, the chiefs of Ai furvey'd   845
The fun's pure fplendor loft in cloudy fhade ;
The fun, their god, his fmiling face withdrew,
And round the world a fearful darknefs flew :
Hence unapprov'd they deem'd the doubtful day,
And fcann'd, with careful looks their homeward way : 850
As thus they backward gaz'd, the driving rain
Rufh'd, with impetuous fury, o'er the plain ;

Fierce down th' expansion streaming torrents shower'd,
And blood-stain'd brooks along the champain pour'd.
The clash of arms, the long-resounding cries   855
Wav'd o'er the world a hoarse, tumultuous noise ;
From heaven's huge vault loud-rolling thunders came,
And lightnings blaz'd insufferable flame.
Then sad, dishearten'd, from the dreadful fire
Ai's generous leaders bade their host retire.   860
Reluctant, slow, disdaining base defeat,
From Israel's sons the grisly ranks retreat ;
Surpriz'd, fierce Israel see their backward course,
Hang o'er their rear, and press with gathering force ;
Intenser shouts ascend ; the lightning's flame   865
Casts o'er the shields a strong alternate gleam ;
Loud thunders roll ; the fields all quake around ;
And the rain rushing roars along the ground.
Then Zimri's piercing voice, with stern commands,
Restrains the fury of his eager bands.   870
So fierce the thousands burn for raging war,
Even single warriors urge their foes afar ;
'Till near the chief, they see the standard rise,
While yet the tempest fills the midway skies,
Then deep-embosom'd in th' obscuring rain,   875
Their foes untroubled cross the homeward plain.

  Mean time the winds were pass'd, the storm was o'er,
And streaming torrents ceas'd from heaven to pour ;
Strait to the camp, by Zimri's voice compell'd,
The bands slow-moving cross'd the spacious field.   880
With joy, the chief revolv'd the troubled day,
The fate, and influence of the fierce affray ;
Ai, in fierce conflict, fail'd the wreath to gain,
And Israel, dauntless, trod the skirmish'd plain ;
He saw the host again to combat won   885
Their hopes new-kindled, and their terror gone ;
Thence his own bosom boding fear dispell'd,
And promis'd triumph on the future field.

And now the Youth they pass'd, as, with fond eyes,
He saw the varying fate of combat rise ; 890
To him, deep-pondering, blew the storm in vain,
Scarce heard the peals, or mark'd the battering rain :
'Till Ai, retir'd, the doubtful strife resign'd,
And calm'd the tumults of his anxious mind.

Then gentler scenes his rapt attention gain'd, 895
Where GOD'S great hand in clear effulgence reign'd,
The growing beauties of the solemn even,
And all the bright sublimities of heaven.
Above tall western hills, the light of day
Shot far the splendors of his golden ray ; 900
Bright from the storm, with tenfold grace he smil'd,
The tumult soften'd, and the world grew mild.
With pomp transcendant, rob'd in heavenly dies,
Arch'd the clear rainbow round the orient skies ;
Its changeless form, its hour of beam divine, 905
Fair type of truth, and beauty ; endless shine,
Around th' expanse, with thousand splendors rare,
Gay clouds sail'd wanton through the kindling air ;
From shade to shade, unnumber'd tinctures blend;
Unnumber'd forms of wonderous light extend ; 910
In pride stupendous, glittering walls aspire,
Grac'd with bright domes, and crown'd with towers of fire,
On cliffs cliffs burn ; o'er mountains mountains roll :
A burst of glory spreads from pole to pole :
Rapt with the splendor, every songster sings, 915
Tops the high bough, and claps his glistening wings :
With new-born green, reviving nature blooms,
And sweeter fragrance freshening air perfumes.

Far south the storm withdrew its troubled reign ;
Descending twilight dimm'd the dusky plain ; 920
Black night arose ; her curtains hid the ground ;
Less roar'd, and less, the thunders solemn sound ;
The bended lightning shot a brighter stream,
Or wrapp'd all heaven in one wide, mantling flame ;

By turns, o'er plains, and woods, and mountains, spread
Faint, yellow glimmerings, and a deeper shade.   926
'From parting clouds, the moon out-breaking shone,
And sate, sole empress, on her silver throne ;
In clear, full beauty, round all nature smil'd,
And claim'd o'er heaven, and earth, dominion mild; 930
With humbler glory, stars her court attend,
And bless'd, and union'd, silent lustre blend.

All these bright scenes revolv'd, his raptur'd mind,
With sweet transition, heaven in all divin'd ;
Where, round the prospect, grandeur, beauty, glow'd,
They shone, the grandeur, beauty, of a God ;   936
God look'd through all, as, with resplendence gay,
They rais'd, and bore him from himself away.

THE

CONQUEST of CANÄAN:

BOOK IV.

ARGUMENT.

Morning. Tribes assemble. Story of Achan. Embassy from Gibeon. Story of Mina, Joshua gives her to Elam, prince of Gibeon, in marriage, and makes peace with the Gibeonites. Feast. Joshua's prayer. Cloud descends on the tabernacle. Elam sollicits leave to return to Gibeon. Joshua consents. Sports of the Israelites. Conduct of Hanniel. Walls built around the camp. Story of Helon.

THE CONQUEST OF CANAAN.

BOOK IV.

NOW the third sun illum'd the azure main,
And Israel anxious gather'd on the plain.
In every face suspense and grief appear'd,
Each son was doubted, and each parent fear'd:
Brothers on brothers cast a side-long eye,   5
And trembling fair-ones press'd the rising sigh.
   Mid the wide concourse great Eleazar shone,
The sacred minister of Heaven's high throne.
White were his aged locks, and round his face
Calm contemplation cast a solemn grace;   10
O'er his pure vesture shining unguent spread,
And breath'd the fragrance of th' Arabian shade:
Full on his breast the star-bright Urim glow'd,
And o'er his brow beam'd HOLINESS TO GOD.
   The sacred rites perform'd, he bent his way   15
To the bright dome that mock'd the rising day.
The train with reverence bow'd.   Around his head
Red spires of lambent flame serenely play'd;
On the clear splendors gaz'd the crowd around,
And deep attention hush'd the shady ground.   20
   Now in the sacred place the Priest ador'd,
And thus his voice Jehovah's smiles implor'd.
O thou, whose wisdom built the bright abodes,
Great KING OF KINGS, and sovereign GOD OF GODS,

Almighty Father hear ! Let grace divine   25
Shower on our hoft, and cleanfe from every fin !
Thou feeft, Omnifcient Mind ! what guilt unknown
Pollutes our race, and dares infult thy throne:
Thou feeft ; and oh may thy all-gracious voice
That guilt declare, and bid thy fons rejoice !   30

He fpoke.   A rufhing found of winds began,
·Sung in the vail, and thro' the temple ran ;
A fapphire flame, unutterably bright,
Shot from the gloom, and wrapp'd the walls in light ;
The dome all trembled ; earth beneath it fhook;   35
And o'er the ark a voice in thunder fpoke---
To Ifrael's thoufands, from th' Eternal throne,
This mighty mandate by thy voice be known.
Of Judah's race, a wretch, by madnefs driven,
With impious hand, hath dar'd the wrath of Heaven :
Stones fhall his houfe deftroy, and flames devour ;   41
I A M commands ; let all my fons adore.---
Nor more ; an awful darknefs round him fpread,
Still as the gloomy manfions of the dead.

All fad, all flow, return'd the mournful prieft,   45
And ftrong impatience every eye exprefs'd---
What the decree of Heaven ! the Leader cried---
With folemn voice, the facred Seer replied---
Of Judah's race, a wretch, by madnefs driven,
With impious hand, hath dar'd the wrath of Heaven :
Stones fhall his houfe deftroy, and flames devour ;   51
I A M commands ; let all his fons adore.

He fpoke ; and forrow gloom'd the plain : in hafte,
So Jofhua's voice decreed, the lots were caft ;
The wretch, fo long conceal'd, arofe to view,   55
And *Achan*'s name to fearful vengeance drew.
Forth from the crowd, with languid fteps, and flow,
The victim ftrode, and look'd unutter'd woe :
His ufelefs hands hung feebly by his fide ;
His tottering knees their wonted aid denied ;   60

His front was clouded with a wild difmay;
For haftening ruin darken'd o'er his way.

  And thus the youth forlorn---My hated name
Sinks in the mifery of undying fhame.
Pafs'd is the day of grace: my dimmed light   65
Fades in the fkirt of everlafting night.
From the rich fpoils my hand a ftore convey'd,
Help'd by the night, and fafe in covert laid.
Beneath my tent the mifchief may be found,
Where fpreads the flooring o'er the fecret ground. 70
Why did my heart refift that lovely fair,
Who fweetly warn'd me of the tempting fnare?
Hear, all ye warriors! fly the fatal road,
And learn, that vengeance waits the foes of GOD!

  Great Joshua heard; and tho' his feeling mind 75
To crimes was gentle, and to mifery kind;
Fierce on the youth he caft a dreadful eye,
That wither'd all his ftrength, and bade him die.
And could no honour, and no law, controul
The groveling wifhes of thy gloomy foul?   80
How durft thou, impious, face th' Almighty rod,
Put forth rebellious hands and fteal from GOD?
Didft thou not know, weak man! th' avenging Sky
Trac'd thy dark footfteps with all-fearching eye?
Didft thou not fear, amidft the gloomy deed,   85
Its vengeance burfting on thy guilty head?
Didft thou not fear the ftings of confcious fhame?
The thunder's terror; or the lightning's flame?
Go, raife to Heaven the fad, repenting eye,
A Heaven that hears, when Mifery lifts her cry! 90
Perhaps foft Mercy yet may lend an ear,
While thy fun glimmers in his laft career.
Not pity's wifh, but folly's, hides from view
The wretch, whom Juftice' awful feet purfue.
Go then, unpardon'd, fink in fhame forlorn,   95
Of Heaven the victim, and of earth the fcorn;

A warning lamp, o'er guilt's benighted way,
To light bewilder'd error back to day.

    He spoke.   The victim, with dread horror pale,
Walk'd trembling onward to a distant vale ;   100
His look of anguish ask'd a hand to save,
And Pity's eye pursued him to the grave.

    Mean time around their Chief the princes stood,
And kind compassion in their bosoms glow'd :
When rob'd in fair attire, two strangers came,   105
And bow'd respectful, at the Hero's name.
One, pass'd his strength, was grac'd with manly scars,
Crown of the brave, and palm of glorious wars ;
Tall was his frame, his countenance roughly kind,
And his calm front with honest boldness shin'd.   110
Dress'd in light robes, as flowers adorn the wild,
In nature's prime his young companion smil'd
Sweetness ineffable.   Devoid of art,
His eye, soft-glowing, look'd the friendly heart.

    Hail strangers, hail ! the mighty Hero cried,   115
Whose port bespeaks a nation's fairest pride.
Bring your kind hands the peaceful branch from far ?
Or pant your bosoms for the fate of war ?
The elder chief replied---From Gibeon's king
Our friendly hands no hostile message bring.   120
Tho' once in fight renown'd, now silver age
Serenes his brow, and cools ambition's rage.
'Tis his first glory, Gibeon's weal t' encrease,
To soothe sad woe, and widen human bliss.

    Pass'd are five morns, since round th' extended plain,
With fond impatience, rush'd a chosen train,   126
O'er rocks, and streams, the nimble deer pursued,
Trac'd the wild marsh, and scour'd the devious wood.
From the lone mansions of the unpierc'd shade,
At once deep cries our wondering ears invade.   130
Led by the unknown voice, we nimbly hied
Thro' the thick grove, and strait the scene deseried.

'Twixt two rough favages, whofe hungry eyes
Lower'd death, and ruin, o'er their helplefs prize,
Fair as the ftar of morn, a lovely maid,   135
In pangs of terror, call'd in vain for aid.
Her robes embroider'd loofely met the view ;
Her hair, unbound, in wild diforder flew ;
All pale fhe ftood, and to the pitying fky
Stretch'd her white hands, and rais'd a piercing cry.   140
In vain, on terror's wings, the caitiffs flew ;
His eager fword this generous hero drew ;
Their heads in twain the fteely vengeance clave,
And hungry vultures yield the horrid grave.

    To Gibeon's domes we led the beauteous fair,   145
Repos'd on down, and nurs'd with tendereft care.
Pleas'd with our pains, her fweet, angelic tongue
Strange truths divine, with heavenly mufic, fung.
Of nature's Sovereign Lord, the tale began,
How earth was form'd, and how created man ;   150
How the tall mountains heav'd their cloud-wrapp'd fpires
And heaven was ftarr'd with thoufand thoufand fires.
Then too fhe told how, rous'd to fearful ire,
JEHOVAH bade the delug'd world expire ;
Thy nation's rife ; the rod of Sovereign power,   155
That fhook proud Egypt's realms from fhore to fhore,
The cleaving main ; the wonders of the wild,
Where hard rocks flow'd, and fands with verdure fmil'd ;
Food, fhower'd from heaven, perfum'd the morning blaft,
And quails in millions peopled all the wafte.   160
In thefe dread fcenes, Aradon's mighty mind
The clear difplays of boundlefs power divin'd ;
Scenes nobler far than ancient fages knew,
Than age e'er taught, or airy fancy drew.
At once, infpir'd with eager zeal to learn   165
What wondrous truths the glorious fcheme concern,
This prince, his only hope, the monarch chofe,
And join'd with me, his pleafure to difclofe.

                        N

Sweet peace by us his friendly heart demands ;
His gold he proffers, and his warlike bands ;   170
At thy requeſt, to arms the thouſands fly,
With thee we conquer, or with thee we die.
Shouldſt thou conſent, ſome bright, and generous Sage,
Fam'd for pure manners, and grown wiſe with age,
Skill'd with unſeen, yet all-perſuaſive art,   175
'T' inform the mind, and ſoftly win the heart,
Whoſe tenets, nobly rais'd o'er pride, and ſtrife,
Grace the fair conduct of a virtuous life,
He aſks, to ſpread Religion's ſacred ſway,
To lure his ſons to heaven, and point the way.   180
And O what price immenſe canſt thou demand !
What golden hoards ? or boundleſs breadth of land ?
One precious prize our grateful hands reſtore,
Unbought by gems, or loads of ſhining ore,
In thy own tent, behold thy favorite fair,   185
Child of thy choice, and darling of thy care !
  Thus ſpoke Hareſhah.   While glad ſmiles expreſs'd
The Leader's joy, he thus his chiefs addreſs'd.
Even now, propitious, on our lengthen'd toils
Behold th' all-watchful Eye complacent ſmiles !   190
In other realms our growing fame is heard,
Our triumphs number'd and our Guardian fear'd.
But ſay, brave princes, ſhall theſe bands be tied ?
And Gibeon's ſons to Jacob's heirs allied ?
Shall ſome bleſs'd ſage her thouſands teach to riſe   195
To peace, to truth, to virtue, and the ſkies ?
Your choice I wait---he ſaid.   Quick Hanniel roſe,
Whoſe life was conteſt, and whoſe joy t' oppoſe.
To ſave the ſuppliant race his wiſh inclin'd,
For Heaven had form'd him with a feeling mind :   200
But well he knew how fair his matchleſs art
Could gild the latent miſchiefs of his heart ;
How thouſands on his words inchanted hung,
Touch'd by the magic of his wily tongue.

All paths with him were smooth, that shew'd a name, 205
Tho' slaughter'd nations pav'd the road to fame.
Thrice rose the chief to thwart the Leader's choice,
And thrice strange faltering seiz'd his opening voice ;
Far round he casts his keen, experienc'd view,
And peace, the wish of every bosom, knew ;   210
With shame his dauntless front was cover'd o'er,
And the cheek blush'd, that never blush'd before.

Pleas'd the great Leader saw his failing eye,
And voice, in vain, attempt a base reply,
Then smiling thus---Uutaught the wiles of art   215
I see mild aspects speak the friendly heart.
Yes let fair Peace, o'er Gibeon's happy land,
Raise her sweet voice, and lift her sacred wand.
'Gainst hostile realms alone our falchions rise,
Foes to high Heaven, and victims of the Skies.   220
But far remov'd from Israel, very far,
Be every wish t' extend the waste of war :
To sooth vain pride with conquest's dreadful name ;
To pamper avarice with the spoils of shame ;
To take one hour from man's too hasty doom,   225
Or force one widow to a husband's tomb.
From death's sad scenes, and battle's horrid toils,
The real hero's generous mind recoils :
When swords alone can plead the righteous cause,
The crimson steel his hand reluctant draws ;   230
Grief walks his partner to the dreadful plain,
And glory's mansions prove the haunts of pain.

'Tis Israel's boast, the human weal t' increase ;
To stretch the reign, and nurse the arts, of peace ;
The fierce, the wild, to tame ; the weak defend ;   235
Late to begin, and soon the strife to end ;
To teach vain man the bliss to virtue given,
And with new saints t' enlarge the bounds of heaven.

But now, brave chiefs, to Joshua's tent repair---
My fond heart pants to find the lovely fair---   240

Her sire, in Edom's realm, our nation join'd,
Urg'd by the dictates of a virtuous mind:
Her, a sweet babe, his hand indulgent bore,
To virtue form'd, and nurs'd in sacred lore.
As some bright lilly, daughter of the morn,   245
Swells its young leaves, and bids its splendors burn ;
Fair, and more fair, th' expanding beauties glow,
Dance in the sun, and shame the driving snow ;
So, born for heaven, still brightening to the view,
From truth to truth, from charm to charm, she grew ; 250
Soft was her temper ; all her thoughts refin'd ;
Beauty her form, and virtue was her mind.

    Now at the tent arriv'd, the fair they found ;
With many a lovely maid incompass'd round ;
With smiles of joy, their friend the virgins hail'd,   255
And gentle tears on every cheek prevail'd.
When first her Sire appear'd, around his form
She cast, with sweetest grace, each snowy arm ;
Pleas'd the great Hero eyed his lovely child,
And gave the fond embrace, and o'er the charmer smil'd.

    Sweet maid! he cried, where rov'dst thou from the plain ?
With tears we sought thee, but we sought in vain.   262

    Far in the wood, replied the fair, I stray'd,
No care disturb'd me, and no fear dismay'd ;
Charm'd with the flowers, that, undistinguish'd, smil'd
With solitary beauty round the wild.   266
A plum'd musician, on her verdant throne,
Hymn'd, with soft transport, to the falling sun.
Slow I approach'd ; the bird before me flew ;
I heard the sound ; how could I not pursue ?   270
So long I wander'd, day forsook the sky ;
I gaz'd, and gaz'd ; but found not where to fly.
In different paths, I roam'd the woody plain ;
But faint, and trembling, still return'd again.

    Line 243, *Her, a sweet babe,*] This epithet is given merely from
tenderness.

The wolf began to howl ; and all around,   275
The hungry panther fhook the fhuddering ground ;
Loud roar'd the approaching lion's dread alarms,
And death rufh'd by me, in a thoufand forms.

    The long, long, difmal night at length was gone ;
And cheerful day with pleafing beauty fhone.   280
Hufh'd was the world, fave where, along the wood,
Rung the foft current of a filver flood.
Down verdant banks, with trembling fteps I ftray'd ;
Each breeze alarm'd me, and each leaf difmay'd ;
Till, near the confines of the lonely ftream,   285
Ro fe two barbarians, as the tyger grim.
My hated garb difpleas'd their favage eyes,
And female weaknefs bade their luft arife.
O why was ftrength to mifcreant villains given ?
Why lovely virtue left unarm'd by heaven ?   290
Why muft the helplefs fair-one's glory ftand
A prey, for every monfter's brutal hand ?
Thus mourn'd my heart ; when Elam rufh'd to fight,
Clave the dire foes, and calm'd my wild affright ;
At once low-whifper'd Virtue's heavenly friend---   295
Weak are the fair, that heroes may defend.

    She fpoke. The blufh that gives the brighteft charm,
Glow'd in her face, and told her heart's alarm.
Skill'd in the fcience of the human foul,
Th' experienc'd Chief beheld her paffions roll,   300
Smil'd at th' expreffive language of her eye,
The dancing bofom, and the deep drawn figh.

    On Elam's face he turn'd a fearching view,
Trac'd his young flame, and all his wifhes knew.
Oft on the virgin glanc'd his earneft gaze ;   305
She glance for glance, and blufh for blufh, repays ;
Their eyes prove faithful to the melting heart,
Waft the fond wifh, and all the foul impart.

Line 287. *My hated garb,*) She wore the Ifraelitifh drefs.

No pride of beauty wak'd his young defires;   310
Nor eye that fparkles, fraught with lambent fires ;
Nor cheek, that gaily fhines with morning glow ;
Nor downy bofom, dipp'd in fpotlefs fnow.
He figh'd for charms of nature more refin'd,
The Maker's image, in the fair one's mind ;
Such charms, as found in heaven, delight improve,   315
And plac'd in angels prompt an angel's love.

   Thus while they paus'd ; with fweet, and modeft grace,
Fear in his eye, and blufhes o'er his face,
The trembling youth began---O Chief divine !
My parent's voice thou heard'ft, difdain not mine.   320
To this bright maid my wifhes would afpire---
O blame not ! frown not on the fpotlefs fire !---
Thou know'ft the joy her virtues yield to thee ;
Then think her hand were paradife to me.

   Pleas'd the Chief faw his eyes with fondnefs fhine,   325
And mien all modeft, merit's faithful fign,
And thus---O fair ! 'tis thine alone to choofe.
Say, muft this heart fo foon its darling lofe ?
Canft thou to Elam yield a willing hand,
And feek a guardian in a diftant land ?   330

   With voice fincere, unus'd her thoughts to hide,
And bofom frank, the virgin's lafting pride,
The guife, low-creeping Cunning muft approve,
Fair mark of worth, and friend to virtuous love,
The maid replied---O fire ! 'tis blifs to me,   335
To be by him belov'd, approv'd by thee.

   The Chief return'd ; Blefs'd heir of fpotlefs fame !
Thy choice and wifdom ever afk the fame.
Receive, brave Elam ! Jofhua's favourite care,
As angels virtuous, and as Eden fair.   340
Her hand, her heart fhall heal thy bleeding mind,
Warm'd with pure love, and grac'd with truth refin'd,
Thy fainting ftrength, thy languid eye infpire,
Improve thy joys, and wake the hero's fire,

Charm, with foft tendernefs, thy griefs away,   345
And gild alike the darknefs and the day.
And thou, brave Elam ! ftill, as morn returns,
While early tranfport in thy bofom burns,
On firm foundations let thy fondnefs reft,
Nor cold indifference canker in thy breaft.   350
Know, all the vows by heedlefs lovers given,
Though oft on earth forgot, are feal'd in heaven :
Then let thy fond connubial actions fhow
'Truth was the language of the lover's vow.
And thou, my child, to Heaven thyfelf approve ;   355
Act all the foft commands of duteous love :
So fhall your lives ferenely dance away,
And blifs unclouded light the fetting day.
But now, brave friends, let pleafure round us roll ;
Enjoy the genial feaft, and fhare the bowl ;   360
Three days, with me, and every pleafure, ftay ;
The fourth glad morn fhall gild your homeward way.'
    Thus he.   The feelings of each grateful breaft
With manly dignity the chiefs confefs'd.
In converfe mild they fate.   With bufy care,   365
Th' attendant train the cheerful feaft prepare ;
With kindly warmth the fmoaking cauldrons glow,
And fweet thro' ether rifing odours flow.
    So vaft, fo various, was the Leader's mind,
It rov'd through every region, unconfin'd ;   370
From fcenes fublime, with foft tranfition, ran
Thro' all the duties, all the weal, of man ;
At once his friends, his race, his Maker, ferv'd ;
At once his own domeftic blifs preferv'd ;
In nice dependence rang'd the fervant train,   375
And o'er his houfe bade beauteous order reign.
Thro' all their minds Religion's influence ran---
Men, true to Heaven, he knew were true to man---
Her fons he chofe ; and with all-bounteous fway,
Rewarded, rul'd, and led in virtue's way :   380

Hence, rich return of all his watchful toil,
No murmur pain'd him, and no houshold broil.
Peace round his mansion shed her influence mild,
And cheerful, friendly, each domestic smil'd.
    Now the lov'd maid had 'scap'd from savage bands, 385
With twofold pleasure, wrought their active hands.
So just, so gentle was her angel mind,
To want so bounteous, and to all so kind,
Her, as the Leader, each alert obey'd,
And thought it bliss to please the heavenly maid,   390
    Mean time, selected for the genial feast,
To Joshua's tent came many a princely guest;
Their courteous hearts the noble strangers greet,
And hail the fair with gratulation sweet.
    O'er a vast board a wide pavilion spread,   395
With grandeur shin'd, and cast a pleasing shade.
There sate the guests; there cates delight the soul;
There wines inspiring tinge the spacious bowl:
They taste, enjoy, and, with light converse gay,
In calm oblivion roll their cares away.   400
    O'er all great Joshua shone, with aspect mild,
Cheer'd every guest, and with soft splendor smil'd:
Touch'd by his eyes, each heart with rapture glow'd,
And sweet complacence every face o'erflow'd.
So round th' immense the sun's broad glories stream, 405
Spread boundless life, and pour the etherial flame;
Warm'd with pure light, the golden planets roll,
And smile soft-beaming joy from pole to pole,
In endless pride, at beauteous distance, rise,
Swell the great pomp, and glad the earth, and skies. 410
    There, like the day-star, beauteous Irad shone,
His splendors lessening in the nearer sun;
Full on the Chief a sparkling eye he turn'd,
And as he gaz'd, with bright ambition burn'd,
Mark'd all the glories of his awful face,   415
His solemn grandeur, and his matchless grace;

While hoary Hezron watch'd with boding eyes,
And saw, well-pleas'd, the future hero rise.

There too, in transport brighten'd Caleb's pride,
With tears, embracing Elam's lovely bride ;   420
Yet felt soft pain, to see her favourite's charms,
The destin'd treasure of a stranger's arms,
To see her days at distance doom'd to roll,
And mingling friendship soothe no more the soul.

In easy converse pass'd the hours away ;   425
Each face shone cheerful, and each heart was gay ;
In glad succession went the goblets round,
And blended voices gave a jocund sound.

Mean time throng'd numerous round the Leader's door,
The stranger, orphan, widow, and the poor ;   430
Call'd from each tribe, by Joshua's kind command,
A rare-felt joy inspir'd the friendless band ;
They feasted, sang, and in the dance combin'd,
Pour'd forth the raptures of th' oblivious mind :
Then, moving various, o'er the camp they spread,   435
Each bliss imploring on the Leader's head.

When now the feast was o'er, the sun drew nigh
The gilded borders of the western sky :
Forth to the temple march'd th' illustrious train,
The thousands gathering o'er th' extended plain.   440
From a tall rock, amid the silent crowd,
The suppliant Hero rais'd his voice aloud---

O thou, whose hand illum'd yon rolling fire,
Stretch'd the wide plains, and bade the hills aspire,
Rul'd by whose power, the stars unnumber'd rise,   445
And swift-wing'd lightnings flame athwart the skies,
Storms ride majestic o'er th' etherial plain,
And wake the sleeping thunders of the main !
Empires, at thy command, arise, and fall ;
And flight and triumph hasten at thy call !   450
Disclose, O Power Divine ! thy sovereign voice---
Does combat please thee ? combat is our choice---

O

Does peace delight thee ? peace alone we prize,
Led by thy will, and guided by thine eyes.
By thee this land to Abraham's race was given,　　455
'Till suns withdraw, and stars are lost in heaven:
If now the bright possession God ordain,
And crowns await us, on the crimson plain,
By some great sign th' eternal smiles display,
And point our footsteps to the fierce affray !　　460

   At once a hollow wind began to roll,
As distant thunders rumble round the pole ;
The fields grew black, the forests felt th' alarm,
And swift through ether rush'd a cloudy storm,
High heaven all trembled with the dreadful sound,　　465
And peals on peals, convulsive, shook the ground.
Far round the sacred dome the darkness spread ;
The sun's clear splendor vanish'd in the shade:
Red flames burst forth ; the conscious mountains nod,
And the world smokes beneath th' approaching God.

   In silent awe, the camp astonish'd stood ;　　471
And each burn'd fiercely for the day of blood.
Fix'd in still wonder, gaz'd the stranger pair,
And mark'd, with anxious mind, the darkening air,
The dome, invelop'd in the sable shroud,　　475
And peals deep-murmuring in the hollow cloud:
With solemn look, each freqnent eyed his friend,
And felt, instinctive, half-form'd prayers ascend.

   Mean time the Leader every chief commands---
Two days, let peace refresh the fainting bands;　　480
The third glad sun, awak'd by trumpet's sound,
Shall light our falchions to the deathful ground.
Sleep, hapless Ai ! thy last returning day
Soon gilds thy turrets with a pitying ray.
And let the chief, th' important charge who owns,　　485
Of all our wealth, our wives, and blooming sons,
Bid a long trench wind through the tented ground.
And guardian walls the spacious camp surround.

He fpoke.   With joy th' attendant chiefs obey'd,
And round the camp the glad commands convey'd.   490
The fquadrons ardent wait th' appointed morn,
Cleanfe their blue fhields, and polifh'd coats adorn.
So Jofhua will'd ; for well the Hero knew
How glittering fteel allur'd the ravifh'd view ;
Thence prais'd the chief, in fhining neatnefs arm'd,   495
Averfe from toys, but with true beauty charm'd ;
And thence in glorious panoply he blaz'd,
A great example, acting all he prais'd.

Now round the world pale Eve her fadnefs threw;
Still, folemn darknefs cloudy curtains drew ;   500
Through the wide camp the Leader trac'd his way,
To learn what wifhes mark'd the bufy day.
Ai, full in view, each heart to combat fir'd,
And with gay profpects every breaft infpir'd.
No thought of Egypt boding minds embrac'd ;   505
No childifh fear even vulgar fouls difgrac'd :
In deep oblivion funk the painful wound,
And fierce impatience hop'd th' embattled ground.
Pleas'd the great Hero heard th' exulting ftrain,
And wandering, liftening, fought his tent again.   510

When now the morn look'd mildly from the eaft,
To Jofhua Elam thus his voice addrefs'd---
O Chief of Ifrael, crown'd with grace divine !
Let health's green garland round thy temples twine,
To blefs mankind be ftill thy lov'd employ ;   515
To ferve thy Maker ftill thy facred joy ;
No hour of thine to wafting grief be given ;
Let each m ore brightly roll, and antedate thy heaven !
But now, his years impatient of delay,
My hoary father hopes our homeward way.   520
Indulge, great prince, our eager wifh to bear
The rapturous tidings to his longing ear.
His foul rejoic'd will fmile at nature's pains,
And life flow fwifter through his icy veins.

Bid us with speed our destin'd path resume,   525
And bless a parent, sinking in the tomb.

He spoke.   Hareshah join'd the youth's request:
Even Mina's eyes a secret wish confess'd.
In love's kind heat, like ice in summer's ray,
All former ties, dissolving, pass away ;   530
To new-found friends the soul oblivious flies,
New objects charm us, and new passions rise.
The Hero saw, and kindly bade depart
The lov'd, the long-lost favourite of his heart ;
With arms impassion'd clasp'd the bright-eyed fair,   535
Kiss'd with fond look, and dropp'd a tender tear.
On gay-dress'd camels, toward the setting day,
With converse sweet, the lovers bent their way ;
Like two fair stars, that shed a lonely light,
And sink in clouds, above the mountain's height.   540
Two seers their steps attend, to point the way,
That ends in mansions of unchanging day.

And now, o'er all the camp, the raptur'd throng
Crowd the wide plain, and wake th' enlivening song.
Here cheerful thousands bid the walls ascend ;   545
And broad, and deep, the lengthening trenches bend.
Here the strong arm the falchion learns to wield,
Or hurls the javelin o'er the measur'd field.
With shouts of praise the conquerors oft are crown'd,
And clanging bucklers swell th' applauding sound.   550
Part, join'd in crowds, in mimic fight engage,
Range their small hosts, and sport with seeming rage ;
From force unequal here the vanquish'd fly ;
There, with deep groans, dissembling victims die.

Mean time all-watchful.   Hanniel, round the plain,
From crowd to crowd, inspir'd the busy train.   556
He knew the plot, the generous Youth disclos'd,
To dark suspicion saw his name expos'd ;
To wipe disgrace, his influence to recall,
And, with light, secret snares, to gather all,   560

From tent to tent he urg'd his active way;
And blam'd with words severe, the wild affray.
Me, cried the hero, Israel's thousands know
A fair unchanging friend, or open foe.
To generous war since Israel's voice is given, 565
To war I fly, and hope the smiles of Heaven.
Rouse then to arms; for glorious fight prepare;
Each thought of peace, each terror vile forbear:
Let glory's fire each warrior's breast inflame,
And deathless deeds shall brighten Jacob's name. 570

Thus he. The wile the thoughtless thousands drew,
Snar'd by soft words, and caught by gilding shew;
For war, invigor'd, glow'd th' undaunted mind,
And kindling eye-balls with new lustre shin'd.
No walls they need, to stay th' impending foe; 575
Yet, with light labour, swift the barriers grow;
Hope high in view display'd unmeasur'd spoil,
Sooth'd every pain, and lessen'd every toil.

As thus serenely pass'd the cheerful day,
And care, and grief, oblivious roll'd away, 580
At once shrill rang, from eastern woods afar,
The cry of foes, and growing sound of war.
The sporting warriors, prompt at dread alarms,
Ceas'd from each game, and brac'd for fight their arms;
O'er eastern fields, with rapid steps they hied. 585
And bands conjoining swell'd th' embattled pride.

From the wood hastening, flew, with wild surprize,
Two timorous youths, and rais'd lamenting cries,
With trembling voice, they said---Of nought afraid,
Through yonder grove, with easy course, we stray'd; 590
A savage band, by twining shrubs conceal'd,
Burst on our path, and half enclos'd the field.
Amaz'd we flew. Snar'd by the tangling vine,
Our heedless Partner fell; of Simeon's line;
Helon his name: they seiz'd him fallen; in vain 595
Uplifting cries, and bore him o'er the plain.

Quick, at the sound, a warrior rais'd his voice---
'Tis my own son; the spring of all my joys---
Haste, haste, brave friends, my darling Helon save;
Nor yield your faithful Shallum childless to the grave.
The train, inspir'd, with nimbler footsteps flew;   601
Each press'd his shield, and each his falchion drew;
The youths, before them, shew'd the sadden'd way,
Where the fell heathens bore their hapless prey;
Where the close thicket wrapp'd the ambush'd force,   605
And bending shrubs, and footsteps mark'd their course.
Thence the glad train, with ease, the foe pursued,
And hoping, hastening, scower'd the devious wood.

Now, where all-anxious through the favouring shade,
Their hapless prize the heathens swift convey'd;   610
Weening, ere morn, through Oran's camp to bear
The youth, with tidings of th' expected war,
The heroes rush'd: his friends glad Helon knew;
Loud rose his voice; the warriors eager flew;
While the bold heathens stay'd their useless flight,   615
New-brac'd their shields, and strung their nerves for fight.

Shrill through the woods the clash of arms arose;
These, fix'd to hold, and fierce to rescue, those;
The forest shook.   In front, confess'd to view,
Full on the heathens raging Shallum flew.   620
One with his lance, and one with griding steel,
He flew: the victims gave a hideous yell.
To his son's voice he wing'd his furious course;
Nought stay'd his speed, and nought withstood his force.
Where two huge heathens struggling Helon led,   625
He wildly sprang: one flew; the other bled:
With frantic joy he seiz'd his raptur'd hand,
And urg'd him trembling toward the friendly band.
There scarce arriv'd, a javelin pierc'd his side;
He groan'd, he sunk, grew pale, and fainting died.   630
Aghast, his darling's fate the sire beheld,
Then rush'd delirious round the woody field;

On the fled heathens ftretch'd his raging courfe,
O'ertook, and fingly drove the gather'd force :
Three fierce he flew ; the reft, in devious ways,   635
Fled o'er the field, and 'fcap'd the hero's chace.
At length return'd, with a deep, burfting groan,
In ftrong embrace he clafp'd his haplefs fon,
Prefs'd to his bofom, bore him o'er the plain,
And, mid the weeping warriors, fought the camp again.

THE

CONQUEST of CANÄAN:

BOOK V.

ARGUMENT.

THE CONQUEST OF CANÄAN.

BOOK V.

NOW funk the fun beneath the weftern main,
    And deepening twilight fhaded every plain :
To the known tent untroubled Irad fped,
And forth, with proffer'd hand, Selima led.
Through fouthern fields they trac'd their eafy way,   5
And love, and rapture, chang'd the night to day.
The weftern beam decay'd : th' expanding fky
Spread clear, and boundlefs, to th' attentive eye :
Scarce fill'd, the moon afcends the vaulted even,
And flow behind rolls on the pride of heaven ;   10
With joy, th' unenvious planets round her play,
Join their glad beams, and fwell the mimic day ;
From ftar to ftar the mingling luftre flies ;
Unmeafur'd beauty clothes the lucid fkies ;
Hufh'd in calm filence fleeps the world ferene,   15
And floating fplendor gilds the fhadowy fcene.
    Round the mix'd glories of the fpacious fky
The pair inftinctive turn'd a raptur'd eye,
From fcene to fcene with rifing wonder ran,
And mild, with accent fweet, the maid began---   20
In yon broad field what fcenes of glory fhine !
The bright effufions of a fource divine !
Great as the hand, that form'd yon lucid way !
Fair as the morn, that op'd immortal day !

In earliest youth, when first my feeble mind   25
In nature's works celestial power divin'd,
To those gay regions fancy stretch'd her flight,
And rov'd, and sported, mid the gems of light.
For whom, I cried, ascend yon glowing fires ?
What favourite first-born of th' angelic choirs ?   30
Those azure curtains ? that sublime abode ?
A tent of glory for some darling God !
Say, loveliest Prince ! for thy superior mind
Walks, with sure step, in wisdom's path refin'd,
Why rove so far th' unnumber'd flames on high ?   35
Why cast their endless beauty through the sky ?
Is yon blue frame, that limits morn and even,
The sapphire pavement of some nobler heaven ?
Are stars but gems of unborn light, that spread
With dust of gold the streets where angels tread ?   40
Or if for man these works of glory shine,
For earth-born reptiles furniture divine :
Say why so strange the acts of Heaven appear,
There such bright pomp, such wondrous meanness here.

    The Youth return'd---Fair as those lucid eyes,   45
All lovely maid ! thy bright ideas rise.
In vain proud man, with self-applause runs o'er
His arts of Egypt, and his Eastern lore,
Thy soul, on nature's pinions, takes her flight,
And, self-instructed, gains a nobler height.   50

    When from the deep, ascended earth, and heaven,
To man, sole heir, the mighty boon was given.
Unlike his sons, no guilt his mind deform'd ;
His life, his limbs, no fierce diseases storm'd ;
Nor death's cold poison pal'd his growing bloom,   55
Nor knew his feet the journey to the tomb.
Young beauty's purple splendor round him play'd ;
Immortal Health his vigorous limbs array'd :
Life, eldest heiress of th' empyreal sky,
Smil'd on his cheek, and blossom'd in his eye.   60

Array'd in endless light, his infant mind
Shone with fair truth, and glow'd with grace refin'd;
Her robe sky-tinctur'd, Virtue round him threw;
Unchanging jubilee his passions knew;
Heaven's living lamp, with clear, and constant shine,
Sunn'd the pure regions of the world within. 66

   Far other glories then arose to view;
Parts answering parts, and beauties ever new.
With strong, bright charms the heaven angelic shin'd;
The varying prospect charm'd th' inchanted mind; 70
Soft strains of rapture bade all ether ring;
The gales, all fragrance, shed the light of spring;
From stars, from moonbeams, life's sweet influence flew,
Inspir'd the streams, and glow'd in fostering dew;
Bade with strong life the purpling fruits refine, 75
And warm'd the bosom with a youth divine.

   Then reign'd fair Love, th' immortal bliss of heaven;
Then social angels came on clouds of even:
Here trac'd new wonders of th' omniscient Mind,
Strange to their world, and first on earth design'd;
In countless forms, where love and beauty glow'd, 80
And stamp'd a rival of the bright abode.

   His hand such nature to the man assign'd,
His form so temper'd, and so wrought his mind,
All gave delight; where spring display'd her prime; 85
Or where blank winter froze the desert clime:
The vale's soft pride; the flower's etherial form;
The mountain's grandeur, and the solemn storm.

   But when foul guilt debas'd the beauteous mind,
The skies grew dim, and sickening nature pin'd. 90
With converse sweet, no more kind angels came:
No blissful morning shed th' eternal beam;
No more from starry realms life's influence fell,
And peace, and Eden bade the world farewell.

   Yet still with clear, though faded lustre, glow'd 95
The love, the greatness, of a bounteous God.

What though cold east winds wither'd all the plain ;
Though blasts, and mildews shrunk the golden grain ;
Pale evening's, skirts the frost, and damp o'erhung ;
Air bred disease, and worms the fruitage stung :   100
Still o'er the mountains stars serenely rise ;
Still the soft moonbeam trembles from the skies ;
The sun, fair image of unborrow'd day,
Lights heaven, and earth, and cheers the boundless sea ;
Reviving seasons, crown'd with lustre, roll,   105
And plains of plenty glad th' expecting soul.

These splendid scenes surprize thy curious mind ;
For worms too noble, and for foes too kind.
But not too noble, or too kind, they shine,
The works of wisdom, power, and love, divine.   110
From morn's gay bounds, to skirts of distant even,
They teach the hand, and spread the name, of Heaven ;
In beauty, grandeur, make JEHOVAH known,
But mark, with faded charms, a world undone.
Yet these, could man the common bliss pursue,   115
Would gentle peace, and smiling joy, renew,
Light, with soft-beaming hope, the cheerful day,
And drive grim war, and cankering hate, away.

Thus spoke the Prince.   The tender maid replies,
While her sad bosom heaves unbidden sighs.   120
Fair scenes of bliss thy living words disclose,
Realms of gay youth, and times of sweet repose.
Oh had our sire ! but hence, ye wishes vain !
No fancied joy shall edge returning pain---
Yet too, too blissful is the fond employ,   125
To nurse gay hope, and dream unreal joy ;
Abroad in fields of airy light to roam,
And fly th' envenom'd grief, that lurks at home.
Ah, had the fatal fruit, untasted hung,
What bliss had brighten'd ! and what glory sprung ! 130
In gentlest union these bless'd hands had join'd,
One wish inform'd us, and one soul intwin'd ;

On some lone hill our envied mansion stood,
There rich perfumes in morning breezes flow'd;
Sweet Peace around it wav'd her balmy wing,   135
And Youth unchanging dress'd eternal spring.
There, O bless'd lot! each innocent employ
Had form'd, and cherish'd mild, domestic joy:
The walk all-pleasing, virtuous love refin'd;   139
Our flocks, our prospects, sooth'd th' improving mind;
For me, the garden op'd its spicy bloom;
For thee, soft vesture whiten'd o'er the loom:
Our growing bliss the sun delay'd to see,
And the poor heathen been as bless'd as we.
Ah dire reverse! while round this field of gore,   145
War's hoarse rough-grating clangors ceaseless roar;
While sons, and fathers, in one hour are slain,
And each bright youth must tempt the fatal plain;
While the sad virgin sees, with wearied eye,
No hope remains her, but to weep, and die;   150
While pain, and grief, and half-form'd joy invade,
And suns gay-rising set in mournful shade.

  Kind, tender maid! the smiling Prince return'd---
The hapless fall how sweetly hast thou mourn'd!
Thy voice, all music, wins the raptur'd ear;   155
Yet more persuasive drops that melting tear.
But, O bright maid! by strong affections driven,
Let no fond wish oppose the choice of Heaven.
To man's first guilt ten thousand ills adjoin'd,
Writhe the torn limbs, and agonize the mind: 160
Pain, famine, toil, the sword, the ruthless wave,
Care, envy, broken faith, sad sorrow, and the grave.
Yet God's high acts unerring wisdom guides,
And boundless love his every choice decides.
Hence all events, and hence all beings right,   165
Best in their places, to best ends unite.
Hence from small ills unmeasur'd good shall flow;
Hence joys unnumber'd spring from every woe:

Through the vast whole th' eternal glories shine,
One great I AM, all-beauteous, all divine.   170
   Thus the great Prophet sung ; and oft my sire
With these bless'd truths my tender heart would fire,
When, won to virtue, on his lips I hung,
And learn'd pure wisdom from his friendly tongue.
   Heaven's high behest, had faithless man obey'd,   175
A peaceful earth his eye had still survey'd ;
Mild hours and seasons soft o'er nature run ;
His sons, in millions, spread to lands unknown ;
To Eden's bowers the filial nations come,
Hail'd their great sire, and own'd their happier home.
While from his throne, supreme of all below,   181
He saw well-pleas'd, his mighty kingdom grow ;
His subjects children, love his potent sway,
And one vast houshold spread to every sea.
   But, sprung from earth, and still to earth confin'd,   185
No fairer bliss had flow'd for poor mankind : ·
No law had given the high, stupendous claim,
To soar, and brighten in th' immortal flame.
Now to those climes where, 'twixt delight and pain,
Expands, untravers'd, night's eternal main,   190
Worms, born of dust, may point their lofty way,
And seize the bliss of ever-rising day.
   Oft on the flower, embosom'd in perfume,
Thou seest gay butterflies in beauty bloom ;
With curious eye, the wondrous insect scan,   195
By Heaven ordain'd a threefold type of man.
First from the dung-hill sprang the shining form,
And crawl'd to view, a hideous, loathsome worm ;
To creep, with toil, his inch-long journey's, curs'd ;
The ground his mansion, and his food the dust :   200
To the next plant, his moment o'er, he drew,
And built his tomb, and turn'd to earth anew.
Oft, from the leaf depending, hast thou seen
Their tombs, with gold bedropp'd, and cloth'd in green ;

There flept th' expectant, 'till the plastic beam   205
Purg'd his vile drofs, and bade his fplendors flame.
Then burst the bonds : at once in glory rise
His form etherial, and his changing dies,
Full on the lucid morn his wings unfold,
Starr'd with strong light, and gay in living gold;   210
Through fields of air at large the wonder flies,
Wafts on the beams, and mounts th' expanded skies,
O'er flowery beauties plumes of triumph waves ;
Imbibes their fragrance, and their charms out-braves ;
The birds his kindred, heaven his manfion, claims,   215
And shines, and wantons, in the noon-day flames.

So man, poor worm ! the nurfling of a day !
Springs from the duft, and dwells in humble clay ;
Around his little mole-hill doom'd to creep,
To drag life's load, and end his toil with fleep.   220
In filence to the grave his form defcends,
And waits the trump, that time and nature ends,
There ftrength imbibes, the beam of heaven to bear :
There learns, refin'd, to breathe its fragrant air ;
Of life the bloom, of youth the fplendor, gains,   225
And, cloth'd in beauty, hopes empyreal plains.
Then, wing'd with light, the deathlefs man shall rife,
Sail through yon ftars, and foar from skies to skies ;
See heavens, o'er heavens, beneath him leffening roll,
And feel the Godhead warm his changing foul;   230
From beauty's fount inhale th' immortal ray,
And grow from light to light, in cloudlefs day ;
Mid morn's fair legions, crown'd with grace, be known,
The peer of angels, and of God the fon.

But O what fcenes in that far region glow !   235
What crowns of patience ! what rewards of woe !

From yon tall hill, when morn's inviting air
To woodland wandering lur'd thy chofen fair,
Thou know'ft how fweet gay profpects to defcry,
And catch new Edens with the ravifh'd eye.   240

In living green, the lawns at distance lay,
Where snowy flocks mov'd round in vernal play ;
High tower'd the nodding groves ; the cliffs sublime
Left the low world, and dar'd th' assaults of time ;
Huge domes heav'd haughty to the morning fires,　245
And the sun trembled round a thousand spires :
All heaven was mild ; and borne from subject vales,
A cloud of fragrance cheer'd th' inchanting gales.

　Such pleasing scenes if this drear earth supply,
What scenes, what glories bloom beyond the sky !　250
There with strong life the plains immortal glow ;
There Beauty bids her streams of rapture flow :
There changing, brightening, reigns th' extatic power ;
Smiles in each fruit, and burns in every flower ;
In solemn domes, with growing pride, aspires ;　255
Gems with fair stars, and robes in living fires ;
Round the trees wantons ; on the mountains blooms ;
Charms in new songs, and melts in strange perfumes.
And O, of liquid light what seas extend !
What skies impurple ! and what stars ascend !　260
But cease, my tongue ! nor headlong rush too near
The sun, that kindles heaven's eternal year.

　When great Messiah shall those gates unbar,
Where grief recedes, and pain, and death, and war ;
Then freed from dross, from every stain refin'd,　265
And dress'd in all the elegance of mind,
To her own mansion shall thy Soul aspire,
And add new raptures to the sainted choir.
With love divine thy heart has learn'd to glow ;
Smil'd at each joy, and wept at every woe ;　270
In each soft station amiably stood,
And shewn the bright ambition to be good ;
The best, the loveliest daughter, sister, friend ;
Thy life all virtue, and the heavens thine end.
Scarce, of thy years, can blooming cherubs claim　275
A purer conscience, or a fairer name.

Pleas'd as he spoke, an aged Form drew near,
The moon-beams whitening o'er his silver hair.
His quivering limbs a tatter'd garb array'd ;
A staff his flow, and faltering footsteps stay'd---   280
Oh youth! he said, in wealth thy lot is cast ;
Let humble Poverty thy bounty taste.
Large as thy treasure be thy heart to give ;
Thy bread impart, and bid my children live.

   Sire! cried the Youth, to Hezron's tent repair ;   285
The poor, unfriended, never enter'd there.
To share his wealth the Heaven-sent strangers come ;
There orphans, beggars, find a constant home.
His pious acts in sweet memorial rise,
And prayers of thousands bless him from the skies.   290

   Return'd the sage. To life's far distant end,
On thee may Judah's envied bliss descend !
From Asher's race I spring, nor of thy sire,
Nor thee, fair Prince ! or clothes, or food require.
My highest wish the gifts of Heaven exceed ;   295
Though small my portion, yet far less my need.

   But O lov'd Youth ! my faithful counsels hear ;
Let hoary Age command thy listening ear.
Thy growth, thy beauty, nobler than thy peers,
Mine eyes attentive mark'd from earliest years :   300
I saw thy limbs in fair proportion rise,
And thy face smile the image of the skies.
Thy mind all-lovely, every voice proclaim'd ;
For sense distinguish'd, and for virtue fam'd ;
Bounteous and brave thy heart ; thy tongue discreet ; 305
Thy manners courteous, and thy temper sweet.

   Oft on these plains when gathering armies spread,
The long van darken'd, and proud ensigns play'd ;
Absorb'd, I saw thee war's gay splendors view,
Trace the deep files, and moving chiefs pursue ;   310
I saw the martial flame instinctive rise,
And growing lightnings tremble in thine eyes ;

I saw, and smil'd ; and Israel's voice approv'd,
That destin'd empire to thine arm belov'd.

But still, impell'd by strong desire to find   315
If Fame well sung the beauties of thy mind,
I watch'd thy steps, when evening hid the main,
Assum'd these rags and sought thee on the plain.
For know, fair Prince ! in Truth's unbiass'd state,
The proud are little, and the lowly great ,   320
From man, man claims, of high, or low degree,
The courteous manners, I have found in thee.

Now o'er thy head have twice ten summers run ;
The Youth is ripen'd, and the man begun :
Thy shapely limbs are sinew'd into force,   325
To hurl the dart ; to speed the nimble course :
Yet on what plain in triumph hast thou stood ?
When, bold and active, dar'd the strife of blood ?
No scar of thine attests the patriot wound ;
Thine arm inglorious, and thy wreaths unbound: 230
Should'st thou, when Joshua sleeps, the sceptre bear ;
How shall thy untaught mind conduct to war ?
How know what counsels wisdom bids embrace ?
What strength to arm ? the ambush where to place ?
Where on the field to stretch the dreadful wing ?   335
Or with what words of fire the languid arm to string ?
Rise then, brave Youth ! from ease unhonour'd rise !
Let sun-bright glory tempt thine eager eyes !
When next approaching combat threats the field
Seize the strong lance, and grasp the sheltering shield ;
If Hezron grant, the van's bright station claim,   341
And leave the foremost in the chase of fame !

Ill fits vile ease a Prince of worth divine,
Whose countless graces fair as angels shine ;
At home, unnotic'd, stretch'd in sloth, to lie,   345
While friends, while fathers toil, and bleed, and die ;

Line 323. *Twice ten summers*) This is a mistake of the Sage.

To fhare the fpoils diftain'd with others' gore,
A mean, falfe plunderer, when the battle's o'er.
Then while to war thy bold companions run,
While deeds of glory, wreaths of life, are won;   350
On the dread fword while Ifrael's caufe fufpends;
While empire victory, ruin flight attends;
While in full view the field of promife lies,
And the brave arm fhall win th' unmeafur'd prize;
Demand thy fhare, thy fhare of danger claim;   355
The toils of danger give the crown of fame.
To thee, through tribes, through nations yet to come,
Let grateful Ifrael owe her profperous doom;
Her endlefs rule; her land in beauty drefs'd;
Her ftream of glory, and her ages blefs'd.   360
Thus, in far diftant times, when Jofhua's name
Shall pafs, all-fragrant, down the tide of fame;
When future heroes to their fons fhall tell
How Hezron triumph'd, and how Sihon fell;
Combin'd with theirs, thy deeds fhall waft along,   365
Swell the glad theme, and mingle in the fong.
  No fhameful floth, no dread of manly toil,
No mean, falfe with to fhare in others' fpoil,
No love of eafe, the generous Youth replied---
To tents confine me, and to Hezron's fide.   370
Far other with my glowing mind infpires;
Fame wings my thoughts, and war my bofom fires.
When Glory's fons affembling hofts array,
Th' extatic view bears all my foul away.
My pulfe beats high; my briftling hair afcends;   375
My heaving heart a thrilling anguifh rends:
Sighs, prayers, and tears confefs the growing pain;
But fighs, and prayers, and melting tears are vain.
By love, beyond my higheft claim impell'd,
My fire conftrains me from th' embattled field.   380
Youth, frowns the chief, to ruin heedlefs flies;
From arms refrain, 'till years fhall make thee wife.

Go tell thy fire, the kindling fage return'd,
Thy hated abfence Ifrael long have mourn'd.
In forceful language, afk their wondering eyes,   385
Why funk in floth, their darling Irad lies,
Their voice demands thee to th' important plain,
To generous toils, and glories bought with pain:
They pant, they burn, to fee thy fplendors fhine,
Thy falchion triumph, and thy garlands twine.   390
Not fame alone, but duty points the way,
And truth and virtue chide the dull delay.

This faid, the Ancient o'er the plain withdrew,
And, fading from the moon-beam, left the view.

As loft in filence ftood the wondering pair,   395
Or maz'd, bewilder'd, rov'd they knew not where,
A cloud afcending eaftern fkies o'erfpread,
Involv'd the moon, and wrapp'd the world in fhade:
A dim-feen luftre cloth'd all heaven around,
And long, black fhadows floated o'er the ground.   400
As deep and folemn the far whirlwind roars,
Or waves run rumbling under cavern'd fhores,
With murmuring noife, o'er weftern mountains came
A broad, and dark-red meteor's awful flame:
Far o'er the woods, and plains, its fanguine hair   405
Stream'd wild, and dreadful, on the burden'd air.
As eaftern groves its leffening light abforb,
Like thoufand thunders, burfts the rending orb;
Wide-fhooting flames the glimmering fky furround;
A gloomy glory fpreads the twilight ground;   410
Loud o'er the world a long, hoarfe echo roars,
And fad Canäan groans through all her fhores.

Quick to the camp return'd th' aftonifh'd pair,
And half, in broken flumbers, loft their care.
O'er anxious Irad hovering vifions play'd,   415
Call'd up fair fcenes, or difmal terrors fhed;
Oft from his couch, in act to fmite, he fprang,
And oft his voice in fhouts imperfect rang.

When firſt through broken clouds the morning ſhin'd,
In purpoſe firm he fix'd his doubtful mind ;   420
At Hezron's feet, with graceful reverence ſtood,
And claim'd the bleſſing, e'er with joy beſtow'd.
With dawning ſmiles, he bleſs'd his lovely ſon,
And ſweet complacence round his aſpect ſhone.
Will Hezron bend his ear ? the favourite cries---   425
Speak, my belov'd---th' indulgent ſire replies.

  Thou know'ſt my boſom feels the warrior's flame,
Sighs for gay arms, and pants for generous fame ;
For Iſrael weeps, to aid her cauſe aſpires,
And burns tumultuous with reſiſtleſs fires.   430
When next our hoſt the ſhining falchion wield,
Bleſs'd ſire ! command me to th' embattled field.
Youths, o'er whoſe heads a few more months have run
In ſport, the peers, the rivals of thy ſon,
In glory's bright career with heroes join,   435
And their fair names even now begin to ſhine.
Grant, beſt of parents ! grant one bliſsful day,
And threefold duty ſhall thy love repay.

  Why doſt thou bring---the anxious ſire replied---
The dread requeſt, my love has oft denied ?   440
Why muſt thy ſire his favourite treaſure loſe ?
Why will thy heart the path of danger chooſe ?
That path, conceal'd where various evil lies,
And the brave periſh, while the daſtard flies.
More circling ſummers have thoſe youths beheld ;   445
Th'accuſtom'd age commands them to the field.
Scarce nineteen ſuns thine infant eyes have ſeen ;
Secure from ſhame, enjoy thy hours ſerene.
Let truth, let wiſdom be thy virtuous care ;
And the ſweet converſe of thy darling fair.   450
Still with thy partners draw the mimic field ;
The javelin hurl, the heavy falchion wield :
So taught their uſe, ſhalt thou, when battles join,
With fairer names, with veteran heroes ſhine ;

In marfhal'd hofts a nobler office claim,   455
And ftride more fwiftly in the chafe of fame.

Return'd the favourite---To thy faithful fon
Whene'er thy choice, indulgent fire, was known,
No counter choice unduteous words confefs'd,
But my fole anfwer was obedience blefs'd.   460
When laft mild evening clos'd the cheerful day,
O'er fouthern plains I trac'd my carelefs way ;
There as I gaz'd the works of Heaven around,
A chief, of Afher's race, my footfteps found---
Youth, cried the hoary fage, the changing fun   465
Beholds, well pleas'd, thy riper years begun.
The fcenes of dangerous war thy breaft demand,
And thy lov'd nation afks thine aiding hand ;
Their eyes require thee on the hoftile plain,
Nor let a nation claim thy aid in vain.   470
Go tell thy fire, while friends, while brothers die,
'Tis fhame, 'tis guilt, in torpid eafe to lie.
His duty bids him drefs thy limbs in arms,
And thine ftrait fummons to the trump's alarms.
Hafte, virtuous Youth ! thy nation's voice obey,   475
And fly, where Glory points her envied way.
Ah fire belov'd ! to fhame, to fatal fhame
Yield not thy darling Irad's opening name.
Think, beft of parents ! with what ftings of gall,
Contempt and fcorn a generous mind appall.   480
Save me from piercing fcorn ; from ruin fave ;
From daftards fnatch me ; rank me with the brave ;
Thy nation's call, more loud than thunders hear ;
Though Irad fail, let Ifrael gain thine ear.

With anxious look, th' unwilling fire replies,   485
The tears faft-ftreaming from his reverend eyes---
O fon belov'd ! beyond expreffion dear !
The ground of every joy ! and every fear !
This painful tale difparts my troubled foul ,
And bids my tears in large effufion roll.   490

How can my heart to favage war refign
My wealth, my boaft, my glory, all that's mine;
The child, the joy, the image, of my mind;
The beft, the only trace, I leave behind;
To prayers long-tried, all-fervent, kindly given;   495
The richeft bounty of indulgent Heaven?
  From infant years thy lovely form to raife,
To lure thy mind to all that merits praife;
'Gainft fatal fnares thy youthful heart to arm,
With truth illumine, and with virtue warm,   500
Ten thoufand fighs I breath'd, ten thoufand prayers,
Watch'd countlefs nights, and felt unnumber'd cares.
Each opening wifh, each rifing thought, I fcann'd;
Each new-born virtue nurs'd with foftering hand:
The flower etherial faw, with rapture, bloom,   505
Glow with ftrong light, and charm with choice perfume,
And each glad morn beheld my praifes rife,
A grateful tribute to the bounteous fkies.
  As, touch'd with joy, thy beauties I behold,
Thy limbs invigorate, and thy thoughts unfold;   310
Thy pure complacence eye the all-lovely Mind;
Thy love, thy goodnefs flow to all mankind;
Thy aims expand beyond the flight of youth;
Thy tongue unvarying yield the voice of truth;
Thy cheerful bounty make the poor thy care;   515
Thy fpotlefs mind affect fo bright a fair;
Thy fweet obedience every wifh forerun,
And my blifs double in my darling fon;
Too blefs'd, I wifh, my pains, my toils review'd,
Each pain repeated, and each toil renew'd.   520
  But chief, when that bright fair, who gave thee breath,
Sunk, pale and haplefs, in the arms of death,
Thy hand fo gently footh'd her long decay;
So fweetly guileful lur'd her pains away;
Whole nights, whole days, fuftain'd her drooping head;
Dried her fad tears, and watch'd her weary bed;   526

Like some mild angel, sent from pitying skies,
Shed dewy slumbers on her languid eyes ;
Illum'd the grave, seren'd the rugged way,
And cheer'd each fainting Hope of future day ;   530
Me from myself thy matchless duty stole,
And chain'd thee lovely to my inmost soul.

Now to far regions is that parent gone,
And, but for thee, thy sire were left alone :
From thee remov'd, no second self I know ;   535
And, O bless'd favourite ! solitude is woe.

When wing'd, my sweet companion trac'd her flight,
A wildering gloom obscur'd the cheerful light ;
Each joy was banish'd from my hapless doom,
And not a wish remain'd me, but the tomb.   540
Her tent, forsaken, seem'd in shades to mourn ;
Her empty seat implor'd her bless'd return :
Friends grac'd my board ; her vacant place I view'd ;
Down rush'd the tear, and every pang renew'd.
Through distant fields I roam'd ; the fields were sad :
No more her presence bade the flowers be glad :   546
A solemn twilight round all nature spread,
Drear as dun caves, that house the silent dead.
Alone in crowds I stood, in fields alone ;
My hope, my friend, my lovely solace gone.   550
But thou wast left.   In thy angelic face
Smil'd her lov'd image, glow'd her matchless grace :
To thee I flew ; and, in thy duty, view'd
Her power to charm, her wish to bless, renew'd.
That peace, the world beside could never give,   555
I found in thee, and lov'd again to live.
Too rich, too great, I own my Heaven-lent store ;
On earth, if thou may'st live, I ask no more.

Shall then thy sire that dread persuasion hear ?
Or feel the urgence of that forceful tear ?   560
Ah ! how can Hezron thy lov'd life destroy,
And yield th' insatiate grave my only joy ?

For, O fond Irad ! all the pride of state,
Fair dreams, and painted bubbles, of the great,
No real joy, no gentle peace, contain,   565
But gay deceit, and undiscover'd pain.
Whate'er in Wisdom prompts a wish to live,
Soft, calm domestic scenes alone can give.
Should'st thou be slain, even these must ceaseless mourn ;
No joy betides me, and no hopes return ;   570
A poor, despairing stranger, here I stay,
'Till Death's loud voice shall summon me away.

But ah ! to combat Israel Irad calls---
The piercing sound my struggling heart appalls---
Was all my bliss for Israel's weal bestow'd ?   575
And is a nation's voice the voice of GOD ?
Go then, my son, may he thy bosom guard,
To triumph lead thee, and with fame reward ;
Bright, and more bright, extend thy prosperous doom,
Or speed my footsteps to an early tomb.   580

Thus the great chief ; and rising as he spoke,
In his right hand a sword suspended took ;
Forth from the sheath the blade refulgent drew,
And his sad eye-balls kindled at the view.
Behold, brave youth---with earnest voice he cried---   585
Thine is the sword, thy sire's, thy grandsire's pride ;
By death of kings, and generous chiefs, renown'd,
With wreaths ennobled, and with triumphs crown'd.
When Egypt's sons, on proud Sabea's plains,
By Moses guided, pour'd their countless trains ;   590
High in his haughty car a chieftain rode,
Bore down whole troops, and roll'd through brooks of blood ;
Deep in his breast, while thousands round him fell,
Thy generous Grandsire lodg'd this shining steel ;
Then ceas'd the fight ; Sabea's millions fled,   595
And the earth groan'd beneath the piles of dead.

Line 589. *Egypt's sons*) See the account of the event referred to
in Josephus.

To Jahaz' deathlefs field when Sihon drew,
When combat thicken'd, and when dangers grew,
This arm, this falchion clave the monarch's fide,
And low on earth abas'd his impious pride.   600

From Hezron's hand the honour'd gift embrace,
Dread of thy foes, and glory of thy race;
And while thy arm their weapon learns to wield,
Let the fame fpirit prompt thee to the field,
Each wild excefs, each ufelefs danger fhun;   605
But firft in virtue's courfe aufpicious run:
Outftrip thy peers; To Jofhua's height afpire;
Let real glory all thy wifhes fire:
Let mine, my fire's, my tribe's, my nation's fame
Imbibe new fplendors from thy added name.   610
Yet not one fear my boding mind alarms,
Left Irad's deeds diftain his parent's arms;
I know thy generous mind; and, forc'd to yield,
Affur'd, behold thee grace th' embattled field.
And oh! wilt thou, whofe hand from every foe   615
My life preferv'd, and footh'd in every woe,
My darling fon defend! from thee he came;
Scarce born, I gave him to th' eternal Name;
Thine are his virtues; round his youthful head
A guardian fhield may thy good angel fpread.   620

Thus fpoke the chief. In Irad's feeling foul
A ftrange, tumultuous joy began to roll:
As oft t' unfold his grateful heart he tried,
The fuffocated founds in filence died.
Down dropp'd the fword; and ftrait, with homage due,
The Youth enkindling from the tent withdrew;   626
Quick to the lovely fair-one trac'd his way,
And ftrove the tumult of his thoughts t' allay.
Her in the tent, with maidens compafs'd round,
Select companions of her fports, he found.   630
There, fweetly welcom'd with inftinctive fmiles,
He fmooth'd his face with new, but harmlefs wiles,

And, while foft art her tender mind prepar'd,
His own defign, his fire's confent declar'd.
With guarded lips he fpoke ; but dire furprize   635
Pierc'd her fad heart, and gloom'd her ftarry eyes ;
With one deep figh, fhe felt her ftrength decay,
Slid to the ground, and breath'd her life away,
Quick to her aid the Youth impaffion'd flew :
And, with the virgins, bade her life renew ;   640
Again reviv'd the fplendor of her eye,
And ting'd her cheek with health's tranfcendent die.
O beft belov'd ! with tender voice he faid---
Let not fuch anguifh wound my beauteous maid !
Let cheerful hope thy timorous thoughts infpire,   645
And thine eye languifh with a brighter fire !
      When o'er my head a few fhort days fhall roll,
My haftening feet muft reach th' appointed goal ;
To manhood grown, the law, from heaven reveal'd,
Refiftlefs calls me to th' imbattled field.   650
If Ifrael's fons my falchion earlier claim,
And kindly fummon to the path of fame,
Why fhould'ft thou mourn ? 'tis duty points the way ;
When duty calls us, fafety bids obey.
      Thou know'ft when evening laft the fkies attir'd, 655
The fage, reproving, generous thoughts infpir'd ;
Firft from his mouth my nation's choice I knew ;
And fwift to war my foul obfequious flew :
No place, no hope, to vile delay was given ;
The call of nations is the call of Heaven.   660
Led by his voice, I truft his guardian care ;
With equal eafe he faves in peace, and war.
The fame good hand, that thro' the woodland fhade,
To friends, to fafety, lovelieft Mina led,
Though thoufands fall, may Irad's bofom fhield,   665
And wing th' averted javelin through the field.
      Thus he, with fofteft voice, and fondeft eye---
Then ftopp'd ; and anxious, hop'd the maid's reply.

She, plung'd in grief, and loft in dread amaze,
Sate filent, folemn, fix'd in mournful gaze: 670
With tendereft action on her looks he hung,
And thus vain folace tunes again his tongue.

    But, doom'd to fall, fhould Heaven my life demand,
And death betide me from a heathen's hand,
I fall in virtue's caufe.   Far happier doom,   675
In that blefs'd path, to find a fpeedy tomb !
Than, loft in fports, or funk in fhameful eafe,
To drag a worthlefs life, and fwell in glorious days.
And O bright maid ! without one guilty fear,
My thoughts can view refiftlefs death draw near.   680
In that far clime, where joy extends her reign,
My pinion'd foul fhall fpring to life again ;
Strong with empyreal youth, fhall trace her way,
And join the nations of immortal day.

Thence, when thy form is fummon'd to the tomb,   685
Perchance my fpirit, wing'd with light, fhall come,
Hail thy releafe from toil, and grief, and pain,
And raptur'd guide thee o'er the tracklefs main ;
In bonds etherial there our fouls be join'd,
And prove th' extatic nuptials of the mind.   690

    With filent, fad, and difcontented air,
And face averted, fate the liftening fair.
While the deep woe her feeling bofom mourn'd,
With a long, heavy figh, fhe thus return'd.

With boding heart I heard the fage's tale,   695
But felt fond hopes the dire defign would fail ;
That Hezron's choice, fo often tried in vain,
Would ftill confine thee from the fatal plain.
Yet thy lov'd maid, with gentle words, defign'd
To change thy wifh, and footh thy eager mind,   700
But my foul trembled at the dreadful light,
And every fenfe was loft in wild affright.

    Now to dire fate my fondeft hope muft yield,
While empty fame allures thee to the field.

But O bless'd youth! by soft intreaties won,   705
Where duty calls not, hideous danger shun.
Let not thy ardour fame's high impulse feel,
Tempt nearer fight, and try the deathful steel.
The fatal front to veteran warriors give;
Be thy rich boon, thy bless'd reward, to live.   710
I know thy bosom burns with glory's fire;
I know what visions war's bright beams inspire.
I fear, would Heaven the cause were less to fear,
Lest thy bold footsteps headlong rush too near;
Lest, wing'd with zeal, on instant death thou fly,   715
And leave thy hapless maid to weep, and die.
    For ah! on Irad all my joys suspend;
Grow with thy bliss, and with thy life extend.
Should then dread war compel thee to the grave,
The sad, untimely portion of the brave,   720
Whither, ah whither can Selima fly?
Where find a friend, to bid her early die?
Robb'd of thy face, the world's a desart drear;
The house of pain, and grief, and cankering care;
Forlorn, and friendless, life's lone path I tread,   725
And ask no lot, but with the silent dead.
Nor all those joys, thou know'st to paint so fair,
Can sooth sad woe, or lighten dark despair.
With thee conjoin'd, I claim my only doom,
Alike well-pleas'd, or here, or in the tomb.   730
Scarce would my soul, without thee heaven explore,
Where the first joy shall be to part no more.
    Oh, would the Chief thy anguish'd maiden hear,
And mark thy station in the humbler rear!
There no fell heathen would thy life annoy;   735
Nor fatal danger threat Selima's joy:
'Till age, 'till art, from sure experience won,
Had taught thee caution's every wile to shun.
And then, ah then might peace our days serene;
War cease to rage, and foes no more be seen;   740

Bliss, in glad streams, around our land extend,
And every sigh, and grief, and terror end.

Thus spoke the saddening maid. With pleasing guile,
The tender Prince recall'd her vanish'd smile;
With tales amusive lur'd her grief away,   745
And cheer'd her soul with hope's inlivening ray.

Meantime, through Israel spread the rumour far,
That matchless Irad join'd the coming war.
Charm'd with the tale, a bold, and generous train
Of youths, his rivals, throng'd the vacant plain;   750
And there, with one glad voice, the hero chose
To guide their footsteps 'gainst th' expected foes.
To him too youths the flattering message bare;
With modest grace, and sweet, becoming air,
Surpriz'd he heard, and while their hearts he won,
Assum'd the trust, and own'd the honour done.   756

And now decay'd the sounds of busy day;
The sun descending beam'd his final ray;
In starry grandeur rose the boundless night,
And temper'd ether with a milder light.   760
As through the host a general silence flow'd,
To Zimri's tent the watchful Leader strode,
And thus---Brave chief, to Ai direct thy course;
Thy sole command awaits a chosen force:
Through the deep forest steer thy southward way,   765
Where stately portals hail the setting day.
When first the clarion's voice to conflict calls,
Forsake thy ambush, and ascend her walls;
O'er all her domes let sudden flames aspire,
And her proud turrets sink in hostile fire: 780
Then through her northern gates direct thy way,
And lead thy squadrons to the fierce affray.

I go---the chief replied. The moon's broad round
Look'd in full lustre on the tented ground;
Fair o'er the shadowy hills she gently rose,   785
And shew'd a path for Ai's exulting foes.

In glimmering steel, a long, refulgent train,
Stretch'd in just files, and dazzled all the plain.
Slow to the wood their fading steps they press'd,
The Chief, in silent joy, retir'd to rest.

THE

CONQUEST OF CANÄA·N:

BOOK VI.

ARGUMENT.

Morning. Army assembles under the command of Hezron, and Joshua. Irad sollicits, and obtains a post, in the front of the western division. Orders. Israelites march. Army of Ai. Characters of Oran, and Carmi. Battle. Feigned retreat of the Israelites. Hanniel's disobedience, and overthrow. Joshua rescues him. Signal of return to battle. Joshua's address. Battle renewed. Joshua retires, and gives Caleb the command. Exploits of Irad. Exploits of Hezron, and of Caleb. Death of Ludan. Oran. Death of Hezron. Exploits of Carmi. His death. Irad rallies Judah. Joshua descends to battle, kills Oran, and puts the Heathens to flight. Zimri, having set Ai on fire, comes out upon the rear of the enemy. Final rout, and overthrow of the Heathens. Irad's distress at the fate of his father. Interview of Irad and Selima. Evening.

The CONQUEST of CANÄAN.

BOOK VI.

NOW dawning light conceal'd the worlds on high,
    And morn in beauty cloth'd the cloudlefs fky:
Loud o'er the field the trump's fhrill found began,
And fwift to arms the ftartled thoufands ran;
From all the camp burft forth the numerous throng,   5
Shook their tall fpears, and wak'd the martial fong;
Wide wav'd their plumes, refulgent flafh'd their fhields,
And fpiry banners trembled o'er the fields,
South of the camp, in two deep fquares they ftood,
And fierce for combat, fac'd the plain of blood.   10
    Before the weftern band great Hezron rofe,
Joy of his race, and terror of his foes:
Averfe from pomp, in ufeful fteel array'd,
Pleas'd, his juft ranks the mighty chief furvey'd;
Pleas'd to the well-known field of combat drew;   15
When duty call'd, his foul no terror knew
    Of equal ftrength battalions eaftward ftood,
And high in front exalted Jofhua ftrode.
By nature fafhion'd millions to controul,
In peace, in war, the great all-moving foul,   20
His mind expanded look'd exiftence through;
His heart undaunted danger never knew;

With calm endurance, toils and fears engag'd,
Climb'd as they rose, and triumph'd as they rag'd;
Patient, serene, as ills and injuries tried,   25
Meek without meanness, noble without pride,
Frank yet impovious, manly yet refin'd,
As the sun watchful, and as angels kind.
His Maker first, his conscience next he fear'd,
All rights kept sacred, and all laws rever'd;   30
Each wandering friend, with faithful friendship blam'd;
Each foe applauded, as fair merit claim'd:
Alike his kingdom wealth and want approv'd;
The noble reverenc'd, and the peasant lov'd.
His form majestic, seem'd by God design'd   35
The glorious mansion of so vast a mind:
An awful grandeur in his countenance sate;
Calm wisdom round him cast a solemn state:
His deathful arm no single force withstood;
His speed, his skill, no vigor could elude;   40
His piercing eye his mighty soul display'd;
His lofty limbs resplendent arms array'd;
With varied lightenings his broad falchion shone,
And his clear buckler mock'd the rising sun.

     Fair in the front of Judah's manly train,   45
A young gay band, adorn'd the gladsome plain.
Bright was their steely mail; their polish'd shields
With dazling splendor streak'd the smiling fields;
Soft breezes sported through their plumy pride;
Their trembling falchions glitter'd by their side;   50
Equal their bravery, and their thirst of fame;
Their age, their stature, and their arms the same.
     In the fair front, more beauteous than the morn,
When cloudless splendors orient skies adorn,
First of his race exalted Irad stood,   55
His soul inflam'd, his falchion drawn for blood;
On Joshua's steps his ceaseless eye was turn'd,
Charm'd with the pomp, that round the hero burn'd;

Tall was his stature, lofty was his mien,
His eye refulgent, and his brow serene : 60
Topp'd with two snowy plumes, that play'd in air,
A silver morion crown'd his auburn hair :
Far o'er the train his form sublimely shone,
By nobler arms, and manlier beauty, known.
So, when calm spring invests the sparkling plain, 65
And night sails silent up th' etherial main,
Round the broad azure stars unnumber'd glow,
And shadowy lustre robes the world below :
Thron'd in the western heaven young Hesper shines ;
His silver car to nether realms declines ; 70
O'er the gay mountains smiles his living eye,
And sinks, in splendor, down the gladsome sky.

From host to host the Chief majestic strode,
Inspir'd their hopes, and steel'd their souls for blood ;
Their perfect ranks his skilful eyes divide, 75
And his great bosom swells with manly pride.
As tow'rd the western square he bent his way,
Where hoary Hezron led the long array ;

To meet his steps impatient Irad ran,
And bent one knee before the godlike man ; 80
And thus---To youth will Joshua lend an ear ?--
---Speak my brave son ; thine every wish declare---
---With gentle voice, he said---The Youth replied---
See that fair train, inwrapp'd in steely pride !
In war, though young, our bosoms pant to shine, 85
And feel the wish, that brighter glows in thine.
Give, best of men ! this brave, though youthful band
In the bright front of charging fight to stand.
Oh, by my father's toils in fields of blood,
Whose love this freedom, and this sword bestow'd, 90
Indulge this ardent wish ! nor let thy frown
Quench a young flame, that emulates thy own.

I grant thy wish---the mighty Chief replied,
Smiling superior o'er his manly pride,---

Go, first of youths, defend thy Maker's laws,   95
And lift the falchion, in thy country's cause.
May God's good hand thy tender footsteps guard,
With caution bless thee, and with fame reward !

He spoke, and kindly raptur'd Irad rear'd ;
His swimming eye the grateful mind declar'd ;   100
Swift he return'd, on high his shield display'd,
Shook his blue sword, and thought the fight delay'd.

Near the bless'd scene enraptur'd Hezron stood,
And life ran nimbler thro' his languid blood ;
Charm'd with the kind regard, to Irad given,   105
He kneel'd to earth, and bless'd all-bounteous Heaven,
That Heaven which gave, his every wish to crown,
The Chief to Israel, and to him the son.

Now, rang'd for combat, wait the warrior bands,
And his brave leaders Joshua thus commands---   110
'Till this right hand exalt the javelin bright,
Let every rank conduct a mimic flight :
Slow, firm, and close, be mov'd the fair retreat ;
Nor wing'd with ruin wild, and foul defeat :
Meantime a missive death let arrows rain,   115
And slings unnumber'd tempest all the plain.
But when the javelin's beams in ether burn,
Swift to the fight let every rank return ;
Each vigorous arm the sword's broad terrors rear,
Or hurl the vengeance of the slaughtering spear ;   120
Brace firm the spacious shield ; disdain to fly ;
Rush to glad conquest, or with glory die.

He spoke: o'er southern plains, in long array,
To Ai's high walls the squadrons bent their way.
Undaunted Ai, th' approaching storm beheld,   125
And rous'd her heroes to the darkening field ;
Her chiefs command, her northern gates unfold,
Bright arms burst forth, and hosts to fight are roll'd ;
Like gloomy clouds, the blackening thousands rise,
And shrill-voic'd clarions thunder in the skies: 130

Two warlike chiefs th' embattled heathens guide,
Their forms majestic cloath'd in golden pride,
Wrapp'd in blue mail, insufferably vain,
With cruel front, that frown'd a stern disdain,
Around, dark Orán cast a sanguine eye,   133
Wav'd his broad shield, and dar'd th' avenging sky.
Grim in the van, with lofty stalk, he strode,
And shook his spear distain'd with drops of blood,
Blood, by his hand, in ancient battles shed,
In wasted realms, and fields bestrew'd with dead: 140
Sheath'd, in his hall the crimson'd weapon lay,
Lest cankering time should cleanse the stain away;
There, oft retir'd, he turn'd it o'er, and o'er,
And with fierce transport view'd the purple gore,
There call'd to mind the orphans of his spear,   145
Smil'd horrid o'er the scene, nor knew to drop a tear.

Behind him darkly roll'd a cloudy band,
Rous'd to the war from many a distant land,
With various arms in one great host combin'd,
And various banners streaming on the wind.   150
'Gainst Joshua's host the chief imperious strode,
And with fond prescience hail'd the scenes of blood;
A gloomy smile array'd his shaggy brow,
And thus his horrid joy began to flow.
Bless'd be the Gods, who gave this rapturous hour!   155
For this their fires shall many a youth devour;
While their gor'd children bleeding parents view,
And tears in vain their lifeless forms bedew.
Warriors rejoice; yon troop forgets the day,
When Ai's brave squadrons swept their host away;   160
Soon shall our spears be bath'd in brooks of blood,
And fields grow fruitful with a genial flood.
'Gainst Judah's hosts, inclos'd in burnish'd arms,
With matchless bravery and unrival'd charms.
Ai's dauntless sons to fight young Carmi led,   165
And now the helm first sparkled on his head.

T

Mov'd by his ceaseless sighs for martial fame,
His royal sire the parent's fears o'ercame.
Reluctant sent him to the deathful plain,
And fondly hop'd his lovely steps again.   170
There pleas'd with fame's imaginary charms,
He clasp'd the phantom in his eager arms,
On the bright glories turn'd a raptur'd eye,
And gaz'd, and gaz'd, and fancied bliss was nigh.

  Now, mid the grandeur of the deep array,   175
A dreadful space in gloom tremendous lay :
No banners wave in air, nor trumpet's sound ;
But silent terror saddens all the ground.
Loud burst the clarion's voice, and trembling far,
Shoot the broad ensigns o'er the frowning war ;   180
As thousand stars thro' kindling ether stream,
Bright showers of arrows cast a transient gleam :
From slings tempestuous countless pebbles rain,
Whizz thro' the skies, and whiten all the plain ;
The shrill helms clatter, death pursues the wound,   185
And prostrate heroes cloth'd the sprinkled ground.
So, when red summer burns the sultry pole,
O'er darkening hills a cloud's black volumes roll ;
Hoarse rush the winds ; hoarse drives the rattling hail,
Batters the craggs, and tempests all the vale ;   190
Deep groan the forests, torne their branches fall,
And one tumultuous ruin buries all.
Ere the loose combat long suspense had hung,
" Retire," the great command around them rung ;
Then, closely wedg'd, recedes the yielding fight,   195
And well-feign'd terror clothes the mimic flight.
Swift tow'rd their yielding foes the heathens spring,
Their bucklers blaze, their flashing lances sing :
Oft they rush forward, oft the bands retreat ;
For Israel's host disdains a base defeat ;   200
From ranks behind unnumber'd arrows shower,
And stones unnumber'd down the concave pour ;

Thick fall the foremost, clanging arms resound,
And streams of crimson die th' embattled ground.

   Meantime, fierce Hanniel, burning still for fame, 205
And sickening still at Joshua's envied name,
Deem'd this the destin'd hour, to pluck the crown
From the Chief's head, and plant it on his own.
Oh heaven, he cried, shall Israel ever flee,
The dupe of cunning, and the coward's prey ? 210
Must these pain'd eyes again our ruin view,
Curse our wild counsels, and our follies rue ?
Come every generous chief, whose bosom brave
To foul disgrace prefers a hero's grave,
Join Hanniel's path ; and soon proud Ai shall see 215
A few, bold warriors yet disdain to flee.
Whate'er my voice commands, my hand shall dare,
My deeds unspotted, as my dictates fair ;---
Far nobler doom, to fall in manly fight,
Than share, with titled names in splendid flight.--- 220
This said, his course the hero forward bends,
No chief applauds him, and no chief attends :
Two vulgar warriors, sad rebuff to pride !
Alone rush on, and clamour at his side.
Their dauntless course their raptur'd foes descry, 225
And well-aim'd lances glitter thro' the sky ;
Thick round the warriors, sinks the hissing steel,
And death's cold hand the brave attendants feel ;
In Hanniel's thigh expands a painful wound,
And the stunn'd hero raging bites the ground. 230

   Swift to his aid, impassion'd, Joshua flew,
Tho' well proud Hanniel's dark designs he knew,
Heard all the vaunts, the close injustice saw,
And felt th' infractions of his prudent law :
Yet now the chief lay weltering in his gore ; 235
Foes in distress to him were foes no more---
O'er the pale form he threw his guardian shield,
And bore him languid thro' the dreadful field :

Thick shower the stones, the flashing javelins sing;
And his bright arms with ceaseless murmurs ring.   240
Borne by four warriors o'er the distant plain,
Reluctant Hanniel sought the camp again :
There friendly plants his dying strength renew,
And sleep's soft influence aids the balmy dew.
While Joshua thus---Hence taught, ye warriors, know, 245
Wild, headstorng wishes guide to certain woe,
In peace, laws only claim a righteous sway ;
In war, one voice commands, the rest obey.
Proud disobedience Heaven consigns to shame ;
The path of duty leads alone to fame.   250
He spoke---With awe the silent squadrons heard,
The precept reverenc'd, and the teacher fear'd ;
Each saw, abash'd, the terrors of his frown,
And pleas'd, condemn'd rebellion, not his own.

   Meantime, brave Irad, on the western plain,   255
With pangs retir'd from Ai's contemptuous train.
As oft th' imperious taunt his rage inspires,
And his scorch'd bosom flames with eager fires,
Their utmost strength his vengeance promps to try,
He longs, he pants, to bid th' insulters fly :   260
Oft toward the host his course instinctive turns ;
His drawn sword trembles, and his buckler burns ;
But still his soul, in child-hood taught t' obey,
Restrains the wish, and backward turns his way.

   Now with pure splendor glow'd meridian light,   265
And Ai triumphant chas'd th' imagin'd flight,
When gay in dazzling arms, great Joshua turn'd :
His eyeballs sparkled, and his bosom burn'd :
The glittering lance his mighty hand uprear'd :
Loud rose his voice, and distant squadrons fear'd.   270
Behold, he cried, yon sheets of smoke ascend !
What heavy volumes round the skies extend !
Brave Zimri's conquering arm, while Heaven inspires,
Bursts Ai's proud portals, and her turrets fires ;

Now wheel your courfe ; to active vengeance fpring : 275
Brace the ftrong hand : the bloody falchion wing ;
See, Heaven's propitious finger points the way !
Fear chains their limbs, and terror yields the prey ;
O'er our glad courfe commencing grory fmiles,
And boundlefs treafures crown triumphant toils.   280

He fpoke ; the warriors eyed th' exalted fign ;
And thrilling bofoms own'd the voice divine ;
Swift wheel'd, the ranks to combat vigorous rife ;
Red lances fhower, and fhouts convulfe the fkies.
An equal ardour Ai undaunted brings,   285
Fronts the dire foe, and fierce to danger fprings---
As, borne by warring winds, thro' ether roll
Two rifing ftorms, and cloud the northern pole :
O'er fome dark mountain's head their volumes driven
With floods of livid lightening deluge heaven ;   290
Peal following peal, careering thunders fly,
Burft o'er the world, and rend the fhuddering fky.
With equal noife the ftorms of war refound ;
The blackening volumes cloud the hoftile ground ;
Thro' the fhock'd air in mingled tumult rife,   295
The conqueror's triumphs, and the victim's cries.

And now the chief to prudent Caleb's charge,
While the cloud thickens, and the founds enlarge,
Commends the hoft that own his mighty fway,
And bends to diftant rocks his backward way.   300
Here high in air he lifts the lance's beam,
And power divine fupplies a ceafelefs ftream ;
With pointed circles glows the weapon bright,
And cafts th' effulgence of exceffive light.

Long o'er the plain, impatient to purfue,   305
Had panting Irad fix'd an anxious view,
Sigh'd the great Leader's warning voice to hear,
Or catch the radiance of th' expected fpear :
The ready fword his hand all eager prefs'd ;
The well-brac'd buckler glitter'd o'er his breaft : 310

In th' utmoft weſtern ranks he ſilent ſtood
And look'd far onward thro' the field of blood ;
Pain'd, leſt the deſtin'd ſign, forgot ſhould fail,
Or ſome baſe dart the Leader's life aſſail.
But when the ſun-bright point inſtarr'd the air,   315
The blooming hero kenn'd the beam afar ;
To his brave peers, with ardent joy he cries,
And all the warrior ſparkled in his eyes.
Lo, generous youths, on yon delightſome plain
Shines the fair javelin, wiſh'd ſo long in vain !   120
Now ſpurn the hated flight ; to combat ſpring ;
Let virtue rouſe you, and let glory wing.
Now ſhall our ſires, and now the Leader, know
What flames heroic in our boſoms glow ;
Ai now ſhall learn, untaught our ſtrength to ſlight   325
Not fear, but wiſdom plann'd our ſeeming flight,
On their own heads redoubled vengeance feel,
Or fly inglorious from the conquering ſteel.
Riſe then, brave youths, their impious ſcoffs **repay** ;
My arm to triumph leads the envied way.   330
   He ſpoke ; the voice each active hero **warms** ;
With dreadful din they claſh their glittering **arms**,
Full on their dauntleſs foes impetuous fall,
And break reſiſtleſs o'er th' embodied wall.
As winter's ſhrilling blaſt begins to roar,   335
And drives, in gloomy rage, along the ſhore ;
Torne, in it's path, the trees confus'dly lie :
The white waves roll, the boughs tumultuous fly.
Not with leſs force, o'er piles of warriors ſlain,
Pours the bold band acroſs the bloody plain ;   340.
Death leads their way : with youthful vigor light,
They deal ſwift vengeance thro' the duſty fight,
Regardleſs of the ſtorm, that round them flies,
Of dying murmurs, and of conquering cries.
    High in the van exalted Irad ſtrode,   545
And now commenc'd the toils of death and blood.

When first his arm, immingling in the strife,
Drew the red stream, and spilt a human life,
(A lovely youth oppos'd his hapless head,
And with pure crimson died the infant blade)   350
Thro' his chill'd veins a new, strange horror ran,
And half-form'd tears in either eye began ;
In his young heart, unus'd to create woe,
Instinctive sympathy began to glow ;
The dreadful scene he gaz'd, and shook to hear   355
.The hollow groan and see pale death so near.
But soon fresh transports in his bosom rise,
Rous'd by shrill arms, and fir'd by barbarous cries :
Again his spirit claims th' imbattled foe ,
And bids two heroes to his falchion bow ;   360
Thro' cleaving ranks he wings a dreadful way,
And clouds of rolling dust obscure the day.

   Meantime in Judah's van great Hezron sped,
His voice arous'd them and his footsteps led ;
With fix'd firm course, the hoary hero strode,   365
His brown arms purpled with the bursting blood ;
Ranks after ranks against his falchion rise,
And chief on chief in swift succession dies.
For now each breast such active vengeance warms ;
They spurn the trifling toil of missive arms ;   370
Each braces firm the shield, and joys to wheel
The surer vengeance of the griding steel.
Full on great Hezron's course the heathens rush'd,
And the first chiefs by following chiefs were crush'd :
In solemn pomp, against the growing storm   375
The mighty hero rear'd his moveless form.
In vain bright swords around him ceaceless hung,
Troops press'd in vain, and clattering armour rung.
So, on some hill, while angry tempests lower,
In stately grandeur, stands the moss-grown tower ;   380
Loud roar the winds ; impetuous drives the rain,
And all the fury of th' etherial main ;

Still, rear'd to heaven, it frowns with pride sublime,
Spurns the fierce storm, and mocks the waste of time.

Far distant, Caleb swept the crimson plain,   385
Guided the fight, and pil'd the numerous slain;
Round his great arm the cloudy squadrons hung;
Clash'd on his buckler countless weapons rung;
Chiefs after chiefs oppos'd his wasting course,
Met his broad steel, and felt its fatal force.   390

Ludon, the Hivites' prince, his arm defied
All rough with gold, and gay in barbarous pride;
With giant strength the heathen hurl'd his spear,
Its terrors quivering through the parted air;
Loud o'er brave Caleb's shoulders sung the steel,   395
And pierc'd a warrior's breast; the warrior fell;
His blue mail clang'd; to rise he tried in vain,
But writh'd in dying anguish on the plain.
The mighty leader rais'd his sword on high,
Its transient lightnings circling in the sky,   400
Full on the Heathen's neck a griding wound
Sunk; the loos'd head fell spouting to the ground.
Amaz'd, the Hivites saw their monarch lost.
And deathlike murmurs groan'd around the host.

Near the bold leader Oran rear'd his steel,   405
Where the storm thicken'd, and the fiercest fell;
Imperious taunts provoke the rage of war,
Loud threats insult, and tumult sounds afar;
Wedg'd in a moveless throng, the battle grows,
Cries deeper roar, and shriller ring the blows.   410
With joy, unfeeling Oran strides the slain,
And hails the ruins of th' accustom'd plain;
No anguish melts, no wound his pity charms,
No fate impassions, and no groan alarms;
Thro' the red scenes he hews a raptur'd way,   415
And mingling darkness intercepts the day.

Meantime fierce Irad o'er the field is driven,
And boasts th' assistance of a favouring heaven;

Though new to war, with war his bosom glows,
And knows no transport, but the flight of foes.   420
  In scenes of distant death bold Hezron stands,
Dies his blue arms, and pains his aged hands;
Full many a chief his veteran falchion crowns,
Thick flit the shades, and blood the verdure drowns.
Impetuous Carmi springs the chief to meet,   425
Conscious of youth, and light with nimble feet;
His arm all active strews the sanguine ground,
Wakes the deep groan, and deals the frequent wound:
Full on his angry sword the warriors rush,
Impel th' upright, the falling heedless crush: 430
No chief the fury of his arm withstands,
And ruin widens o'er bold Hezron's bands.
Amaz'd, the hero saw the deluge spread,
And wide, and wider rise the piles of dead,
Flight first commence in hosts that own his sway,   435
And proud Ai hail a second conquering day:
From his sad bosom heav'd a heavy groan;
Round the whole war he miss'd his favourite son:
Untaught to droop, he hopes congenial fire
May yet ward shame, and yet the troops inspire.----   440
Where now, he cries, are fled the boasts of morn?
The towering stalk? the brow of lifted scorn?
Then Judah's warriors promis'd deeds of fame,
Hiss'd impious flight, and spurn'd the dastard's shame.
Far other scenes now rend these hapless eyes;   445
The foe advances; and the boaster flies;
Broke but by fear, ye wing inglorious flight,
Giants in words, and maidens in the fight;
Oh had kind Heaven dispens'd a speedier doom,
And this frail form in Bashan found a tomb!   450
Then had these palsied limbs, in peace repos'd;
Unpain'd with shame, these eyes in triumph clos'd;
Pleas'd to the last, survey'd my favourite race,
View'd no base flight, and bled for no disgrace.----

Hence, hence, ye timorous fouls, to Joſhua fly,   455
And tell the Chief, ye ſaw your leader die.

The hero ſpoke ; and urg'd by paſſion's force,
On furious Carmi bent his aged courſe ;
Awful in gleam of arms, the chiefs appear,
Here the bold youth, the white-hair'd hero there: 460
But ere his ſword great Hezron could extend,
Or circling bands their ancient chief defend,
A long, bright lance his wary foe beheld,
And ſnatch'd it glittering on the bloody field ;
Swift through the hero's ſide he forc'd the ſteel ;   465
Pierc'd to the heart, the aged warrior fell ;
There lay, a corſe, beſpread with purple ſtains,
The form, that triumph'd on a hundred plains.

On Ridgefield's hills, to ſhame to virtue dead,
Thus daſtard bands the foe inglorious fled ;   470
When Wooſter ſingly brav'd the deathful ground,
Fir'd hoſts in vain, and met the fatal wound.
In dangers born, to arms in childhood train'd,
From Gallia's heroes many a palm he gain'd ;
With freedom's ſacred flame ſerenely glow'd   175
For juſtice arm'd, and ſought the field for God ;
With ſteady zeal his nation's intereſt lov'd ;
(No terror touch'd him, and no injury mov'd)
Far in the front, with dauntleſs boſom bled,
And crown'd the honours of his hoary head.   480
Bent o'er his foe, the lovely Carmi ſtood,
And view'd, with tears of grief, his burſting blood ;
And thus---Unhappy ſire, he ſadly cried---
Perhaps thy monarch's joy, thy nation's pride.---
How like my father's bends thy hoary brow ?   485
His limbs, his countenance, and his locks of ſnow,
All in thy venerable face I ſee---
Perhaps the parent of a ſon like me---

He ſpoke ; and fiercely wheel'd his bloody ſword,
Sprang to the fight, and many a hero gor'd ;   490

His voice, his eyes the joyful hoſt inſpire,
And through the ſweetneſs flames a dreadful fire.
Active as light, o'er trembling ranks he hung ;
Shouts ſhook the plains, the frighted foreſts rung :
Unnumber'd ſullen groans were heard around ;   495
Unnumber'd corſes cloath'd the purple ground :
From poſt to poſt retir'd pale Judah's train,
And chief on chief increas'd the piles of ſlain.
Dark as an evening cloud, bold Ai was driven,
Gloom'd all the fields, and caſt a ſhade on heaven ;   500
Wide roll'd the ſtorm ; wide drove the duſt along,
And ruin hover'd o'er the flying throng.

Meantime, brave Irad turn'd his ſparkling eyes,
And ſaw in diſtant fields the clouds ariſe ;
Sad flight and terror fill'd the backward plain,   505
And the foe ſhouted o'er his kindred ſlain.
As, when autumnal clouds the ſkies deform,
Burſts the wild whirlwind from the gloomy ſtorm ;
Hoarſe craſh the pines ; oaks ſtiffly ſtubborn fall,
And ſudden thunders liſtening ſwains appall :   510
So, wing'd by Heaven, impetuous Irad flew ;
As ſwift their darling chief the youths purſue ;
Whelm'd in their path, the falling bands expire,
And crowds of warriors from their ſteps retire.

Now, where brave Carmi ſwept the purple ground,
Terrific Irad ſhook his buckler's round ;   516
Alike in years they ſeem'd, alike in arms,
Of equal ſtature, and of rival charms :
Nor this, nor that, the dangerous fight can yield ;
But each demands the empire of the field.   520
From the fierce chiefs the wondering bands retreat ;
Blows following blows their ſounding ſhields repeat ;
Uncleft, each faithful orb the ſtroke rebounds,
Blunts the keen blade, and intercepts the wounds :
'Till Irad's nimble arm, with ſudden wheel,   525
Through Carmi's ſide impels the fatal ſteel,

Pure ftreams of crimfon ftain the fubject ground,
And the freed foul pervades the gaping wound.

Not that fair pride, that foul-fupporting flame,
That lights the fplendors of th' immortal name ;   530
Not all the bravery nature can impart,
Nor the fond wifhes of a virgin's heart,
Nor parents' vows, nor nations' prayers could fave,
The young, bright hero from an early grave.
He fell, with beauty's faireft beams adorn'd,   535
While foes admir'd him, and while Irad mourn'd.
Ah youth, too foon allotted to the tomb ;
Oh had kind Heaven difpens'd a fofter doom,
On thy fair deeds a fweet reward beftow'd,
And op'd the manfions of the blefs'd abode !   540

Thus, where fad Charleftown lifts her hills on high,
Where once gay ftructures charm'd the morning fky,
Ere Howe's barbarian hand in favage fire
Wrapp'd the tall dome, and whelm'd the facred fpire,
In life's fair prime, and new to war's alarms,   545
Brave Warren funk, in all the pride of arms.
With me, each generous mind the hour recall,
When pale Columbia mourn'd her favourite's fall ;
Mourn'd the bright ftatefman, hero, patriot, fled,
The friend extinguifh'd, and the genius dead ;   550
While he, the darling of the wife, and good,
Seal'd his firm truth, and built his name in blood.

Loud as the rufhing ftorm, the din of war
Burft o'er the plain, and fhook the fields afar ;
Fierce Irad rais'd a loud, diftinguifh'd cry---   555
Here fee, my friends, their gafping leader lie.----
Through Ai's wide hoft my fword fhall hew your way ;
Shall Judah's fons alone defert the day ?
Shall Jofhua know you fled ? to glory rife ;
Lift all your arms, and pierce the knave that flies.   560

The hero fpoke : abafh'd the warriors heard,
Rung their blue arms, and high the ftandard rear'd ;

Aloft in air a Lion's gloomy form
Lower'd, like the darkneſs of a ſullen ſtorm ;
Around his head his ſhaggy terrors frown'd,   565
And his red eyeballs gleam'd deſtruction round.
Swift from the bearer's hand fierce Irad drew
The banner'd ſtaff, and mid the heathens threw ;
With joy they ſprang to ſeize the glittering prize,
And ſmiles of triumph ſparkled in their eyes.   570
Shame fluſh'd the cheeks of Judah's glowing train ;
Their boſoms heav'd ; their faces flaſh'd diſdain ;
To ſeize the ſhining ſpoil each warrior ſprang ;
The combat thicken'd ; and all ether rang ;
Far roll'd the darkneſs of the duſty cloud ;   575
Loud roſe their cries, and armour claſh'd aloud.
The blackening tempeſt Ai undaunted kenn'd,
Pleas'd to procure, and ſtubborn to defend ;
Scarce Irad's arm could cleave the firm-wedg'd train,
As fierce he ſtrove the ſtandard to regain ;   580
Through ranks on ranks he forc'd a ſanguine way,
Ere his red falchion won the ſplendid prey ;
With ſmiles, he ſaw the crimſon tumult grow,
And hail'd the vengeance gathering o'er the foe.
    From the tall rock great Joſhua caſt his eyes,   585
And ſaw the varying ſcenes of combat riſe.
To Carmi's force beheld pale Judah yield,
And roſe to ſave the triumphs of the field ;
But ſoon new ſhouts aſcend the clouded ſky,
His friends now triumph, and the Heathens fly.   590
    Now nearer ſcenes his ſearching view demand,
Where mighty Caleb rules the warrior band ;
Fierce Oran's ſword begins inglorious flight,
And his loud clamours animate the fight :
Scarce Caleb's arm the conflict can ſuſtain,   595
His voice arouſe, or deeds inſpire, the train ;
So fierce the heathens throng th' embattled ground,
So thick the warriors fall, the groans reſound.

The Hero view'd, and tow'rd the fainting throng,
Swift as a rapid whirlwind, rush'd along;   602
As 'gainst a mound, when tempests ride the gale,
The raging river foams along the vale:
Down the wall crumbles, and with dreadful reign
Sweeps a wild deluge on the wasted plain.
Bursting upon the dark embodied throng   605
Thus the wide ruin Joshua drove along;
Around his course increas'd the piles of dead,
The brave sunk fighting, and the coward fled.

Now, where unfeeling Oran crush'd the slain,
All grim with dust, and red with many a stain,   610
While smiles of transport gather'd on his brow,
His fierce eye sparkling o'er the bleeding foe,
While high for death he rear'd his sanguine arm,
And a brave warrior bow'd to shun the storm,
Great Joshua's full-orb'd buckler caught the wound,   615
And lightnings darted from the moony round,
Then, by his hand with rushing thunder thrown,
On Oran's helmet burst a mighty stone,
That, bounding onward 'gainst a warrior's side,
Crush'd his strong ribs, and shed a plenteous tide.   620
Stunn'd by the staggering blow, the leader fell,
Writh'd with the pain, and gave a hideous yell;
Furious he lay, with heaving, panting breath,
Roll'd up his whitening eyes, and frown'd in death;
Cursing the shield, which seiz'd his nimble dart,   625
And stopp'd its passage to the warrior's heart:
Swift on his throat descends th' indignant blade,
Bursts the black gore, and leaps the grisly head.

Loud o'er the tumult rose the Hero's cry;
The host all quakes, the distant groves reply---   635
Rush on, bold heroes, conquest crowns the day;
Now spring to fight, and seize the trembling prey.
This arm on Oran drove the final wound;
Let shouts of triumph shake the hostile ground:

Wealth, and fair peace, the generous contest yields, 635
And wreaths of glory bloom in bloody fields.----
As in th' enkindled wood fierce winds arise,
And storms of fire are blown across the skies;
In blazing trains, the towering pines descend,
And rushing thunders all the forest rend: 640
So, loud and furious, Israel throng'd the fight,
And their blue armour flash'd a dreadful light;
O'er the pale rear tremendous Joshua hung;
Their gloomy knell his voice terrific rung;
From glowing eyeballs flash'd his wrath severe, 645
Grim Death before him hurl'd his murdering spear;
Heads, sever'd from their necks, bestrew'd his way,
And gushing bodies round his footsteps lay.

Meantime Ai's sounding portals wide unfold,
And fierce to combat bursting bands are roll'd; 650
In dreadful pomp ascends the widening train;
Battalions on battalions cloud the plain:
There glowing Zimri wings his rapid force,
And eager thousands darken round his course.

Ai's ghastly sons the smoking walls survey'd, 655
And wild amaze each pallid front array'd;
Here lay in gore their brethren, and their sires;
There sunk their mansions in terrific fires;
Before, behind, their foes increas'd alarms; 659
They rais'd one shriek, and dropp'd their useless arms:
Where'er an opening rank receiv'd the day,
Or dust obscure disclos'd a glimmering ray,
Borne by light fear, they left the lingering wind,
They fled, they flew, nor cast a look behind;
Oft on the spear's protended point they ran; 665
While throng'd resistless, meeting man with man,
Steel stretch'd to steel, and shield to shield oppos'd;
On every side the power of Israel clos'd.
So thick they throng'd, no spear could miss its course;
In vain no falchion spent its ardent force: 670

Less heard and less, resounded piercing cries,
And dust besprinkled ceas'd to fill the skies.
So, when tall navies lift imperial sails,
And hope th' indulgence of propitious gales,
When the cold north's fierce wind the main deform, 675
And, fill'd with thunders, rolls the raging storm,
Heav'd from the bottom, foaming billows rise,
And climb, and climb, and roar against the skies;
O'er shiver'd masts unroll the surging waves,
And the pale sailors plunge in watery graves.   680
Swift as a whirlwind, o'er the southern plain,
Impetuous Zimri drove the Hivite train:
With prosperous course, they sped their hasty flight,
Sunk in the wood, and vanish'd from the sight.

    And now, obedient to the Chief's command,   685
Round the tall standard throng'd each wearied band;
A smile of transport every face adorn'd,
Their wounds unheeded, and the dead scarce mourn'd.

    Nor knew fair Irad how his parent lay,
But, fir'd with glory, steer'd his careless way;   690
Near the great Chief he mov'd with conscious grace,
And conscious blushes crimson'd o'er his face;
When, pale and ghastly, on the bloody ground,
Stain'd with black dust, and pierc'd with many a wound,
Stiff gore besprinkling all his locks of snow,   695
And a cold cloud around his reverend brow,
Hezron appear'd: at once his nerves congeal'd;
His frozen lips a dumb, dead silence seal'd;
A moveless statue, o'er the sire he hung,
Nor streaming tears releas'd his marbled tongue.   700
Then round the corse impassion'd arms he threw,
And wash'd the clotted gore in filial dew;
Glu'd to the form with strong embraces lay,
And kiss'd, with quivering lips, the senseless clay.
At length the Chief, soft pity in his eyes,   705
Reach'd his kind hand, and forc'd the Youth to rise:

Four mournful warriors Hezron's body bore,
And their eyes glisten'd with a tender shower.

The sun declin'd ; besmear'd with dust, and blood,
Slow o'er the plain the wearied squadrons trode ;   710
When, fair as Phosphor leads the morning train,
Dress'd in new beams, and beauteous from the main ;
Crown'd with white flowers, that breath'd a rich perfume
And cloth'd in loveliness, of gayest bloom,
Rose in soft splendor Caleb's youngest pride,   715
A thousand maidens following at her side.
In snow-white robes of flowing silk array'd,
First of the virgins walk'd the blushing maid ;
Her long, dark hair loose-floated in the wind ;
Her glowing eyes confess'd th' etherial mind ;   720
A wreath of olive flourish'd in her hand ;
A silver lyre obey'd her soft command ;
With sounds harmonious rang the warbled strings,
And thus the maids, and thus Selima sings.
Who comes from Ai, adorn'd with gay attire,   725
Bright as the splendor of the morning fire ?
Fair as the spring, ascends the lovely form,
And dreadful as the blaze, that lights the storm !
Ye maids, with flowerets strew the conqueror's way,
Strike the loud harp, and sing the dreadful day !   730
To Irad's steps the matchless fair-one came,
Her breast quick-panting, and her cheeks on flame ;
Her beauteous hand the verdant crown display'd ;
Graceful he bow'd, and plac'd it on his head.
Slow to her train the trembling fair withdrew,   735
The charm'd youths following with a moveless view,
So, wing'd with light, and dress'd in strange array,
The mantling glory of the rising day,
With sweet complacence, such as angels show
To souls unprison'd from this world of woe,   740
Parted soft-smiling from our general sire
Some bright-ey'd Virtue, of the heavenly choir,

X

Far in the folar walk, with wanderous flight,
The form celeftial leffen'd on his fight.

    Again the youth his wonted life regain'd ;   145
A tranfient fparkle in his eye obtain'd ;
A rifing glow his tender thoughts confefs'd,
And the foft motions of his melting breaft.
But foon dark glooms the feeble fmiles o'erfpread ;
Like morn's gay hues, the fading fplendor fled ;   750
Returning anguifh froze his feeling foul,
Deep fighs burft forth, and tears began to roll.

THE

CONQUEST OF CANÄAN.

BOOK VII.

ARGUMENT.

Evening described. Irad's dream. He goes out to the walls of Ai. His lamentation for his father. Reflections on the fate of Ai. Appearance of an army. Irad returns in haste, and alarms the Camp. Joshua, at his request, allots him a body of forces, with whom he goes out to attack the Heathens. Battle by the burning of Ai, between Hazor, &c. and Israel. Irad's exploits. He kills Adnor, and pursues Samlah to the eastern part of the host. Uzal. Shelumiel. Jabin's character, and exploits. He kills Shammah, and Seraiah. Jobab. Confusion of the Israelites. Irad returns, and rallies them. He attacks Jobab, with success. Kindling of the neighbouring forest separates the combatants.

The scene of this battle is partly on the plain east of Ai, partly in the forest still eastward, and partly northward of the forest.

THE CONQUEST OF CANÄAN.

BOOK VII.

O'ER the wide world immeasurably spread,
    Night, still and gloomy, cast a solemn shade.
  In heavens half-clouded stars unfrequent hung ;
Scarce heard, the blast with mournful murmurs rung ;
Above tall, eastern hills, the moon's pale eye   5
Look'd sad, and dreadful, from the cheerless sky :
Her cold, wan face, half-hid behind a cloud,
That wrapp'd the mountains in a sable shroud,
With feeble lustre streak'd the shadowy plains,
And edg'd her vapoury robes with dismal stains.   10
All, but the savage race, to sleep retir'd,
And the last gleams of western skies expir'd.
  Stretch'd in his tent, unhappy Irad lay,
And sad oblivion bore his toils away.
In that still hour, when rapt on eagle-wings,   15
To distant climes bewilder'd fancy springs,
A death-like slumber seal'd his tearful eyes,
And thus unreal scenes in vision rise.
  Through lonely fields, in russet gloom array'd,
Lost in mute grief, with weary steps he stray'd.   20
A shadowy light, like evening's dusky ray,
Spread o'er the world, and form'd a twilight day.
Before his wandering path, a northern grove
Shed midnight round, and pierc'd the clouds above :

Slow wav'd the tall, dark pines : a hollow found   25
Roll'd through the wood, and shook th' autumnal ground,
Dull-murmuring fell the sullen, swelling streams,
Lulling to sleep, and blue in glimmering beams.
With broad, black horrors o'er its bosom spread,
An eastern mountain rear'd its shaggy head ;   30
High hung the hoary cliff ; the cedars height,
Less seen, and less, withdrew beyond the sight.
Strange unknown scenes the regions wild display,
And solitary music slowly dies away.

From the thick grove, in dark-brown robes reveal'd,
A form stalk'd solemn o'er the shuddering field ;   35
Of other worlds he seem'd ; nor cast an eye
On the brown plain, or on the gloomy sky.
Regardless of the scenes that round him mourn'd,
On Irad's path his sad, slow steps he turn'd ;   40
Pale stood the Youth ; the stately shape drew nigh ;
Gash'd was his cheek, and fix'd his lofty eye ;
Like a light flame, low hung his beard of snow,
And death's cold terrors hover'd on his brow.
'Twas Hezron's self. With weak, but solemn sound,   45
As sullen graves beneath the foot resound,
His voice began---On fate's dark verge I stand,
Whence thickening dangers roll across thy land.
Night wraps the world ; approaching storms arise,
Hang o'er thy race, and cloud the southern skies.   50
My mouldering bones a colder night detains,
Clos'd in the tomb, and bound in icy chains :
But the wing'd spirit fairer climes surround,
And heaven unfolding bids her songs resound.
Faintly he spoke. By strange, immortal spell,   55
His wounds grew smooth, his sightless garments fell :
His pallid face a sudden beauty fir'd,
And with strong life his changing eye inspir'd ;
O'er his white robes a purple splendor ray'd ;
Long glittering pinions loosely round him play'd ;   60

In dreadful pomp, sublime the Vision stood,
And living fragrance breath'd along the wood.
   At once the hero, startled, rais'd his head ;
Still was his tent, and all the tumult fled :
Again to sleep he clos'd his wearied eyes,   65
And broken slumbers o'er his toils arise.
   Sudden, his name re-echoing from the walls,
A wild, and visionary murmur calls---
Irad awake ; my voice thine ear invades,
From the dark mansions of imprison'd shades ;   70
In southern plains the clarion's thunders rise,
And shouts of triumph fill the rending skies.
   Swift from his couch the Youth astonish'd rose,
(While every vein the dreadful murmur froze)
With active hand his arms around him brac'd ;   75
With nimble feet the glimmering champain pass'd,
And tow'rd Ai's flames, that rag'd with awful force,
Suspense, but fearless, steer'd his lonely course.
Still o'er his head the airy phantom hung ;
Irad awake---the voice unreal rung :   80
Sad grief, and anxious doubt his thoughts oppress'd,
But love's soft whispers still disturb'd his breast.
   Now solemn silence sail'd along the air ;
No bird complain'd ; no echoing voice was near ;
Save the flow murmur of the passing gale,   85
That swept the plain, and sounded through the vale.
The flames dark-glimmer'd on the hero's shield,
And cast long shadows o'er the pallid field :
Round the dread scenes he turn'd regardless eyes,
And thus began, with intermingled sighs---   90
   And art thou fled forever ? this thine end,
Thou best of parents, and thou surest friend ?
And could'st thou fall, a prey to murdering war ?
What cruel demon drove my feet so far ?
Was no kind angel hovering o'er the throng ?   95
Where look'd the Power, thy virtue serv'd so long ?

Thy foul fo pure---thy life fo firmly juft---
Scarce Heaven's own law could more demand from duft,
Why, O thou righteous Mind ? but ceafe my tongue,
Nor blame the dread decree, that cannot wrong.   100
Mine the fole fault---and mine the fingle blame---
Wild with the magic of that phantom, fame.
Didft thou for this the guilty fhield beftow,
To leave thee naked to the fatal blow ?
Didft thou for this the fword accurs'd impart,   105
That fhould have plung'd beneath the murderer's heart ?
Far other love, far other faithful cares
Nurs'd my young limbs, and watch'd my rifing years ;
My early fteps, from pleafure's flippery road,
Lur'd with foft fmiles, and led them up to GOD ;   110
Thy own bright actions prompting to purfue,
To virtue charm'd me, and to glory drew;
With Jofhua's felf my wifhes forc'd to vie,
Boaft of mankind, and chofen of the Sky.

　　Pale, in the vifions of the guilty bed,   115
Thy form affrights me, and thine eyes upbraid.
There fcenes of dire diftrefs thy words unroll,
Doom'd for my life, and opening on my foul.
Or does thy mind its lov'd employ purfue,
To guard from ill, and hidden dangers fhew ?   120
Perhaps thy thoughts, beyond the filent tomb,
Watch, as in life, thy nation's fecret doom ;
Some rufhing fate unknown difcern afar,
Some threatening ambufh, or fome wafting war.

　　Perhaps the firft of maids thy care demands,   125
And claims her fafety from aerial hands.
Ah ! knew the fair what crimes to me belong,
Her lovely voice had fpar'd th' applauding fong ;
A breaft more pure her melting arms embrac'd,
And the bright garland worthier temples grac'd.   130
　　Thus fpoke the chief, when now his fteps were nigh
Ai's awful flames, that wav'd acrofs the fky ;

All pale, and gloomy, climb'd the dreadful blaze,
And smoky volumes curl'd above the rays ;
A dreary gleam enroll'd the shady ground,   135
And the brown land-scape faintly rose around:
Touch'd by the solemn scene, the hero cried---
Where hapless Ai ! is now thy towery pride ?
Where now thy manly sons, whose sinewy arms
Rose, a strong bulwark 'gainst impending harms   140
Where now the heaven-topp'd spire ? the gilded wall ?
Thy kings, thy heroes ? whelm'd in ruin all---
Destruction's clouds sail'd blackening o'er thy light,
And wide oblivion's never-ending night.

Where yon tall dome shoots forth the greedy flame,145
Perhaps some hero hop'd a deathless name.
Oft when return'd from war, his tender race
Climb'd his fond knee and ask'd the sweet embrace :
Oft, with a parent's glistening eye, he view'd
His face, his virtues in their forms renew'd.   150
Perhaps some daughter, darling of his care,
Beam'd, like Selima fairest of the fair :
And could those flames some lovely maid destroy,
A nation's glory and a parent's joy ?
Could babes, sweet-smiling, claim no hand to save, 155
But find, unwept, a furnace for a grave ?

Thus mourn'd his generous heart the doom severe,
And paid lost Ai the tribute of a tear.
Like ocean's long, deep roar, a rushing sound
Burst from the wood, and pour'd along the ground ; 160
At once wide trembled o'er the awful fields
The sudden gleam of spears, and helms, and shields,
Impetuous roll'd unseen the rattling car,
And banner'd terrors wav'd th' approach of war.
Loud rung bold Irad's voice ; the dreadful sound   165
Stopp'd the long host, and shook th' affrighted ground ;
Thrice, like the burst of thunder, hoarse he cried ;
Thrice, stood the host ; and thrice the sky replied :

Y

The cry wav'd solemn through the winding vales ;
Night shook, and murmurs fill'd the rushing gales.   170
The southern guards soon caught the boding sound,
And spread th' alarm the startled camp around ;
Loud as tall billows rend the rocky shore,
Rose the sonorous clarion's bursting roar :
Swift to the camp the hero wing'd his way,   175
Rous'd all the host, and scatter'd wild dismay---
Arm, warriors, arm ! to instant battle fly !
The foe's at hand ! ye combat, or ye die.
Swift to these tents unnumber'd bands repair ;
Hark ! how the trumpet fills the troubled air !   180
In southern fields ascends the wasting war,
And fierce as whirlwinds rolls the rapid car.
Arm, ere our camp be wrapp'd in one broad flame,
And Israel's manly thousands want a name,

　　Thus, round the host, his animating cry   185
Urg'd sleep's oblivious hand from every eye ;
Each waking mind the strange alarm appalls ;
Arm, warriors, arm ! each startled hero calls :
From tent to tent the wild confusion flies ;
Shouts rend the plains ; groans murmur ; shrieks arise ;
A rushing noise invades the listening ear ;   191
In swift succession half-seen forms appear ;
Shrill rings the rattling mail ; the trump's big sound
Cleaves the dun heaven, and shakes the gloomy ground.
Round a broad flame, that, by the Chief's command,
Shoots lofty spires, and gleams along the sand,   196
Deep throng the squadrons ; high the standards stream,
And wave, and glimmer, in the livid beam.
There, while the terrors of the lovely fair
Froze every breast, and breath'd a wide despair,   200
A quickening glow the Leader's voice inspir'd ;
Hush'd were their cries ; their lessening fears retir'd ;
Through every bosom thrill'd a new delight,
And brac'd each sinew for the manly fight.

Now, rang'd in ranks, the host expectant stood, 205
Prepar'd for combat, steel'd to death and blood ;
Sudden, before the Chief, with panting breast,
The generous Youth preferr'd his bold request---
Near Ai's red flames I steer'd my careless way,
Robb'd of wish'd slumbers, and to grief a prey, 210
When sheath'd in gleaming arms, a mighty train,
Pour'd from the wood, and cover'd all the plain :
On foaming coursers, chiefs impel the war,
Or whirl the terrors of the wasting car.
And wilt thou, Chief divine, from Irad hear 215
The dictates of a mind, that knows no fear ?
Shall this young arm again the lance command,
And lead to fight a strong, undaunted band,
To Ai's wide ruins wing our active course,
And tempt the fury of barbarian force ? 220
Shall thine unconquer'd sword the camp defend,
And ward the fate, if shame our steps attend ?
Safe in thy prudence shall the race endure,
And Joshua's name our wives, and sons secure.
Lo, dress'd in steel, we wait thy ruling breath ! 225
Counsel is ruin, and delay is death.
Go, in JEHOVAH's name---the Chief replied---
Forth stalk'd the Youth, and warm'd with martial pride ;
O'er southern fields the bands appointed steer'd,
Squar'd in just ranks, and not a warrior fear'd. 230
    Now where Ai's sons bestrew'd the plain, they came,
Faintly illumin'd by the distant flame ;
No foe appear'd : the world more gloomy grew,
And, lost in clouds, etherial realms withdrew ;
Save where lone stars diffus'd a feeble beam, 235
Like the far taper's solitary gleam :
Slow winds breath'd hollow through the dark profound,
And deepening horror brooded o'er the ground.
    East of proud Ai, an ancient forest stood,
And southward far was stretch'd the lofty wood ; 240

North lay fair plains ; and next the walls, array'd
With scatter'd trees, a spacious level spread.

   Now near the burning domes, the squadrons stood,
Their breasts impatient for the scenes of blood :
On every face a death-like glimmer sate,   245
The unbless'd harbinger of instant fate.
High thro' the gloom, in pale and dreadful spires,
Rose the long terrors of the dark-red fires ;
Torches, and torrent sparks, by whirlwinds driven,
Stream'd thro' the smoke, and fir'd the clouded heaven.
As oft tall turrets sunk with rushing sound,   251
Broad flames burst forth, and sweep the etherial round,
The bright expansion lighten'd all the scene,
And deeper shadows lengthen'd o'er the green.
Loud thro' the walls that cast a golden gleam,   255
Crown'd with tall pyramids of bending flame.
As thunders rumble down the dardening vales,
Roll'd the deep solemn voice of rushing gales :
The bands admiring gaz'd the wonderous sight,
And Expectation trembled for the fight.   260

   At once the sounding clarion breath'd alarms ;
Wide from the forest.burst the flash of arms ;
Thick gleam'd the helms ; and o'er astonish'd fields,
Like thousand meteors, rose the flame-bright shields.
In gloomy pomp, to furious combat roll'd   265
Ranks sheath'd in mail, and chiefs in glimmering gold ;
In floating lustre bounds the dim-seen steed,
And cars unfinish'd, swift to cars succeed :
From all the host ascends a dark-red glare,
Here in full blaze, in distant twinklings there ;   270
Slow waves the dreadful light, as round the shore
Night's solemn blasts with deep concussion roar,
So rush'd the footsteps of th' embattled train,
And send an awful murmur o'er the plain.

    Tall in th' opposing van, bold Irad stood,   275
And bid the clarion sound the voice of blood,

Loud blew the trumpet on the sweeping gales,
Rock'd the deep groves, and echoed round the vales ;
A ceaseless murmur all the concave fills,   (hills.
Waves thro' the quivering camp, and trembles o'er the
    High in the gloomy blaze the standards flew ;   181
Th' impatient Youth his burnish'd falchion drew ;
Ten-thousand swords his eager bands display'd,
And crimson terrors danc'd on every blade.
With equal rage, the bold, Hazorian train   285
Pour'd a wide deluge o'er the shadowy plain ;
Loud rose the songs of war, loud clang'd the shields,
Dread shouts of vengeance shook the shuddering fields ;
With mingled din, shrill, martial music rings,
And swift to combat each fierce hero springs.   290
So broad, and dark, a midnight storm ascends,
Bursts on the main, and trembling nature rends ;
The red foam burns, the watery mountains rise,
One deep unmeasur'd thunder heaves the skies ;
The bark drives lonely ; shivering and forlorn,   295
The poor, sad sailors wish the lingering morn :
Not with less fury rush'd the vengeful train ;
Not with less tumult roar'd th' embattled plain.
Now in the oak's black shade they fought conceal'd ;
And now they shouted thro' the open field ;   300
The long, pale splendors of the curling flame
Cast o'er their polish'd arms a livid gleam ;
An umber'd lustre floated round their way,
And lighted falchions to the fierce affray.
Now the swift chariots 'gainst the stubborn oak   305
Dash'd ; the dark earth re-echoes to the shock.
From shade to shade the forms tremendous stream,
And their arms flash a momentary flame.
Mid hollow tombs, as fleets an airy train,
Lost in the skies, or fading o'er the plain ;   310
So visionary shapes, around the fight,
Shoot thro' the gloom, and vanish'd from the sight ;

Thro' twilight paths the maddening coursers bound,
The shrill swords crack, the clashing shields resound.
There, lost in grandeur might the eye behold   315
The dark-red glimmerings of the steel, and gold;
The chief; the steed; the nimbly-rushing car;
And all the horrors of the gloomy war.

Here the thick clouds, with purple lustre bright,   319
Spread o'er the long long host and gradual sunk in night;
Here half the world was wrapp'd in rolling fires,
And dreadful vallies sunk between the spires.

Swift ran black forms across the livid flame,
And oaks wav'd slowly in the trembling beam:
Loud rose the mingled noise; with hollow sound,   325
Deep-rolling whirlwinds roar, and thundering flames re-
    As drives a blast along the midnight heath,   (sound.
Rush'd raging Irad on the scenes of death;
High o'er his shoulder gleam'd his brandish'd blade,
And scatter'd ruin round the twilight shade.   330
Full on a giant hero's sweeping car
He pour'd the tempest of resistless war;
His twinkling lance the heathen rais'd on high,
And hurl'd it, fruitless, through the gloomy sky;
From the bold Youth the maddening coursers wheel,   335
Gash'd by the vengeance of his slaughtering steel,
'Twixt two tall oaks the helpless chief they drew;
The shrill car dash'd; the crack'd wheels rattling flew;
Crush'd in his arms, to rise he strove in vain,
And lay unpitied on the dreary plain.   340

   Now Samlah's hands to war the chariot guide,
Fair, beauteous, tall, fam'd Hamor's youngest pride;
O'er Achsaph's towers he stretch'd a potent sway,
And saw surrounding realms his rod obey.
Adnor, an elder birth, proud grandeur spurn'd;   345
Lord of his soul, inferior realms he scorn'd;
Nor felt one pang, nor shew'd one envious frown,
When doating Age to Samlah gave the crown.

Round his young steps he cast a kind survey,
And taught the blessings of an equal sway;   350
The pride of arts allur'd him to pursue;
To wisdom form'd him, and to virtue drew;
To reason's rules his stormy passions wrought,
And shone, a pattern of the truths he taught.

From Jabin's loins a matchless virgin sprung,   355
And every voice with Salma's praises rung.
Her, Adnor led to share his brother's throne,
And made, delighted, Samlah's bliss his own.
Five weeks the prince beheld in transport glide,
Bless'd in the beauties of his lovely bride: 360
Heedless of war he dwelt, 'till Jabin's voice
Rous'd him to arms, and call'd to ruder joys.

Now, where bold Irad scatter'd blood and fate,
In the same car the friendly brothers sate;
When Adnor thus---Oh fly yon miscreant's arm;   365
Nor tempt the terrors of the sweeping storm!
Its wonted aid my broken spear denies---
With a fierce look, th' impatient youth replies---
Me dost thou urge to base, unmanly flight?
Leap from the chariot; hide in covering night?   370
Shall Salma hear? shall Samlah's growing name
Waste with the pangs of never-ending shame?
He said, and furious, urg'd his rapid car,
Crush'd the firm ranks, and shouted to the war;
On Irad's course he drove; the hero turn'd,   375
And a brown glimmering from his buckler burn'd:
'Twixt the bold leaders pour'd an ardent band;
Sword clash'd on sword, and hand rose up to hand;
They fell; new squadrons o'er their corses rise,
And louder tumults echo from the skies.   380
Imperious Samlah lifts a haughty cry---
Hence, on your lives, presuming dastards fly!
Who dares transgress shall find a sudden doom:
Give Samlah place---give kings, and heroes room---

He spoke.   His friends, all anxious for their king,   385
Still crowd the war, and swift to danger spring;
Loud sung the vengeance of his pointed steel,
And a bold veteran, deeply wounded, fell;
Enrag'd, the bands on either side retreat,
And leave the furious monarch to his fate.   390
    Swift from the chariot faithful Adnor sprang;
On Irad's shield his rushing falchion rang:
The Youth's quick wheeling, thro his shoulder glides;
Drops the cleft arm, and gush the living tides.
He sunk; and Irad, touch'd with pity, cried---   395
Ah youth! whose bosom glows with generous pride,
To scenes of endless gloom thy spirit flies;
Wing, wing thy voice, for pardon, to the skies!
Oh, Sire of all, may this brave warrior's mind,
In life's fair climes, some lowly mansion find!   400
    He spoke.   The chief his answering mind address'd---
If soft compassion warm thy friendly breast,
Oh hear! nor spurn a dying brother's prayer!
Let Samlah's tender years thy pity share!
Oh may a sire, a bride, thy bosom move!   405
The charms of beauty, and the calls of love!
Thus the kind youth, and fainting, as he cried,
He liv'd for Samlah, and for Samlah died.
So frown'd dread night on Abraham's fatal plain,
When thou, Montgomery, pride of chiefs, wast slain.
Spare, sons of freedom! spare that generous tear;   411
To heaven resign, nor name the doom severe---
Great, brave, and just, toward Columbia's shame,
He hunted toil, in fields of growing fame;
Alive, fair Victory ne'er forsook his side;   415
He liv'd in triumph, and in glory died.
Still bards shall sing, to earth's remotest clime,
He bled for all, and every heart for him.
    Glued to his side, t' untimely fate a prey,
There bright Macpherson breath'd his life away.   420

Round the fair youth in vain soft graces glow'd,
And science charm'd him to her sweet abode;
In vain fond parents hop'd his steps again,
And worth approv'd, and realms admir'd, in vain.
Yet patriot virtue writes the glory high,   425
With such a chief, in such a cause, to die.

   Soft spoke the chief---O youth! thy virtuous bloom
Ask'd a lot milder, and a later tomb.
Is there no blissful seat, by Heaven assign'd
To the fair efforts of a clouded mind?   430
To life well-acted, can no grace supply
A sweet remission, and a happy sky?
But thou, base coward, claim'st th' avenging sword;
Could'st thou look on, and see thy brother gor'd?
That best of brothers, whose concluding breath   435
Restrains the falchion, and delays thy death?
Pale Samlah heard, and o'er th' embodied wall
He rush'd, regardless of his brother's fall,
From rank to rank with panting breast he flew,
Where the war open'd, and the coursers drew;   440
Behind, fierce Irad drove his dreadful way,
And left at distance far the pallid ray;
Ten thousand spears around him pierce the gloom;
Ten thousand warriors rush to hastening doom;
Through the black ether smoky volumes flow,   445
And with brown light their skirts all-umber'd glow;
Far o'er conflicting trains the sheets descend;
The deep night thickens, and the shades extend.

   There Uzal brave a stubborn fight maintain'd,
And crown'd with matchless strength, retreat disdain'd;
Dan's mighty chief---On Ai's inglorious plain,   451
When vanquish'd Israel left their kindred slain,
His stiff, strong buckler brav'd the fierce affray,
Shelter'd the flight, and cover'd all the way.
Now, in the centre, shrill his armour rung,   455
Where the darts shower'd, and where the javelins sung,

But still his dauntless footsteps onward drove ;
Nor throng'd battalions could those footsteps move.
On all sides round, a thousand twilight forms
Invade the war, and strike their ringing arms ;   460
Here, 'gainst the chief, prepar'd to pierce his foe,
The lance unheeded aim'd the fatal blow ;
There, whilst the warrior listen'd to th' alarm,
High o'er his helmet hung th' uplifted arm.
Unnumber'd bucklers twinkle round the field,   465
In light now dreadful, now in shades conceal'd.
Still more remote, involv'd in deeper gloom,
Where hands unnotic'd dealt the frequent doom,
Shelumiel fought ; the prince of Simeon's trains,
Fam'd in the contests of a thousand plains.   470

   Meantime, dark Hazor's sons to battle roll'd,
And vast Madonians, wrapp'd in barbarous gold:
These, with their leaders, near the dreadful ray,
Whirl'd the swift car, and drove their rapid way.
There, dress'd in gold, tremendous Jabin shone,   475
And wing'd the terrors of his moving throne.
He Hazor's realms with mighty sceptre sway'd,
And his proud nod unnumber'd hosts obey'd.
A genius vast, with cool attention join'd,
To wisdom fashion'd his superior mind :   480
No scene unnotic'd 'scap'd his searching view ;
The arts of peace, and arts of war, he knew ;
To no kind wish, or tender tear, a prey ;
But taught by keen discernment equal sway :
Interest, of all his life th' unshaken guide,   485
Unmov'd by passion, and unmov'd by pride.
He first, inventive, to the waste of war
Led the tall steed, and drove the dreadful car,
To arms, beneath the standard, veterans train'd,
And every movement, every feint, explain'd: 490
Close, lest his conduct watchful chiefs should arm ;
Slow to decide, and vigorous to perform :

With firm, fierce bravery forc'd his foes to fly,
And gave one law---to conquer, or to die.

  Now his great mind, by long successes fir'd,   495
To matchless fame, and single rule, aspir'd;
In the same cause, beneath his banner join'd,
His voice, his art, this countless host combin'd,
In night's concealing hour, prepar'd th' affray,
And promis'd triumph, ere the dawning ray.   500
High in his flame-bright car his spear he rais'd;
A crimson glory from his armour blaz'd;
Conquer, he cried, or fall, ye dauntless bands,
The noblest heroes of a thousand lands.

Shall this brave host to Israel yield the night?   505
Few in their numbers; timorous in the fight---
Shall we, inglorious, blot our ancient fame?
Forbid it virtue, and forbid it shame.
Lo here the man, ye chose to guide your path,
Prepar'd for glory, or prepar'd for death;   510
This arm shall guide you through the dastard band;
First in the fight, as first in sway, I stand.

  He spoke, and fiercely wing'd his rapid car;
As fierce the squadrons rush to glorious war;
All dropp'd the javelin: all the falchion wheel'd;   515
A copious slaughter drench'd the glimmering field;
From their dire arms a fearful splendor came,
And o'er their faces wav'd the gloomy flame.
Hand join'd to hand, the vengeful thousands rag'd;
Man challeng'd man, and sword with sword engag'd; 520
The victors rush'd; the pierc'd in anguish cried;
No flight; no fear; they conquer'd, or they died;
For Israel's dauntless sons maintain'd the field,
And chief with chief the dread assault repell'd;
Round the wild region mingled horrors reign'd;   525
Nor those would yield, nor these the victory gain'd.

  First, in the van, imperious Jabin's car
Bore down whole troops, and broke the thickening war.

High o'er the reft his dreadful voice was heard ;
High o'er the reft his lofty form appear'd ;   530
His fhield, a crimfon moon, before him fpread,
And o'er his vifage hovering horrors play'd ;
His fteeds, like rapid winds, impatient flew :
His fword the firft, his fpear the diftant, flew ;
Round the dark chariot countlefs weapons hung,   535
And groans, with fullen murmur, ceafelefs rung ;
Rank after rank he turn'd to hated flight,
And joyful Hazor throng'd the ftubborn fight.

    Before this dreadful path, two heroes fought,
And warm'd with vengeance, countlefs wonders wrought.
Sons of one fire, that in the defert fell,   541
When impious Korah bade the hoft rebel.
The helplefs orphans generous Caleb bred,
In arms inftructed, and to combat led.
With mutual flame their friendly bofoms lov'd ;   545
In peace together liv'd, in war together mov'd.

    Now, fide to fide, the manly heroes ftood,
And fable torrents from their falchions flow'd ;
When Shammah thus---thou beft of friends, behold
Yon heathen's car, in gloomy terror roll'd.   550
How his fierce courfers wing their rapid way !
How his keen falchion cleaves the yielding prey !
Say, fhall our force the mighty Chief defy,
His arm experience, and his falchion try ?
Or death, or triumph, fhall the deed await ;   555
And what is death, in Ifrael's dubious fate ?

    To prove fierce danger for his maker's laws,
And proffer life to fave his country's caufe,
Thou know'ft, brave chief, Seraiah quick replied---
The good man's duty, and the brave man's pride.   560

    He fpoke, and fiercely plunging thro' the war,
Hew'd a wide path, and burft upon the car;
Nor Shammah ftay'd. On Jabin's fpacious fhield
His rapid lance Seraiah's hand impell'd ;

Thro' the thick orb the point no paſſage found,   565
Its ſhade dark-quivering in the flamy round.
With a ſhort flaſh, acroſs the thickening air
The furious Heathen drove the greedy ſpear ;
Swift on Seraiah's helmet ſunk the ſteel ;
His red arms rang ; the hero groan'd and fell.   570
With pangs, bold Shammah ſaw his brother's doom,
And wheel'd his fiery falchion thro' the gloom ;
From Jabin's hand a ſecond javelin ſped,
Sung thro' his ear, and pierc'd his guſhing head ;
Shrill roſe the conqueror's ſhout ; and all around   575
The plains remurmur, and the woods reſound.

Now, more remote from Ai's decreaſing light,
Slow mov'd a giant to the dreadful fight.
As when dun ſmoke, o'er all th' horizon ſpread,
Pours round the ſetting moon a crimſon ſhade,   580
Diſtain'd with blood, her broad, and dreadful eye
Looks death, and ruin, from the ſhuddering ſky :
So gleams the circuit of his flame-bright ſhield,
And caſts wide terror thro' the quaking field,
A beam-like ſpear commands his horrid way,   585
And all, before him, ſhun the dire affray.

And now fierce Iſrael's ſons, with ſad ſurprize,
To find brave Irad turn'd their boding eyes.
Far round they gaz'd ; his form no more appear'd ;
They liſten'd ; but his voice no more was heard.   590
Then every boſom ſudden fears appal ;
Their nerves all ſtiffen, and their falchions fall ;
A timorous fight their frozen hands ſuſtain,
And ſighs, and backward looks, confeſs their pain.
With ſhouts of triumph, ſwift the Heathens roll'd,   595
And a bright terror flaſh'd from flamy gold ;
A thouſand moony ſhields before them burn'd ;
Ranks fell at once, and troops to flight were turn'd ;
Each fatal ſtep increas'd the piles of ſlain,
And boundleſs ruin ravag'd all the plain.   600

As when a storm in midnight pomp extends,
And a broad deluge on the world descends,
From steep to steep, disdaining every goal,
Swell'd with hoarse thunders, mountain-torrents roll ;
The vales all echo to the dreadful sound ;   605
The torne rocks roar ; the cracking trees resound.

Meantime bold Irad far had cross'd the fight,
And Samlah vanish'd with auspicious flight :
Round the dread region gaz'd the Youth serene,
And eyed the grandeur of the solemn scene.   610
Unnumber'd phantoms crowd the dusky war ;
The half-seen hero, and unfinish'd car :
Black were the shades, as midnight in the tomb,
And floating glimmerings spread a fearful gloom.
Now roll'd the distant cries an awful sound ;   615
Now nearer clamors shook th' embattled ground.
At once, from western fields, a shout ascends ;
The plains all tremble, and the concave rends :
Quick turn'd the chief, while sad alarms inspire,
And saw dark forms, that pass'd along the fire ;   620
Slow tow'rd the camp the shouting squadrons move,
And long pale spires tremendous wave above.

Ah wretch ! he cried---to childish heat a prey !
How soon wild passion drove my steps astray !
What chief, less vain, shall lay th' increasing fear ?   625
Who cheer the bands, my presence ought to cheer ?
Ah ! should disgrace, and dire defeat, ensue,
No more this guilty face shall Joshua view ;
These eyes ne'er open on a host undone,
But death, or glory, by this arm be won.   630

Thus as he spoke, he cross'd the deep array ;
To his known form they yield an easy way :
Red flash his arms ; and high above the field,
Gleams the drear lustre of his orbed shield.
So, pale, and dreadful, thro' the midnight shade,   635
Sails a broad meteor o'er the mountain's head :

Dim rife the cliffs; and on the kindling air,
Stream the long terrors of its fanguine hair.
His voice refounding thro' the gloomy fight,
Reviv'd their ftrength, and turn'd th' increafing flight.
Fly, daftards, fly; defert your Maker's laws;　641
Your name difhonor; yield your country's caufe;
But come, ye friends of Ifrael's injur'd name,
Sons of the fkies, and heirs of deathlefs fame!
Know, round the diftant plains, by chiefs infpir'd,　645
By virtue prompted, and by vengeance fir'd,
Bold, manly warriors, never taught to yield,
Cleave their fell foes, and fweep the dufty field;
Let this bright pattern every breaft inflame;
Here lift your fwords, where Irad leads to fame.　650

　Thus every rank his voice invites to arms;
His prefence actuates; his example charms;
From band to band, with nimble courfe, he flies,
Wheels the long hoft, and wakes intenfer cries;
Thick flafh the falchions; thick the javelins rain;　655
And fhooting banners tremble o'er the plain;
In every fcene, alert, the youth appears;
Each chief, each rank, his cry with tranfport hears;
Shouts fiercely burfting liftening earth appall,
And hovering Conqueft yet fufpends her fall.　660

　And now bold Irad, thro' the thickeft war,
Drove the tall chief, and darkly rolling car,
When, lo! the giant full before him ftood,
Involv'd in death, and cover'd o'er with blood:
Like fome vaft wave, approach'd the horrid form,　665
Heedlefs of fpears, and raptur'd with the ftorm.
His wonderous fize th' admiring Youth beheld,
And fnatch'd a lance that glitter'd on the field;
Loud rang the weapon on the monfter's brow;
Backward he quick recoil'd, and bending low,　670
Stood ftaggering.　Irad wav'd his dreadful fword,
Springing impetuous; fwift between them pour'd

Two gloomy chariots, of their lords defpoil'd,
And fierce around them thoufand heroes toil'd:
No more the chief could find his deftin'd prey,   675
But turn'd, and mingled in the fierce affray.

Now loud, and folemn, thro' the roaring vales
Swell'd the hoarfe murmurs of the founding gales,
With deep confufion fhook the cliff's tall brow,
And rufh'd tempeftuous on the world below;   680
From grove to grove the blaft impatient flies,
Rends the ftiff oak, and howls along the fkies,
On Ai's broad flames, with wild dominion, falls,
And pours ten thoufand thunders round her walls.
More wide, more bright, the folding fires afcend,   685
Heave the dun fmoke, and far in ether bend;
The glittering brands, by rapid whirlwinds driven,
Stream, like dim meteors, o'er the blacken'd heaven;
Swift through the woods red paths expanding roll;
Long heavy volumes thicken round the pole;   690
From all the concave fparks in torrents rain,
And fiery tempefts rufh along the plain.

Far through the groves the furious flames had fpread,
And thoufand fires rofe fcatter'd in the fhade,
Ere Hazor's bands (fo eager rag'd the fight)   695
Beheld, with fad amaze, the fearful fight.
Then Jabin's voice, terrific, bade retire,
And the glad warriors fled the widening fire.
Ifrael purfued; but Jabin's deathful arm
Whole troops repell'd, and brav'd the wafting ftorm:700
With the fierce giant, o'er the rear he rofe,
And cool'd the vengeance of his ardent foes,
Then to the fight, that ftill, with dreadful fway,
Rent eaftern plains, brave Irad wing'd his way.
Part of the foes, that in the wood remain'd,   705
Had fled the heat, and fafe recefses gain'd;
Part, lodg'd in open fields, maintain'd the war,
And fhouts rebellow'd tore the murmuring air.

Sudden, o'er all the bands, resounds a cry---
Fled are our friends ; we conquer, or we die :   710
Lo round the wood the kindling torrents burn ;
Fix here our ranks ; no warrior can return---
  Then fierce despair the dauntless bosom fir'd,
Wing'd the keen falchion, and the arm inspir'd ;
The chiefs exhorted, threaten'd, shouted, cried ;   715
The ranks rush'd onward, met the steel, and died ;
For Israel's sons a moveless fight maintain,
Glued to the field, and cleaving man to man ;
Brave Irad's dreadful voice the heroes arm'd,
Strung every nerve ; and every weapon warm'd ;   720
On friend, and foe, alike the blind sword fell ;
And the son sunk beneath the parent's steel.
Wild, and more wild, the ruin rag'd around ;   (ground ;
Shouts rung ; groans murmur'd ; thunders rock'd the
Through the rent concave rush'd the loud acclaim,   725
Swell'd with the roaring wind, and fierce resounding flame.
At length a heathen's voice---Retire, retire,
Where yon black opening parts the raging fire---
Quick, at the sound, along the glimmering shade,
Thro' the wide forest panting heroes fled,   730
In different courses, where the moory ground
Cleft the deep blaze, and form'd a verdant mound.
Swift as the rapid blast, the youthful train
Nimbly precipitated o'er the plain ;
On every side, the flames, with wild career,   735
Roar'd near their path, and added wings to fear ;
None turn'd a gazing eye ; but, with bless'd flight,
Stream'd thro' the grove, and scap'd the vengeful light.
  Behind, his path pale age more slow dragg'd on,
And wish'd, in vain, impending fate to shun ;   740
Now here, now there, with feeble steps, they turn'd ;
And here, and there, the fire terrific burn'd.
From tree to tree it flew ; and all around
The moulder'd pines, with hoarsely rushing sound,

Fell thundering. Kindled ruins hedg'd their path; 745
Behind them swift pursued the blazing death ;
Before, beside, and bending o'er their head,
The bright, and scorching splendors fiercely play'd ;
Weak, and more weak, the cries of anguish came,
Drown'd in the roaring fury of the flame.   750

   To the dire forest Israel's sons pursued,
And heathen blood their reeking swords imbrued ;
Then by the chief's command return'd from fight,
Th' attentive squadrons eyed the wondrous sight,
Far sound the dreadful region, trees on high,   755
Wave their tall blazing summits in the sky ;
Thro' the dark air, in crimson terror, sail
Broad sheets of flame, and bend along the gale ;
Loud, and more loud, the raging whirlwind pours ;
From wood to wood the rushing deluge roars ;   760
Then, up vast eastern hills with fury driven,
Rolls o'er aerial cliffs, and kindles heaven :
The mountain groves, a long, long ridge of fire,
Shoot their tall flames, and thro' the clouds aspire.
O'er dim-seen rocks, brown plains, and glimmering streams
Floats the pale lustre of the trembling beams ;   766
The camp astonish'd casts a quivering gaze,
And distant towns are lost in dumb amaze :
Retir'd the squadrons, range in dread array,
And watch the splendors of approaching day.----   770

THE

CONQUEST OF CANAAN:

BOOK VIII.

ARGUMENT.

Morning. Joshua joins Irad. Jobab's character, and challenge. Irad accepts it, and kills Jobab. Battle. Irad kills Samlah, and engages Jabin. His death. Judah routed with great slaughter. Death of Uzal, and Shelumiel. Caleb, with a large division, marches out, rallies Judah, and renews the battle. Irad's death throws the whole army into confusion. Joshua inspirits them, and makes great havoc of the enemy. Zimri's exploits. He kills the king of the Hittites, and routs them. Joshua kills the king of Shimron, and routs the centre. Jabin, perceiving the other divisions of the army defeated, orders a retreat, which is performed with regularity. Joshua's lamentation over Irad. Scene of Selima's distress at the sight of his corpse. Evening.

THE CONQUEST OF CANÄAN.

BOOK VIII.

O'ER mifty hills the day-ftar led the morn,
   And ftreaming light in heaven began to burn;
Wide fcenes of woe the boundlefs blaze difplay'd,
Where the fteel triumph'd, and the deluge fpread.
On wafted plains unnumber'd corfes lay,   5
And fmokes far fcatter'd climb'd upon the day,
Still clouded flames o'er eaftern mountains rife,
And Ai's broad ruins fadden all the fkies.
   When lo! in glimmering arms, and black array,
Like ftorms low-hovering in th' etheriatl way,   10
Far round the north a gloomy cloud afcends,
Its horror deepens, and its breadth extends.
Compact and firm, as mov'd by one great foul,
A front immenfe, the widening fquadrons roll;
Thick fhoot the fpears; the trembling helmets beam,
And waving bucklers caft a moony gleam.   16
As the dire comet, fwift through ether driven,
In folemn filence climbs the weftern heaven;
His fanguine hair, portending fearful wars,
Streams down the midnight fky, and blots the ftars;   20
Pale death and terror light the dufky gloom,
And quivering nations read their fudden doom.

So in the flaming van great Joshua rose,
And shot red glories on the wondering foes.
At his command the trumpet sounded high,   25
Aerial ensigns dancing in the sky ;
Near and more near, they trac'd a dreadful way,
Join'd Irad's host, and stretch'd in long array.

    From Hazor's ranks that now before the wood,
In three embattled squares, refulgent stood,   30
Great Jobab strode. In Madon's realms he reign'd :
Red was his eye, his brow with blood distain'd ;
A beam his spear; his vast, expanded shield
Shot a bright morning o'er the crimson field ;
His head sublime a mighty helmet crown'd ;   35
His quivering plumes with sable horror frown'd ;
Six cubits from the earth, he rais'd his frame ;
His wish was battle, and his life was fame.

    Proud was his father ; prouder was the son :   39
Nought mov'd his pride ; the tear, nor piercing groan :
Unmatch'd his force, he claim'd a matchless fame,
And every combat deck'd his brightening name.
Princes, his captiv'd slaves, before him bow'd,
Stalk'd in his train, and round his chariot rode ;
While their fair partners, first in triumph led,   45
Held the rich cup, or grac'd the brutal bed.
Oft had surrounding realms his aid requir'd,
Ere Zimri's hand Ai's hapless turrets fir'd ;
But still their prayers, and still their gifts were vain,
Till Joshua's glory rous'd his fierce disdain.   50
Else had no proffer mov'd his haughty mind,
That deem'd himself the champion of mankind,
When the joint wishes of the various band
To nobler Jabin gave the first command.
But Joshua's triumphs fill'd his anguish'd ear ;   55
Fir'd at the sound, he snatch'd the deathful spear,
Resolv'd at once to prove the hero's might,
And claim, alone, the wreaths of single fight.

'Twas he, when Irad rais'd his dreadful voice,
And inmoft Hazor trembled at the noife,   60
When prudent Jabin urg'd a nightly ftorm,
Ere the Youth's voice the flumbering camp fhould arm :
Bade his vaft fquadrons in the wood delay,
Nor lift a fpear, till morn fhould lead the day.
Shall this brave hoft th' unmanly path purfue,   65
Fight ambufh'd foes, and bafely creep from view ?
Shall Jobab, like the thief, to conqueft fteal,
And bravery call, what coward minds can feel ?
    And now, from Jabin the proud chief demands,
To lead, as firft in place, the central bands.   70
He, coolly wife, refigns the fhadowy name,
And, pleas'd with fubftance, boafts a nobler fame.
    Forth from the hoft, in fteely pomp, he ftrode,
And 'twixt th' embattled lines fublimely ftood.
His towering ftride, vaft height, and awful arms   75
Chill'd all his foes, and fcatter'd wide alarms :
When thus the chief---Ye fons of Ifrael know
The dauntlefs challenge of no common foe.
If in your hoft three heroes can be found,
(Be Jofhua one) to tempt this dangerous ground,   80
Here fhall they learn what ftrength informs the brave,
And find no God can fhield them from the grave.
    Stung with the infult caft upon his God,
To the great Leader Irad nimbly ftrode,
And thus---Shall yonder heathen's haughty cry   85
Dare Ifrael's hoft, and Ifrael's God defy ?
Let me this boafter whelm in inftant fhame,
Avenge my nation's caufe, my Maker's name.
    Exalted Youth! the fmiling Chief replied,
This elder arm fhall crop his towering pride.   90
Scarce in thy breaft has manhood fix'd her feat ;
Blot not thy bloom, nor urge untimely fate.

Line 60) See Book 7, Line 165.

Brave as thou art, his ſtrength muſt win the fight,
And Iſrael's glory ſink in endleſs night.

Think not, he cried, of Irad's tender age,   95
Nor heed the mockery of yon heathen's rage.
This hand, though young, ſhall boaſt a conquering day ;
Blind is wild rage, and pride an eaſy prey.
Here too ſhall Joſhua's potent prayers be given,
And the bleſs'd aid, that Virtue hopes from Heaven. 100
Should Irad periſh, none the wound ſhall know ;
Should Joſhua fall, our race is whelm'd in woe :
Heaven gave his choſen to thy guardian care,
To rule in peace, to ſave in dangerous war ;
On thee alone our fates ſuſpended lie,   105
With thee we flouriſh, and with thee we die.

Oh beſt of youths ! provoke not haſty doom,
Nor ruſh impetuous to an early tomb.
I lov'd thy ſire, the good, the juſt, the brave---
And ſhall this voice conſign thee to the grave?   110
Swift thy name ripens into matchleſs praiſe ;
My ſon, my choſen, ſtill prolong thy days.
In future fields thy arm ſhall brighter ſhine ;
Thine be the glory, but the danger mine.

Ah grant my wiſh ! th' impatient Youth replies,   115
While two full tears ſtand gliſtening in his eyes---
This arm, unhurt, ſhall bid the monſter bleed ;
Angels will guard my courſe, and Heaven ſucceed.
My ſpear, when night her lateſt darkneſs ſpread,
Had ſunk him breathleſs in the field of dead ;   120
But ſome kind ſpirit ſav'd his life, till morn
Should grace the fight, and Irad's name adorn.
Aid me, oh aid me, Hezron's every friend !
Your voice, your wiſhes, muſt the Leader bend.

Won by his earneſt cries, the generous Chief   125
Forc'd his conſent ; but could not hide his grief.
A ſigh ſteals ſilent from his bleeding breaſt,
As his ſlow tongue permits the ſad requeſt.

Wrapp'd in bright arms, while smiles his joy reveal'd,
The Youth stalk'd fearless o'er the horrid field ;   130
The host, with rapture, view'd his lofty stride,.
The leap alert, the port of conscious pride ;
But each grave chief, by long experience wise,
With faltering accent, to his comrade cries---
I fear, I fear, lest, on the bloody sand,   135
The bold Youth perish, by yon monster's hand.
What bravery can, fair Irad will perform,
But can the opening floweret meet the storm ?
Ah, that such sweetness, such etherial fire
Should fall, the victim of a heathen's ire !   140
Thy votary's course, all-gracious Heaven, survey !
Let some kind angel hover round his way !

Now near the scene bold Irad urg'd his course,
Where Jobab triumph'd in resistless force ;
When the huge warrior, swell'd with angry pride,   145
With bended brow, and voice contemptuous, cried---
Art thou the champion of thy vaunting race ?
Shall this poor victory Jobab's falchion grace ?
Go, call great Joshua, long to war inur'd,
Whose arm hath toils, whose skill hath hosts endur'd, 150
With him, ten chiefs ; this hand shall crush them all ;
Shame stains the steel, that bids a stripling fall ;
Retire, ere vengeance on thy helmet light ;
Fly to yon troop, and save thy life by flight.

His haughty foe the Youth undaunted heard ;   155
Vain, empty threats his bosom never fear'd ;
O'er the vast form he turn'd his smiling eyes,
And saw unmov'd the livid vengeance rise.
Then, with a rosy blush of conscious worth,
Calm from his tongue his manly voice broke forth--- 160
Do threats like these become a hero's voice ?
Can courage find a vent in empty noise ?
To every brave man give the well-earn'd praise,
Nor think on scoffs a bright renown to raise ;

True bravery claims a noble generous fame ;　　165
But the base wretch from vaunts expects his name.
Let shame, let truth, those coward words recall ;
Thou seek'st my life ; I glory in thy fall.
To me thy pride, to me thy threats are vain ;
Heaven sees alone whose arm the prize shall gain.　170
And know, wheree'er may light his angry rod,
I fear no boaster that defies my GOD.

　　Now shield to shield, and lance to lance, they stand ;
With taunts imperious shout the heathen band ;
While hopeless Israel heaven with prayer assails,　175
And grateful incense fills the rising gales.
Stung by the just reproof, with whizzing sound
The giant plung'd his javelin in the ground :
For passion, ever blind, impell'd his arm,
Steer'd a wild course, and sav'd the youth from harm; 180
He, calm and fearless, with a pleas'd surprise,
Survey'd its curious form and mighty size ;
Then 'gainst his foe, with sure, unerring eye
Drove the swift lance, and lodg'd it in his thigh.
Enrag'd, the warrior saw his bubbling gore,　　185
Writh'd with keen anguish, and the javelin tore.
The flesh pursued ; a copious, sable stream
Pour'd from the wound, and stain'd the steely gleam ;
Then high in air he shook his sunlike shield,
And wav'd his falchion o'er th' astonish'd field.　190
With matchless force the vengeful weapon fell ;
The wary hero nimbly shunn'd the steel ;
And while his foe with foaming fury cried,
Oft pierc'd his arm, and wounded oft his side.
Wild, and more wild, the giant's strokes resound,　195
Glance from the shield, and plough the cleaving ground ;
Till, gathering all his strength for one vast blow,
Dark as a storm, he rushes on his foe ;
Lightly the hero springs ; the monster falls,
Like sudden ruins of a turret's walls ;　　　　200

Full on his neck descends the gladsome blade,
And from the trunk disparts the grisly head.

Loud shouts of joy, from Israel's thousands driven,
Burst o'er the plain, and shook the walls of heaven:
Amaz'd the heathens saw their champion lost, 205
And a wide, sullen groan was heard from all the host.

Alert, bold Irad seiz'd the giant's shield,
His sword, his spear, and bore them thro' the field;
At Joshua's feet, with self-approving smiles,
He cast the grandeur of the glittering spoils; 210
The hoary warriors gather'd round his way,
And gaz'd and wonder'd at the curious prey;
Then bless'd the chief, with transport in their eyes,
And own'd th' assistance of auspicious Skies;
While youths unhappy rais'd less ardent prayers, 215
And wish'd the deed, and wish'd the glory, theirs.

Led by soft impulse tow'rd th' imbattled train,
Rov'd sad Selima down the spacious plain.
Afar she stood, and cast an anxious eye,
And strove in vain her favourite to descry. 220
At once, with distant din, the shouts ascend,
And painful fears her tender bosom rend;
Slow tow'rd the camp her lingering steps inclin'd;
But oft the fair-one cast a look behind.

Now the long thunders of the clarion sound, 225
Reclam'd from hills, and plains, and groves around,
O'er the dire field the rushing squadrons driven,
Extend their shady files, and blacken heaven:
High in the central front great Joshua stands,
And shoots wide terror thro' th' astonish'd bands; 230
Mid eastern thousands Zimri towers along,
And Irad shines before the western throng.

Unfurl'd, the sudden banners stream afar,
And, wrapp'd in thunder, joins the dreadful war;
Wide roll the volumes of the dust around, 235
And clouds on clouds envelope all the ground.

As floods, increas'd by long-descending rains,
Pour a brown deluge o'er the wintery plains,
Loud from a thousand hills, the torrents join,
Where azure bonds the river's course confine ;   240
The maddening ice, in boundless ruin driven,
Bursts, like the thunders of a falling heaven ;
The white rocks foam ; the gloomy blasts arise,
Toss the wild stream, and roar along the skies.
So clos'd the squadrons of th' unnumber'd foes ;   245
So stormy shouts and hollow groans arose.

Long in an even ballance hung th' affray,
Nor those would loose, nor these could gain, the day.
'Till Irad's rapid path, like heaven's red fire,
Shot through the ranks, and bade the foe retire ;   250
With joy, their chief surrounding warriors view,
And troops on troops the generous course pursue.

At distance small, proud Samlah's glittering car,
Whirl'd by white coursers, tempts the grisly war ;
O'er all the plain, with piercing sound, arise   255
His stern injunctions, and his conquering cries.
With shouts bold Irad darts along the field,
Now bright in arms, and now in dust conceal'd,
From rank to rank the well-known chief pursues,
And oft his flashing steel in blood imbrues.   260
Vain, impious wretch, he cried, thy nimble flight,
And vain the covert of surrounding might.
Once hast thou fled the swift-pursuing spear,
But fled'st in vain, for vengeance finds thee here.
Learn from this hand what fate betides the knave,   265
Who yields, unmov'd, a brother to the grave.
If now thy feet escape the righteous doom,
Let Heaven protect thee to a peaceful tomb !

In dread amaze astonish'd Samlah stood ;
From his pale face retir'd the freezing blood ;   270
His wild eye star'd ; all bristling rose his hair ;
Quick from his quivering hand the useless spear

Dropp'd; his teeth rattled, and the falling reins
At random trembled on the coursers' manes;
Behind he gaz'd, and found no path to fly;   275
For aid he panted, but no aid was nigh.
Deep in his back was lodg'd the fatal steel;
His breathless form, before the rolling wheel,
Plung'd headlong; mournful rung a pitying groan.
So fair, so mild his beauteous aspect shone: 280
Even Irad, touch'd by Adnor's kind request,
Felt soft emotions stealing through his breast.

   Then swift he wheel'd the lightening of his sword;
Behind him, Judah's host like torrents pour'd;
Shrill rose the tumult of the fields around,   285
Trembled through heaven and wav'd along the ground:
With souls undaunted, both the hosts contend;
Spears fill the air, and shouts the concave rend.

   Far distant, Joshua moves his awful form,
Swells the confusion, and directs the storm.   290
Beyond him, Zimri, swift as rapid fire,
Darts through the fight, and bids the foe expire.
A mingled horror clouds the dreadful plain;
Here rush the fighting, and there fall the slain.

   Now the mid sun had finish'd half his course,   295
When Irad raging with resistless force,
And far before him breathing wide dismay,
On Jabin's chariot drove his rapid way.
Brave youths around him throng'd the crimson fight,
Eyed the bless'd chief, and smil'd a fierce delight;   300
From every sword increasing vengeance fell,
And Death sate hovering o'er the sanguine steel.
Thron'd in proud state, the savage Monarch rode;
Like two red stars his wrathful eye-balls glow'd;
Hoarse from his voice a dreadful thunder came,   305
And his bright armour flash'd a sudden flame.
Two steeds, bedropp'd with gore, and pale to view,
Emblems of death, his smoaking chariot drew.

Cheer'd by his hand, the coursers swiftly sprang;
Beat by their hoofs, the brazen bucklers rang;   310
Tow'rd Irad's path the heathen wing'd his way,
And, boding conquest, snuff'd the fancied prey.

    Unmov'd, th' angelic Youth, with wearied hands
Pav'd his red path, and drove the circling bands---
Stay, lovely hero! stay; thy course forbear;   315
Enough that sword has rul'd the glorious war---
Ah stay, till Israel's sons thy steps surround;
Return, return, and be with glory crown'd!

    Great Jabin stood, and o'er the bloody field
Rais'd the broad terrors of his flaming shield;   320
His grimly brow, all blacken'd o'er with dust,
Frown'd like a storm, and froze the trembling host;
Near beauteous Irad stream'd the sounding car,
And opening squadrons yield the dreadful war.

    The foaming Chief, serene the Youth beheld,   325
And rear'd his javelin o'er the purple field;
Shrill sung the lance along the dusty sky,
Bor'd the strong shield, and pierc'd the Monarch's thigh.
Enrag'd, to earth the haughty Warrior sprang;
His red eyes flam'd; his arms descending rang;   330
With lofty action, each his hand uprais'd;
The falchions flash'd; aghast the squadrons gaz'd;
Two generous youths between them nimbly broke,
And bow'd their lives beneath the fatal stroke.
Their lovely heads (their helmets cleft in twain)   335
Died the keen swords, and spouted on the plain.
More fierce the Monarch's disappointed ire
Glow'd in his face, and blaz'd with gloomy fire.
In Irad, innocence serenely mild,
And beauty's sweetness with soft splendor smil'd;   340
Round his fair forehead beams of bravery play,
Nor stain'd with rage, nor mingled with dismay.

    Again in ether rose the dreadful steel;
Again it lighten'd, and again it fell;

The Heathen's, ringing, leap'd from Irad's shield;
The Youth's in fragments, treacherous, strew'd the field.
Held by a chief, swift-leaping from the band,
A second falchion touch'd his reaching hand,
When---lovelieft Youth! why did thy buckler's bound   350
Shield but thy breast? why not thy form surround?
Where stood thy friends? was no kind hero near,
To guard thy life, and stay Selima's tear?---
From some base arm unseen, in covert slung,
Through his white side a coward javelin sung,   355
He fell---a groan sad-murmur'd round the host,
Their joy, their glory, and their leader lost.

Forth from the train a youth impatient sprung,
Spread his fond arms, and round the hero clung,
With soft endearments stay'd the fleeting breath,
And wish'd to save him from the hand of death.   360
But Jabin's sword, driven through his friendly side,
Stain'd his white armour with a spotless tide:
In kind imbrace their heaving bosoms lay,
And all life's blooming beauty died away.
Through fields of air, their social spirits join'd   365
Wing'd their light way, nor lost a look behind;
While two bright forms, on rosy pinions borne,
Sail'd round their path, and op'd the gates of morn.

Mid countless warriors Irad's limbs were spread,
Even there distinguish'd from the vulgar dead.   370
Fair as the spring, and bright as rising day,
His snowy bosom open'd as he lay;
From the deep wound a little stream of blood
In silence fell, and on the javelin glow'd.
Grim Jabin, frowning o'er his hapless head,   375
Deep in his bosom plung'd the cruel blade;
Foes, even in death, his vengeance ne'er forgave,
But hail'd their doom, insatiate as the grave;
No worth, no bravery could his rage disarm,
Nor smiling love could melt, nor angel-beauty charm.

His hapless fall pale Jarmuth's sons beheld ;
Grief froze their hearts, and fear their nerves congeal'd
The Chief pursues ; their trembling bands retire ;   675
Deep groans ascend, and troops on troops expire :
Wide rolls the dust ; the skies are snatch'd from sight,
And death hangs dreadful o'er the growing fight.

There, thron'd in state, and dress'd in burnish'd steel,
Lachish' fair prince, Japhia, hapless fell.   680
He bade soft songs awake the trembling lyre,
With notes of magic, and with words of fire ;
Such songs, as Moses, uninspir'd, might sing ;
Like him, a bard, a hero, and a king.
But far beyond the pride of pomp, and power,   685
He lov'd the realms of nature to explore ;
With lingering gaze, Edenian spring survey'd ;
Morn's fairy splendors, night's gay curtain'd shade ;
The high hoar cliff ; the grove's benighting gloom ;
The wild rose, widow'd, o'er the mouldering tomb ;   690
The heaven-embosom'd sun ; the rainbow's die,
Where lucid forms disport to fancy's eye.
When rous'd to war, and deeds of deathless name,
Faint shone to him the charms of martial fame :
But fir'd to ecstacy, his soul beheld   695
The stormy grandeur of the troubled field :
The morn, that trembles o'er the steel-bright plains ;
The whirlwind car, wing'd steed, and clashing trains.
Such scenes the warrior sung. The swains around
Hung on th' enchantment of the wildering sound :   700
Soft o'er the lyre the voice of music pass'd,
Wild as the woodland warblings of the waste ;
Each savage soften'd, as the numbers rose,
Forsook his falchion, and forgot his foes.

As dread before him glow'd the Hero's face,   705
His angel pomp, and heaven-descended grace ;
He stopp'd ; he gaz'd ; and with fond fancy warm,
Glued to the solemn glories of his form ;

So Jabin's car with gloomy terror flew,
And crush'd the ranks that near him rashly drew;
Roll'd in one mighty mass, the heathen force,
The swift-wing'd chariot, and the foaming horse,   420
O'er all the lovely band resistless fly,
And countless warriors round their Irad die.
Thus, on the stream's fair bank in beauty rise
Young, towering trees, and feel indulgent skies;
In spring's mild beam their lovely boughs aspire,   425
Wave o'er the flowers, and call the plumy choir:
At once the floods descend, the torrents roar;
The trees lie withering on the wasted shore.

All firmly brave, imbrown'd with dust and blood
'Gainst the rude tempest Judah's veterans stood;   430
Fix'd, even to death, their nation to defend,
With stout, stiff strength, the stubborn ranks contend;
To fate undaunted many a hero springs,
The shouts redouble, and the concave rings.
Full in the front brave Uzal moveless stood,   435
His falchion reeking with incessant blood;
Fight, warriors, fight, or fall---he said, nor more;
But wheel'd his arm, and stepp'd in floods of gore;
Above his feet the purple torrents ran,
And high before him man was pil'd on man.   440
So thick the swords around his helmet hung,
That sword clave sword; aloud his armour rung:
Panting he stood; in floods the sweat distill'd:
Nor moves the Hero, nor the squadrons yield.

From his bright car, that rattling pour'd along,   445
With shouts, and threatnings, Jabin fir'd the throng;
Man leap'd o'er man: from every side they rush'd;
Bold warriors fell, by other warriors crush'd;
'Till, hurl'd by Jabin's hand, a javelin flew,
Pierc'd Uzal's heart, and life's fair current drew,   450
Pleas'd, the great hero gave his parting breath;
My nation own'd my life, and now demands my death.

C c

Thus hung with wounds, a prey to savage steel,
In Princeton's fields the gallant Mercer fell.
When first his native realm her sons decreed,   455
In slavery's chains, with want and woe to bleed,
Check'd, through his bosom fond remembrance ran,
The cause of freedom was the cause of man.
In that fair cause he bar'd his manly breast,
The friend, the hope, the champion, of th' opprefs'd,
From height to height on glory's pinions rose,   461
Bless'd by his friends, and prais'd by generous foes ;
Swift flew the shaft ; the eagle ceas'd to rise,
And mourning millions trac'd him down the skies.

He fell ; the throng, that prefs'd against his shield,   465
Plung'd in one heap, and spread along the field ;
Bucklers on bucklers rang ; steel clash'd on steel ;
Their own swords gash'd them, wounding as they fell.
In one broad ruin lay the mingled crowd,
And cries, and hollow groans were heard aloud.   470
So some tall prop, that bears extended walls,
Mouldering, gives way ; the mossy structure falls,
The long beams thundering echo round the skies,
Earth shakes beneath, and clouds of dust arise.
Thus sunk the warriors, some to rise no more,   475
Some, nimbly bounding, bath'd their spears in gore.

Now haughty Jabin lifts a louder cry,
The tall hills echo, and the fields reply.
Fly, dastards, fly ; death haunts your impious way ;
Your proud name sinks ; your squadrons swift decay :   480
Where now 's the chief, that led your hosts abroad ?
Your far-fam'd bravery, and fictitious GOD ?
Call the dread Power, that cleft th' Egyptian wave,
To mourn your fate, and ope your heads a grave.
Pour on, my heroes, while yon friendly light   485
Shines in the heaven, and joys to view the fight.
He spoke, and onward wing'd his dreadful form ;
Hazor behind him, like an evening storm,

That rides on gloomy blasts above the hills,
And wakes the thunder of the mountain rills,   490
Roll'd blackening.   Israel's sons in sad dismay,
Bent tow'rd the camp their slow, unwilling way.

Enrag'd Shelumiel rais'd his angry voice,
But rais'd in vain; no hero heeds the noise:
Hoarse with shrill cries, and wild with deep despair,   495
He rush'd resistless on the thickest war,
From Jabin's lance a grateful exit found,
Sunk in his arms, and stiffen'd on the ground.

Far from the fight, despoil'd of helm and shield,
Slept beauteous Irad on the mournful field ;   500
Deaf to the groans, and careless of the cries ;
His hair soft-whistling o'er his half-shut eyes.
On either side his lifeless arms were spread,
And blood ran round him from the countless dead.
Even there, two warriors, rushing o'er the plain,   505
O'er crimson torrents, and o'er piles of slain,
Stopp'd, when the lovely form arose to sight,
Survey'd his charms, and wish'd no more the fight.

Ah ! hapless Youth ! cried one, with tender voice,
The Gods' fair offspring, form'd for milder joys !   510
A face like thine the gentlest thoughts must move,
The gaze of Beauty, and the song of Love.
Sleep on, fair hero ! for thy corse must lie
Bare to the fury of a stormy sky.
Thus he.   His friend, by softer passions warm'd,   515
By grief afflicted, and by beauty charm'd,
Cries sadly---No ; for when my steps return,
This bleeding breast thy early fate shall mourn ;
The melting song declare thy hapless doom,
And my own hand erect thy head a tomb.   520

But now, outspread o'er all the northern plain,
In sable grandeur roll'd a countless train,
With trembling spears, with waving bucklers, bright,
And the quick gleams of interrupted light.

When Joshua strode the heathen host to dare,   525
To guard the camp was prudent Caleb's care.
He, coolly wise, had summon'd all the train,
Dispos'd in ranks, and guided o'er the plain,
All arm'd for war, at distance meet to stay,
And wait the changes of the dreadful day.   530
In even scale while dubious combat hung,
And far in southern fields the tumult rung,
Silent, they listen'd to the blended cry,
And heard faint shouts in distant murmurs die.

But now th' approaching clarion's dreadful sound   535
Denounces flight, and shakes the banner'd ground;
From clouded plains increasing thunders rise,
And drifted volumes roll along the skies.
At once the chief commands; th' unnumber'd throng,
Like gathering tempests, darkly pour'd along: 540
High on the winds, unfurl'd in purple pride,
Th' imperial standard cast the view aside;
A hero there sublimely seem'd to stand,
To point the conquest, and the flight command;
In arms of burnish'd gold the warrior shone,   545
And wav'd and brighten'd in the falling sun.

Swift tow'rd the fight approach'd th' impatient throng,
And wider pour'd the thickening dust along;
Loud, and more loud, victorious clamours grow,
And, more distinguish'd, breathe the sounds of woe;   550
Pale Judah's sons a yielding fight maintain,
And many a face looks backward o'er the plain,
When Caleb's mighty voice, in thunder driven,
Starts all the host, and rends the clouded heaven.
What dismal scenes, enrag'd the hero cries---   555
Convulse this heart, and pierce these bleeding eyes!
Shall Judah's race, my brethren and my boast,
Flee, vanquish'd, driven, before a heathen host?
Can men, can warriors own so black a part,
The best of chiefs, your Joshua to desert?   560

Say with what pangs will Heaven the wretches try,
That know no honour, and that feel no tie ?
On yon bright plain, the conquering Chief behold,
Troops wing'd before him, cars tumultuous roll'd,
With Heaven's imperial sword the fight commands,   565
And drives fierce ruin o'er decreasing bands !
Say, shall the Man, who fights, who bleeds for all,
See your base flight, and perish in your fall ?
The Chief, as angels kind, as angels true,
Sink in the doom, he warded long from you ?   570
Fly then ; but know, a few short furlongs past,
Yon camp wild flames, and savage swords shall waste ;
Besmear'd with streaming blood, your parents lie,
And, dash'd on stones, your gasping infants die ;
Your wives, betray'd by such base culprits, feel   575
Abuse, more dreadful than the griding steel ?
No arm, no sword the falling nation save,
But this dire evening ope our common grave.
Can these dread scenes even dastards fail to arm ? 579
Spring from the trance, and burst the sleepy charm ;
Rise, rise like men ; with shame, with vengeance burn ;
Wipe foul disgrace, and swift to fight return.
And ye brave chiefs, that never knew to yield,
Or turn a backward foot from glory's field,
But, led by me, the van's bright honours claim,   585
Smile at fair death, and shrink from torturing shame ;
Lift high th' avenging sword, from pity free,
And cleave the wretch that basely dares to flee.
    He spoke : the sound their manly bosoms fir'd,
Wheel'd their long ranks, and every arm inspir'd ; 590
Even cowards now to generous combat arm'd,
And fainting heroes with new vengeance warm'd :
Fierce Hazor's sons with equal fury driven,
Like one wide cloud, that shades the skirts of even,
Rush'd dark and dreadful : ranks, by ranks impell'd, 595
Felt the keen lance, and heap'd th' streaming field.

Pois'd in a dire suspense, the combat hung ;
Swords clash'd, mail rattled, striking bucklers rung ;
Here his bold ranks great Caleb's arm inspir'd:
There Jabin's mighty hand his warriors fir'd :   600
No more the foaming steeds could trace their way,
So thick the squadrons wedg'd their black array :
Loud tumults roar, the clouded heavens resound,
And deep convulsions heave the labouring ground.

Meantime, great Joshua, lightening o'er the plain,
Hedg'd his dire path with heaps of ghastly slain ;   606
Back roll'd the squadrons ; death's encircling shade
Involv'd his course, and hover'd o'er his head.
At once a quivering voice fair Irad nam'd,
Announc'd his ruin, and the flight proclaim'd ;   610
From ranks to trembling ranks, the mournful sound
Wak'd a sad groan, and breath'd a gloom around,
With livid paleness clouded every face,
Congeal'd each vein, and stopp'd the growing chace.
On the far camp they turn'd a frequent view ;   615
Their fainting falchions scarce the fight renew :
Throng'd in a blackening storm, the foe descends ;
Swift drive the chariots ; far the dust extends :
With smiles, bold heathens hail commencing flight ;
Their lances shower ; their eye-balls flash delight.   620
Loud as old ocean beats the rocky shore,
Loud as the storm's deep-bursting thunders roar,
Vast shouts unrolling rend th' etherial round,
Trembles all heaven, and shakes the gory ground.

Amaz'd, the Hero saw the wild despair :   625
Nor knew the cause, 'till Irad fill'd the air ;
Irad, re-echoing with a fearful noise,
Pal'd the blank face, and froze the faltering voice.
Loud o'er the bellowing shouts resounds his cry---
My sons, my heroes, whither will ye fly ?   630
Will ye pursue the camp ? desert the slain ?
And leave your Irad on the bloody plain ?

Alas! you fly to more tremendous fates;
There ruin seeks you, and base death awaits:
There, in sad horror, will your eyes behold   635
Flames round your camp, your wives, your children roll'd:
Let vengeance rouse, let Israel's name inspire,
Let danger steel you, and let Irad fire,
Turn, turn, this instant seals your final doom;
You gain the day, or fall without a tomb.   640

  He said, and wav'd his broad, ensanguin'd shield;
Turn, warriors, turn, resounds along the field;
A new-born bravery fires the meanest soul:
Thick spears protend; ranks lengthening onward roll:
Less loud fierce whirlwinds through the valley pour; 645
Less loud broad flames the spiry town devour,
When, wing'd by blasts, red conflagrations rise,
Blaze in the cloud-capp'd towers, and scorch the skies.
Black drifts of dust smoke through the vast profound;
Shouts hoarsely rage, and hollow groans resound.   650
As, when through ether's fields dark storms are driven,
The swift-wing'd flame, descending, kindles heaven,
Scath'd by the dreadful stream, the huge pines fall,
And bursting glory wraps the smoking ball;
O'er the tall mountains rolls the voice of God,   655
The plains all tremble, and the forests nod:
So swift, so bright, the rushing hero pour'd;
With every stroke his sword a life devour'd;
Full on his foes he bore resistless storm,
Pale squadrons opening to his angry form;   660
His shield blaz'd horror, and his lofty hand
Fell, with swift ruin, on the lessening band;
Gash'd by his hand, the coursers burst their reins,
And hurl'd their riders on the bloody plains;
Gash'd by his hand, the prostrate riders die;   665
Crack the round wheels, the splendid trappings fly.

  Meantime, far eastward Asher crouds the war,
Nor heeds the terrors of the rattling car.

Swift as on wings of fire a meteor driven,
Mounts o'er the hills, and sweeps the nightly heaven, 670
When the pale wanderer, lost in devious ways,
With bristling hair, starts at the sudden blaze,
Rush'd rapid Zimri through the parting host ;
Mark'd by his eye the hapless foe was lost ;
O'er quivering ranks his sword incessant hung ;   675
Loud in their ears his voice funereal rung
Death's hideous peal ; hard-following on the sound
Sunk the last stroke, and corses cloath'd the ground.

   Now while the Hittites fled the dire alarm,
Their haughty king withstood th' invading arm.   680
Shrill rose the thunders of his piercing cry,
Lost in deaf ears, and echoing through the sky ;
With swifter steps, his warriors urg'd their flight,
And dark behind them rush'd pursuing night.

Fierce on the king's bright car, with rapid force,   685
Resistless Zimri drove his dreadful course ;
The dauntless monarch cast his mighty spear,
That sung, and trembled through th' enlighten'd air ;
Full on brave Zimri's helm the polish'd steel
Clash'd harmless, and to earth, rebounding, fell.   690
Regardless of the shock, the nimble chief
Sprang to the car ; no sword could lend relief ;
Caught by his arm, the heathen beat the ground ;
Wide on his bosom sunk the fatal wound ;
The greedy blade, deep-plunging, gash'd his side,   695
And down his buckler pour'd a bubbling tide.

   Wing'd with fierce ardour, Zimri mounts the car,
And calls his heroes to the crimson war.----
Rush on to conquest, every generous band,
Lo the bless'd triumphs of this happy hand ! ----   700
Here, through his side the sword indignant thrust,
Their furious leader, gasping, bites the dust.----
Fly, miscreants, fly, and let your lives remain
To grace the falchions of a future plain.

From dovelike foes what warrior hopes a name? 705
So cheap the purchase, victory scarce is fame.---
Thus, loud and taunting, rose the hero's cry;
Swift rush his bands; the heathen swifter fly:
High in the chariot, in dread pomp reveal'd,
His gloomy hand the firey steeds impell'd; 710
In dusty clouds the hosts are snatch'd from sight,
And Death, and Zimri, darken o'er the flight.

While thus brave Asher trod the conquering plain,
And drove wild ruin on the heathen train,
In the dire centre, to resistless war 715
Proud Shimron's monarch urg'd the thundering car.
In early youth, he saw fierce Jabin's hand
Seize his fair crown, and rule his fertile land;
Then to the victor's court a captive brought,
In arms was train'd, in arts politic taught, 720
Won by soft wiles, his throne of Jabin held,
And bade his realm imperial tributes yield.
There, fir'd to glory by the monarch's voice,
He mock'd his pattern, and obey'd his choice,
And hop'd from conduct, form'd by rules so just, 725
Alone to reign, when Jabin slept in dust.

Full on his lofty breast the flashing shield
Gleam'd a bright terror through the clouded field:
As when the Sun, o'er scorch'd Peruvia's plain,
Disease, and Death, and Horror in his train, 730
Unveils his crimson face, distain'd with blood,
Burns the brown hills, and sickens every flood.
Loud rang the hero's voice; his lances flew,
And every lance the foremost warrior slew.
On him great Joshua glanc'd a darkening eye, 735
And rush'd impetuous, with a deathful cry:
His sword, swift-circling, hew'd his dismal way,
Fell'd ranks at once, and broke the deep array.
Amaz'd, the heathen cast a look behind,
And thus in doubt, explor'd his mighty mind.--- 740

D d

Shall I refisting dare that arm of death,
And reach his heart, or nobly yield my breath ;
Or with some diftant band the foe engage
Where bravery fails, and turn the battle's rage ?
This arm, this fpear may fpill his hated life ;   745
And O what wreaths fhall crown the happy ftrife !
What bright rewards fhall Jabin's hand beftow !
What matchlefs honours round my temples flow !
I claim the conteft--hence bafe flight and fhame---
To fight is glory, and to die.is fame.   750

   He fpoke ; while Ruin, riding thro' the plain,
Burft o'er his ranks, and mark'd her path with flain :
On Jofhua's helm fhe fate ; tremendous hung
His arm on high, his voice like thunder rung :
Near the bright car he wheel'd his ftreaming blade, 755
And duft around him caft a night-like fhade.
Full on his buckler clafh'd the heathen's fpear,
Pierc'd the thick plates, and flafh'd behind in air ;
Grazing his fide, it cut the folded garb,
And drops of crimfon ftain'd the polifh'd barb.   760
With joy, the king his faithful javelin view'd,
Leap'd from his car, and with his fword purfued.
Then Jofhua's hand uprear'd his falchion high,
Its flames bright-circling in the dufky fky ;
Firft his foe's arm dropp'd on the bloody field ;   765
The fecond ftroke divides his glittering fhield ;
Full on his throat the fierce avenging blade
Sinks ; the freed fpirit flits to midnight fhade.

   "Pour on to glory"--rung the Leader's voice,
The trembling hoft fhrunk backward at the noife ;   770
Sad Shimron's fons beheld their monarch dead,
Rais'd one deep howl, and, wing'd with horror, fled.
Throng'd in a gloomy ftorm, their head-long foes
Round the dire flight with lifted falchions rofe ;
Broad ftreams of blood o'er-ran the fcenes of death,   775
And fullen groans proclaim'd the parting breath,

As boiling Etna rolls a flood of fire
Down her rough rocks ; and plains, and towns expire,
Lick'd by the flames, exhaling rivers rise,
And crumbling groves smoke upward to the skies,   780
Swift pours the blazing deluge on the shore,
The scorch'd main foams, the hissing billows roar :
So fierce and dreadful, flew the victor host,
In night involv'd, in dusty volumes lost.
Squadrons thick-strown were scatter'd o'er the fields, 785
And helms, and swords, and spears, and sanguine shields.
    Huge piles of slaughter gathering round his course,
On Shimron Joshua wing'd his mighty force.
Like two red flames his vivid eye-balls glow,
And shoot fierce lightenings on th' astonish'd foe ;   790
Before, expanded, his meteorous shield
Blaz'd a broad ruin thro' the stormy field ;
Round the wild war his flashing terrors fly ;
Cars burst before him ;---steeds, and heroes die.
So rush'd an angel down the midnight gloom,   795
When Egypt's first-born sunk in one broad tomb ;
High in dark clouds th' avenging Vision hung,
His path, like distant thunder, hoarsely rung ;
Flames shot before him, whirlwinds roll'd around,
Bow'd the tall hills, and heav'd the trembling ground.
Not with less terror blaz'd the Leader on ;   801
'Twas ruin all and one unbounded groan ;
None look'd behind, none turn'd a hearkening ear ;
Nor hills, nor streams impede the full career :
High o'er the ragged rocks they nimbly bound,   805
Dash thro' the floods, and scower the level ground :
First in the tumult, Youth impels his flight ;
Springs o'er the field, and scapes pursuing night :
Pale Age with quivering limbs, and slow-drawn pace,
Feels the keen sword, and sinks beneath the chace.   810
    Far distant, Zimri, like a sweeping storm,
Grim in the chariot rais'd his gloomy form ;

Still on the hindmost fell his fateful sword;
Earth shook, air trembled; heaven with thunder roar'd:
Oft, from the car descending to the plain,   815
He stream'd, like lightening, o'er the ghastly slain,
Then swiftly rose, and on the heathens sped,
His wheels dark-rolling o'er th' unnumber'd dead.

Meantime, with all the rage of combat fir'd,
While throngs of warriors round his steps expir'd ; 820
While now, first disobedient to his call,
The balanc'd victory doubted where to fall :
While Caleb's arm with youthful vigor warm'd,
Sham'd Judah's thousands and their vengeance arm'd ;
From rank to rank impatient Jabin flew,   825
Drove these with threats, and those with praises drew.

But now the eastern plain loud thunders rend ;
The shrill cars rattle ; hoarser cries ascend ;
Progressive clouds, in thickening volumes driven,
Roll tow'rd the south, and shade the dusty heaven.   830
From the tall car the Chief survey'd the field,
And every circling scene at once beheld,
Even the far wood, with sudden flashes bright,
And the dire omens of tumultuous flight.
Around the war he cast a searching view,   835
Saw the day lost, and all its evils knew ;
Deep from his inmost soul burst forth a sigh,
And momentary sadness gloom'd his eye.
But soon his brow resum'd a cheerful grace,
And living ardour fir'd his artful face.   840
Full well the monarch knew that fears begun,
From breast to breast, like glancing lightenings, run ;
That one rank fled instructs a host to fly,
And cowards' eyes teach heroes' hearts to die---
Then, ere his friends the dire event divine,   845
Or Judah's sons their kindred victors join,
A wise retreat his mighty mind ordain'd,
And thus the rage of war his voice restrain'd.

Hear, all ye chiefs, brave Hazor's bands that guide,
Your nation's pillars, and your monarch's pride.   850
Your matchless deeds this raptur'd eye has told,
And fame's bright hand to diftant years enroll'd.
But fee, o'er weftern hills the fun's low fire
Cuts fhort the day, and bids the hoft retire.
Firm be your ranks, man faft inlock'd with man,   855
The rear led onward, fix'd the generous van;
At once let chief with chief infpir'd combine,
And 'gainft the foe extend th' embattled line;
Brace firm the fhield; the movelefs fpear protend;
Join hand and heart, and every rank defend.   860
Your prince behold; when Hazor claims the ftrife,
My wounds are tranfport, and a toy my life.

   The hero fpoke: as by one foul infpir'd,
Swift to their well-known pofts the chiefs retir'd;
At once, by banners rang'd, to brave the ftorm,   865
Firm, dreadful lines th' experienc'd fquadrons form.
Dire o'er the van-guard, fhield with fhield combin'd,
Spear lock'd with fpear, th' undaunted leaders join'd;
'Gainft Judah's hoft, with ridgy terrors bright,
Rofe a long wall, and flafh'd a fearful light.   870
O'er the tremendous fcene the Monarch's car
Pour'd death around, and rul'd the grifly war:
Fierce on the foe, where'er their fteps purfue,
From rank to rank the mighty warrior flew;
Hearts form'd of ftubborn fteel his deeds appall;   875
The diftant tremble, and the nearer fall;
Till Caleb's voice commands the chace to ftay,
And yields his foes an unmolefted way.

   Then, ftill and flow, while Judah's hoft admir'd,
In gloomy ftrength the fullen ftorm retir'd.   880
So, when in heaven propitious breezes rife,
And on the deep the nimble veffel flies,
Shagg'd with brown fhades, that o'er the billows lower,
In grim, dark pomp recedes the clifted fhore;

Lefs feen, and lefs, the awful fcenes decay,   885
And loft in blue confufion fade away.

    With gore all hideous, and with duft imbrown'd,
In the dire front terrific Jabin frown'd ;
His lifted arm prepar'd the fatal blow,
And menac'd vengeance to th' approaching foe.---   890
So, forward driven by earth's convulfive pangs,
The tall, hoar cliff in dubious terror hangs ;
High pois'd in dread fufpenfe, its hovering brow
Lowers fwift deftruction on the world below :
Amaz'd, the fwain, while fudden fears appall   895
Starts, as the tottering ruin feems to fall.
Enjoy, he cried, imperious foes, enjoy
The fancied triumph, combat fhall deftroy :
But know, ye boafters, foon this arm fhall tear
The fhort-liv'd crown, your haughty temples wear ;   900
Soon your vain chiefs, your nation want a name,
And all your glories fink in endlefs fhame.

    But now, fublime in crimfon triumph borne,
The facred ftandard mock'd th' etherial morn ;
Wide on the winds its waving fplendors flow'd,   905
And call'd the warriors from the diftant wood.
Behind great Joshua, Hazor's fons to dare,
Pour the bold thoufands to the weftern war,
Beyond Ai's walls, the leffening heathen train
In well-form'd fquadrons crofs the diftant plain ;   910
Part ftill in fight their fhady files extend ;
Part fill the wood, and part the hills afcend ;
To ceafe from toil the prudent Chief commands,
And balmy quiet fooths the wearied bands.

    Half loft in mountain groves, the fun's broad ray   915
Shower'd a full fplendor round his evening way ;
Slow Joshua ftrode the lovely Youth to find ;
Th' unwilling bands more flowly mov'd behind.
Soon as the matchlefs form arofe to view,
O'er their fad faces fhone the forrowing dew ;   920

Silent they ſtood. To ſpeak the Leader tried,
But the choak'd accents on his palate died.
His bleeding boſom beat with inward pains,
And leaden languors ran along his veins.

Ah, beſt and braveſt of thy race! he ſaid, 925
And gently rais'd the pale, reclining head---
Loſt are thy matchleſs charms, thy glory gone--
Gone is the glory which thy hand hath won.
In vain on thee thy nation caſt her eyes ;
In vain with joy beheld thy light ariſe ; 930
In vain ſhe wiſh'd thy ſceptre to obey ;
Vain were her wiſhes ; vain the deſtin'd ſway.
Oh! Irad, lovelieſt Irad, nature's pride!
Would Heaven, myſelf for thee, for thee had died!
Nor more ; the thoughts lay ſtruggling in his breaſt ; 935
But tears, expreſſive tears forbade the reſt.
Borne by ſix chiefs, in ſilence, o'er the plain,
Fair Irad mov'd before the mournful train ;
Great Joſhua's arm ſuſtain'd his ſword, and ſhield ;
Th' afflicted thouſands lengthening thro' the field. 940
When, crown'd with flowers, the maidens at her ſide.
With gentle ſteps advanc'd great Caleb's pride.
Her ſnowy hand, inſpir'd by reſtleſs love,
Of the lone wild-roſe two rich wreaths inwove ;
Freſh in her hand the flowers rejoice to bloom, 945
And round the fair-one ſhed the mild perfume.
O'er all the train her active glances rov'd :
She gaz'd, and gazing, miſs'd the Youth ſhe lov'd ;
Some dire miſchance her boding heart divin'd,
And thronging terrors fill'd her anxious mind. 950
As near the hoſt her quickening footſteps drew,
The breathleſs hero met her trembling view ;
From her chill'd hand the headlong roſes fell,
And life's gay beauty bade her cheeks farewell ;
O'er her fair face unmeaning paleneſs ſate, 955
And, ſunk to earth, ſhe felt no hapleſs fate.

With anguish Caleb saw her fading charms;
And caught the favourite in his hastening arms.
Reviv'd with piercing voice, that froze his soul,
She forc'd the big, round tear unwish'd to roll;   960
By all his love, besought him soon to lead
Where cruel friendship snatch'd his lovely dead.
In vain the chief his anguish strove to hide,
Sighs rent his breast, and chill'd the vital tide.

To Joshua then, whose heart beside her mourn'd, 965
With gaze of keen distress, the charmer turn'd.---
Oh, generous Chief, to misery ever kind,---
Thou lov'st my fire---support his sinking mind!
Thy friendly wish delights to lessen woe---
See how his tears for fallen Irad flow!   970
He claims thy friendship---generous hero, see,
Lost to himself, his fondness bleeds for me.---
To view the hapless Youth, distress'd, he fears,
Would wound my soul, and force too copious tears.
But lead, oh lead me, where the Youth is borne! 975
Calm is my heart, nor will my bosom mourn---
So cold that heart, it yields no pitying sigh---
And see no tear bedews this marbled eye.

She said, and look'd resistless; soft reclin'd
On Joshua's arm, she forc'd his melting mind. 980
Pressing her hand, he trac'd a gentle way,
Where breathless Irad, lost in slumbers lay.
From the pale face his chilling hand withdrew
The decent veil, and gave the Youth to view.
Fix'd o'er the form, with solemn gaze she hung, 985
And strong, deep sighs burst o'er her frozen tongue.
On Joshua then she cast a wishful look;
Wild was her tearless eye, and rolling spoke
Anguish unutterable. Thrice she tried
To vent her woes, and thrice her efforts died. 990
At length, in accents of ecstatic grief,
Her voice bewilder'd, gave her heart relief.

Is this the doom we dread ?---is this to die ?
To sleep ?---to feel no more ?---to close the eye ?---
Slight is the change---how vain the childish fear,   995
That trembles, and recoils, when death is near ?
I too, methinks, would share the peaceful doom,
And seek a calm repose in Irad's tomb.
This breath I know, this useless breath must fail,
These eyes be darken'd, and this face grow pale--   1000
But thou art pale, oh Youth ! thy lot I crave,
And every grief shall vanish in the grave.
    She ceas'd, the tender chief without delay,
Soft pressing, kindly forc'd her steps away.
Slow tow'rd the camp, with solemn pace, they drew ;
The corse moves on ; the mournful bands pursue.   1006
Pale Uzal follows, virtuous now no more ;
And brave Shelumiel, black with clotted gore.
Unnumber'd tears their hapless fate bewail,
And voice to voice resounds the dreadful tale.   1010
But Irad, matchless Irad, call'd in vain,
Breathes wide a solemn sadness round the plain :
Unhappy, to their tents the host retir'd,
And gradual ; o'er the mountains day expir'd.

THE

CONQUEST of CANÄAN:

BOOK IX.

ARGUMENT.

Evening. Interview between Selima and her parents. Morning. Distress of the Camp. Joshua directs Zimri to bury the dead. Funeral of Irad. Burial of the dead. Hareshah informs Joshua of a combination of the surrounding nations against Gibeon, and solicits his assistance. Story of Elam and Mina. Hareshah is directed to wait until the divine pleasure shall be known. Eveneng. Joshua walks out on the plain, northward of the camp, and hears Selima lamenting the death of Irad. Affected by the scene, he breaks out into a soliloquy on his distress, and is reproved by an angel, who delivers him a message from the Most High, and directs him to prepare for a vision of futurity.

The CONQUEST of CANAAN.

BOOK IX.

NOW sober evening hung her curtains round,
   And gloomy sadnefs brooded o'er the ground.
All pale, and folemn, rofe the languid moon,
And fhed a feeble twilight from her throne.
Sad in her tent, the feeling maiden fate,   5
Fed on her woes, and figh'd her haplefs fate.
Diffolv'd in tears, her tender parents came,
To fhare her grief, and ftay life's parting flame.
Like dull, cold lights, that hover o'er the tomb,
A lone lamp languifh'd round the filent room :   10
Befide her couch, two lorn attendants ftay'd,
And drooping, lingering, eyed th' unconfcious maid.
O'er the fad fcene the pair attentive hung ;
Then round the favourite form all-anxious clung :
Her tearlefs eye-balls fcarce the virgin turn'd,   15
But, fix'd in blank defpair, her flumbering Irad mourn'd.
   Awake ! oh wake ! the tender mother cry'd---
My child ! my darling ! nature's lovelieft pride !
Awake, and hear ! oh hear thy mother's call !
Behold thefe tears for thee in anguifh fall !   20
Ah fee thy fire, with mighty woes opprefs'd !
His fighs hard-burfting from his heaving breaft !

Turn, turn thine eye ! thy haplefs parents fave !
Nor fpeed our footfteps to the dreary grave !

 She fpoke. O'erwhelm'd in bitternefs of fate, 25
Still the fweet maiden unregardful fate :
Fix'd on the parent, droop'd her failing eyes,
And deep, and heavy, heav'd her long-drawn fighs.
Again the mother, loft in fad amaze,
Caft on her woes a ftrong, expreffive gaze, 30
And thus---O child of parents once too blefs'd !
Let not fuch anguifh tear thy bleeding breaft.
Swell not, with other pangs, thy miferies dire,
A dying mother, and a widow'd fire :
The balm of patience fummon to thy foul : 35
Let Heaven's high voice exceffive grief controul.
He call'd, from earth's dark wild, the Youth away ;
And call'd complacent, to the world of day.
To nobler fcenes his mind feraphic flies,
To blifs, to Hezron, angels, and the fkies. 40

 Thus fpoke the parent. Struggling rofe the fair,
And look'd unmeafur'd woe, and blank defpair :
Again fhe languifh'd ; to the couch fhe fell,
And life fad-lingering feem'd to bid farewell.
Pierc'd to the foul, the tender father ftood, 45
And, loft in woes like her's, the darling view'd,
He faw the mild reproof her fenfe recall,
Her ftrength reviv'd her tears in filence fall ;
A beam of glimmering hope his grief allay'd,
And thus, with grave, but gentle voice, he faid--- 50
O child of love ! fweet daughter of delight !
Let not that death-like gaze our fouls affright.
Arife to thought ! to fenfe, and reafon, rife !
Nor dumb and marbled grieve againft the Skies.
Such mighty woes no earthly lofs requires ; 55
Not Irad claims them, nor true love infpires.
All is not loft ; thy parents ftill furvive :
And for thy blifs, and in thy life, they live.

He spoke.   Again the virgin, whelm'd in woes,
With slow, and forceful effort feebly rose.   60
His voice rever'd arous'd her quickening soul,
Loos'd her sad tongue, and taught her tears to roll;
Pressing her mother's hand, with head reclin'd,
She thus disclos'd the anguish of her mind.
O best of parents, e'er to daughter given !   65
Lov'd, next to Irad ! reverenc'd, next ro Heaven !
Let not these frowns your hapless child destroy,
Bereft of every hope, and every joy !
What hand, what power, can Irad's breath restore ?
Those eyes shall beam, that face shall smile, no more ;
That voice ne'er warble music's sweetest sound ;   71
And that pale form must moulder in the ground.
'Tis this, awakes the anguish of your mind ;
But ye can weep, and weep to Heaven resign'd.
Not so your daughter : form'd of feebler frame,   75
Grief rends her soul, and damps the vital flame.
Yet even her heart but shares the common pain,
Partakes the tears of all, and breathes their sighs again.
Far round all Israel cast attentive eyes,
And see for him the general anguish rise.   80
See his own son the childless sire forget ;
The childless mother only weeps his fate :
His fate alone the virgin's shrieks proclaim ;
And the poor, wailing infant lisps his name.
Even lifeless nature mourns him, wrapp'd in gloom,   85
O'ercast with woe and conscious of his tomb.
I saw the sun forlorn, and slow, retire ;
I saw the silent evening sad expire ;
In shades of double gloom ascend the night,
And the stars languish, with a mournful light.   90
How cold yon moon extends her widow'd beam !
Announcing death, and pale with sickening gleam !
How faint her feeble glimmerings spread the plain !
How still, and lonely, light the azure main !

While thus impassion'd, lifeless nature all,   95
In speechless sorrow, mourns the hero's fall;
Shall I, belov'd, beyond all merit dear,
His best Selima, and his chosen fair,
Shall I, O sire! with common anguish weep?
And o'er his grave, with dull indifference, sleep?   100
Dumb fields, and senseless forests would reprove
Such base oblivion of so bright a love.

    Pleas'd, the great sire beheld her thoughts return,
And heard her melting accents Irad mourn;
And thus---O brightest, loveliest of thy kind,   104
Grac'd with each charm, that robes the angel's mind,
More dear than ever child to sire was dear,
As virtue lovely, and as truth sincere!
Think not thy parents on their darling frown,
Or feel a thought less tender than thy own.   110
Like thine, our wishes the bless'd Youth approv'd;
Like thee, we chose him, and like thee, we lov'd.
But O all beauteous daughter! shall thy sire
Behold thee, whelm'd in boundless grief expire?
Or see thy life to hopeless anguish given?   115
Or hear thee murmur 'gainst a righteous Heaven?
Again to earth could thy fond Youth remove,
His heart would chide thee, and his voice reprove;
Bid thee, submissive, to thy Maker fall,
Embrace his hand, and wake at duty's call;   120
Bid thee to him thy patient thoughts resign,
And blame thy wanderings, with a love like mine.
From grief's excess, thy parent would restrain,
Assert Heaven's right, and fix the bounds of pain.

    Ah sire rever'd! the pleading maid returns---   125
No common loss thy hapless daughter mourns.
Search the wide world.   Can all her regions boast
One youth so fair, so bright, so early lost?
How Age admir'd him! how all Israel lov'd!
The world applauded! and the Heavens approv'd!   130

His form was all, the brighteſt thoughts can frame ;
His mind was all, the fondeſt wiſh can claim ;
Whate'er is great, or good, or ſoft, or fair,
Refin'd, or lovely, fix'd its manſion there.
Even he, whoſe hand the ſacred ſceptre bears,　　　135
Is but an Irad, of maturer years.
It is, O 'tis, as if, in yon fair clime,
Some prince of angels, bright in glory's prime,
Tranſcending every peer, in worth ſupreme,
Mitred with truth, and ſunn'd with virtue's beam,　140
In youth's gay morn, in beauty's endleſs bloom,
And life, ſuperior to the potent tomb,
Had clos'd his ſmiles, while Heaven refus'd to ſave,
And ſunk his glories in the dreary grave.
What tears, for ſuch a loſs, would ſeraphs ſhed ?　　145
Tears, rich as theirs, ſhould mourn their rival dead.

　　And where, O where ſhall poor Selima find
One beam of light to cheer her drooping mind ?
All ſad, I wander round the earth, and ſkies ;
But no ſoft ſolace meets my failing eyes.　　　　　150
To friends I fly : thoſe weeping friends I ſee
Sunk in the deep deſpair, that buries me.
For him, O kindeſt, tendereſt mother ! riſe
Thy heart-felt anguiſh, and thy hopeleſs ſighs.
Thy tears, all-gentle ſire ! reſiſtleſs ſhed,　　　　155
Approve my grief, and weep the hero dead.
No cheering hope your fondeſt love can give,
Sooth your ſad child, or make her Irad live :
Then bid me mourn ; this laſt relief beſtow,
And yield my boſom to the peace of woe.　　　　　160

　　Oppreſs'd with grief, the feeling ſire rejoin'd---
Sweet, lovely charmer of thy father's mind !
From earth, from friends, thy hope can never flow ;
Too poor, to yield the balm of real woe.
When real ills invade ; when Want annoys ;　　　　165
When hiſſing Shame, with lingering death deſtroys ;

When pain torments, or sickness wastes our bloom;
Or friends too dear desert us, for the tomb :
This barren world no solace can supply :
But all earth's portion is to weep, and die.   170
Yet there are springs whence hope and comfort rise,
Springs of pure life, and flowing from the skies :
Thence gentle Mercy sends her treasures down,
And bright Religion makes the bliss her own.
To famish'd Want she spreads a boundless store,   175
With that unbless'd, the heir of worlds is poor :
Repentant Shame she bids to crowns aspire,
Grace ever new, and glory ever higher :
On earth, in heaven, her wealth and honours rise,
Ennoble angels, and enrich the skies.   180
Decay and Pain to cheerful peace she leads,
With patience arms them, and with comfort feeds ;
And points the realms, where Health and Beauty bloom,
And Life, with smiles of triumph, braves the tomb.
When Friends, if Virtue's friends from earth retire,   185
And waste the bosom, with corroding fire ;
She sees those friends again immortal live,
Rise from the grave, and dying worlds survive,
To each the form, the mind, of angels given,
Fair sons of light, and habitants of heaven.   190
She too, and she alone, a Friend secures,
That through all times, and in all scenes, endures
At hand, to hear, to love, to bless, to save,
In life, and death, and worlds beyond the grave ;
As heaven o'er earth sublime, all friends above,   195
In power in wisdom, truth, and boundless love.
  In grief, even vast as thine, his hand can heal,
And teach the heart its anguish not to feel.
Bright from the tomb, she sees thine Irad rise
To peace, and life, and glory, in the skies ;   200
One little moment separate from thy arms ;
Again to meet thee, with superior charms ;

To hail thy rifing foul, from realms above ;
To fmile as angels, and as Heaven to love.

 Then, O thou child of truth ! to her controul 205
Refign the tumults of thy troubled foul.
She on thy wounds fhall fhed her healing power,
Thy faith revive, thy wonted peace reftore ;
With fofteft mufic charm the paffing day ;
Bid Heavenly vifions o'er thee nightly play ; 210
The tents of angels round thy curtains fpread :
Invite the guardian cherub to thy bed ;
Calm, with fweet flumbers, every ftormy care,
And dry, with downy hand, the plaintive tear.
She too fhall life's rough path with flowers adorn ; 215
With fpring's mild fplendor, cheer the wintry morn ;
Thy yielding feet, in ftrong temptations fave ;
Welcome grim death, and triumph o'er the grave ;
To brighter fcenes, in happier regions, fly,
And lift to thrones of glory, in the fky. 220

 The parent fpoke. The haplefs maiden fate
Forlorn, and fad, bewailing Irad's fate.
Silenc'd, but not reliev'd, her drooping mind
Fail'd not to figh, nor yet to Heaven refign'd :
At length with vaft, and heavy woes opprefs'd, 225
She funk in flumbers of tumultuous reft.

 Mild rofe the morn ; and, round the tented plain,
The cries of thoufands mourn'd their kindred flain.
In filent woe the hoary parent ftood,
And wail'd his hopes, all funk in fields of blood ; 230
His fons, fweet charm of nature's evil day,
Fair light of age, and life's moft pleafing ftay,
Now left him helplefs, and alone, to find
Some foreign aid to footh a drooping mind.
Strong pangs of forrow fix'd his fpeaking eye, 235
And his rack'd heart heav'd deep the heavy figh.
The pale, fad widow caft a tender view
On her fweet race, and fhed the plaintive dew :

Touch'd with her woes, the beauteous orphans mourn'd,
And artless tears their infant cheeks adorn'd.   240
The bride deplor'd a young, fond husband's doom,
Snatch'd from her arms, and banish'd to the tomb;
Her joys all ended in one dreadful day;
Her brightest hopes forever swept away;
No prospect left her, but long years of woe;   245
No wish, but ransom from these realms below.

These scenes, with anguish, pierc'd the Leader's breast,
Blank'd his fair prospects, and his soul depress'd.
Yet still, before the host, a cheerful grace,
With blameless art, array'd his tranquil face.   250
In all their pains, to him they cast their eyes;
Like a fond sire, he heard their plaintive cries:
From his calm brow they caught the placid smile,
Forgot their miseries, and despis'd their toil.

Now in the silence of his tent, alone   255
He mourn'd their fears, and made their grief his own,
When Zimri came, with anxious care oppress'd,
And Joshua thus his faithful friend address'd.

Hear'st thou what sorrows fill the murmuring air?
The warriors' groans? and terrors of the fair?   260
What tears of anguish every face bedew!
What throngs of orphans crowd upon the view!
Oh heavy, heavy pangs Jehovah's hand
On this sad heart, and on his chosen band!
Ah, where is Hezron? chief of spotless name!   265
His life so virtuous! and so pure his fame!
How soon, O pride of nature, art thou fled
To the dark, lonely mansions of the dead!
How soon to thy compeers, thine angels, given,
All-beauteous Irad! fairest plant of heaven!   270
But still superior grace may point a way,
Through the long darkness to the promis'd day.

These mournful thoughts with prudent care conceal;
Nor let thy guarded brow a pain reveal.

Thy face they watch, the motions of thine eye, 275
Know all thy fears, and number every sigh.
When leaders smile, their looks the host inspire;
Are leaders brave? the vulgar catch the fire;
With us they faint, they tremble, and they grieve;
With us they joy, they dare, they die, they live. 280

But now more solemn scenes thy care demand;
Choose twice ten thousand of the warrior band;
To yonder hapless field thy footsteps speed,
And pay the last, sad honours to the dead.
In one broad pit, our slaughter'd friends entomb; 285
Nor grudge our foes the same unenvied doom:
Let men, let brave men, ne'er refuse the brave
The humble blessing of a peaceful grave.

I go, the darling hero's fate to close,
And bid the matchless Youth a sweet repose: 290
'Tis all we can, the friendly tear to shed,
And raise the light tomb o'er his lovely head.

With soft affections, thus the mighty Chief:
And Zimri slow retir'd, with answering grief.
Meantime, grave warriors, in black robes array'd, 295
And many a youth, and many a lovely maid,
Along the northern green, the Chief pursued;
Flowers grac'd their hands, and tears their cheeks bedew'd.
For now brave Irad clos'd his final doom,
Borne to his darksome, everlasting home. 300

Behind the bier, that slow, and solemn mov'd,
Pensive Selima follow'd him she lov'd;
On the sad coffin fix'd a stedfast eye;
Nor dropp'd a tear, nor breath'd a tender sigh.
Her dark-brown hair a wreath of roses crown'd; 305
Her robes of sable flow'd along the ground:
A flower, just opening to the morning dew,
Blush'd in her hand, and brighten'd to the view.

Now in the grave the breathless Youth was laid:
Sadly serene advanc'd the lovely maid; 310

With speaking eyes, bewail'd her hapless doom,
And dropp'd the floweret in the lonely tomb.
High on the plain the funeral earth was spread ;
The turf's gay verdure flourish'd o'er his head :
Each gentle face deplor'd his lot severe,   315
And spoke th' expressive language of a tear.

Near the fair maiden stood th' exalted Chief,
Fix'd in mute woe, and great in manly grief.
No ill-tim'd comfort would he strive to lend,
Nor ape the flatteries of the specious friend :   320
Yet the soft texture of his heart could feel---
Why should he ope the wound he could not heal ?

As thus their bosoms wail'd his hapless end,
And mourn'd, as each had lost his chosen friend ;
Admir'd why Heaven had made such worth in vain, 325
And why confin'd it to the dreadful plain ;
His generous deeds in deep dispair ran o'er,
And saw him live, and speak, and act, no more ;
Through the sad silence of the solemn scene,
The bands of Zimri crofs'd the gloomy green.   330
Unnumber'd widows, on the field, they found,
Whose sons, whose husbands, strew'd the crimson ground :
Slow mov'd the fair-ones round the dreadful plain,
Wash'd the black gore, and prov'd the countless slain ;
And when the partners of their joys they knew,   335
They cleans'd their stiffen'd wounds in briny dew ;
Wail'd their hard lot, that swept, in life's gay bloom,
Each hope, each rapture, to the sullen tomb ;
With tears of anguish, envied earth its trust,
And grudg'd the grave the lov'd the precious dust.   340

Three days, above the undistinguish'd dead,
Their friends, and foes, the gather'd earth was spread.
A hill of stones, sad wound to human pride !
Just mark'd the place, where countless warriors died.

As there, in future years, the lonely swain   345
Drove his small flock, to feed the grass-grown plain,

Near the rough mafs, in folemn thought, reclin'd,
Thus fad reflections fill'd his pondering mind.
Ah proud inglorious man! whofe infect life
Is loft in pain, in vanity, and ftrife.   350
What mighty toils, to gain immortal fame!
What waftes, what flaughters, build the darling name!
Yet this rude tomb, this fhapelefs pile, contains,
Of chiefs, of kings, the poor, the fole remains.
This prize to win, muft nations then expire?   355
And feats of peace, and joy, be whelm'd in fire?
Oh Heaven, in pity, loofe the ties, that bind
To man's black race, a juft and honeft mind!
    Low funk the fun.   As now the chief return'd
From midft the camp, and haplefs Ifrael mourn'd,   360
Harefhah fad, befide his tent, he found;
Proftrate he fell, and reverent kifs'd the ground.
Uprais'd by Jofhua's hand, again he ftood,
And thus his fear in plaintive accents flow'd.
Hail mighty prince! to thee alone tis given,   365
To tafte the favour of indulgent Heaven;
To guide, with profperous hand, the race he chofe,
And hurl deftruction on refifting foes.
Thou know'ft, with thee how Gibeon's fons are join'd;
What views unite us, and what covenants bind;   370
This, through the circling realms by fame was fung,
And round each realm, th' alarm of vengeance rung:
To wafte her domes the general voice decreed,
And millions hafte t' atchieve the barbarous deed.
Salem's imperious fons, in proud array,   375
And haughtier Hebron, thither bend their way;
In martial pomp unnumber'd Lachifh fhines,
And Jarmuth brave with favage Eglon joins;
With thefe, fierce nations fpeed from realms unknown,
Near the firft glimmerings of the dawning fun.   380
There too, O Prince! tremendous Jabin ftands,
Brings all his chiefs, and leads his veteran bands,

Wings the dread lightenings of the war around,
And rolls his thunders o'er th' embattled ground.   284

 From these dread powers, so numerous, and so brave,
Nought less than Heaven, and thy own hand, can save.
Worne with long years, Aradon's trembling arm
Ill wards the vengeance of so fierce a storm.
And,---O exalted Prince! prepare to hear
A tale more sad than ever pierc'd thine ear---   390
In the dark grave is generous Elam laid,
And near him sleeps the Heaven-instructed maid.

 How fell the lovely pair? the Leader cried;
And, with sad voice, the stranger chief replied.
When cheerful morn walk'd forth in golden air,   395
Rode the young hero, and his blooming fair,
With nimble hounds, that bade the forest roar;
To chace the buck, to wound the bristly boar;
On two white steeds they bounded o'er the plain,
And gayly round them pranc'd a youthful train.   400
No coats of steely mail their limbs invest;
No buckler sparkles o'er the fearless breast;
Thro' sylvan shades they trac'd an easy way:
Each mind was sunshine, and each face was gay.

 At once, with dreadful din before them rose   405
The trump of death, and shout of savage foes.
From the thick covert burst a barbarous throng,
Rang clashing arms, and scream'd a hideous song;
His gallant friends, a young, but chosen few,
The prince, serenely brave, around him drew;   410
With firm, bold breast, they fought, and at his side,
In death they triumph'd, for with him they died.

 As thro' his bosom sung the fatal steel,
He rais'd his hand, and wav'd along farewell:
On the sweet maid his eye all-wishful hung,   415
And half-form'd accents ceas'd upon his tongue.
Quick round the youth a tender arm she threw,
Fell as he fell, and wish'd to perish too.

The quivering form she press'd, in icy death,
Kiss'd his pale lips, and suck'd his parting breath.   420
No more her careless thoughts attempt to fly ;
No more her ear attends the horrid cry :
Close to the wound her snowy hand applied
Withdrew the lance, and stopp'd the purple tide.
A grim barbarian to the fair-one came,   425
Pierc'd her white side, and forc'd the vital stream ;
With one weak gasp, on Elam's bosom laid,
Her bloom all vanish'd, and her spirit fled.

  In distant fields, we heard the trumpet's sound,
And strode impatient to the fatal ground.   430
On the sad scene, by favouring shrubs conceal'd,
A youth, unarm'd, the dire event beheld :
He, drown'd in tears, disclos'd the fierce affray,
And shew'd where Mina, and her Elam, lay.
On the cold earth, the wither'd leaves he press'd ;   435
The fair yet panting at his lifeless breast.
Her hand was feebly laid against the spear,
Still in her side, and in her eye a tear.
So blooms a flower beside th' autumnal stream,
And waves, and wantons, in the solar beam,   440
Nor knows the frost, that in the midnight sky
Lurks for its charms, and bids its beauty die.

  The hapless pair in snow-white robes array'd,
To the same grave our friendly hands convey'd.
Kind youths, and virgins, there at dawn appear,   445
Strew fragrant flowers, and drop the tender tear ;
There the sad wild rose yields its withering bloom,
And melancholy music mourns their doom.
Pierc'd thro' his thigh, and weltering on the ground,
A savage wretch, beneath an oak, we found.   450
By favours won, he shew'd th' impending doom,
What bands are gather'd, and what heroes come.
To spy these realms, he cried, from Hebron's land,
Thro' many a forest rov'd our warlike band..-

G g

Led by bold Hoham, from far diftant fhores,   455
Thence countlefs hofts invade yon fhining towers;
There giant Zedeck's lofty car is roll'd ;
There beams young Piram in refulgent gold ;
High rais'd in air, ten thoufand ftandards play,
And chiefs unnumber'd hail the deathful day.   460

   Thus fpoke the wretch.   As o'er yon mountain's brow
I fteer'd my path, and eyed the world below,
From diftant fields, the trump's approaching found
Wav'd o'er the plains, and fill'd the groves around ;
Swift tow'rd the walls long, dufty volumes came,   465
And dreadful gleams of interrupted flame ;
On high the banners danc'd ; a mighty train,
With lines immeafurable, hid the plain.

   Oh, by the covenant, which thy voice hath given,
By the bleft favour of all-bounteous Heaven,   470
That Heaven, which makes thee his peculiar care,
Aid our weak race, and grant our righteous prayer !

   Thus mourn'd the chief, while Caleb flow drew nigh,
His anguifh'd bofom heaving many a figh ;
His foul, in filence, mourn'd the haplefs pair,   475
All-lovely Irad and his beauteous fair ;
When Jofhua fad the hoary fage addrefs'd---
Great prince, this night Harefhah is thy gueft,
His voice a mournful tale from Gibeon brings,
How 'gainft her walls Canäan arms her kings.   480
Our aid he claims ; an aid by covenant due ;
But ah, what griefs our haplefs race purfue !
Again th' Eternal arm our courfe withftands,
Cuts off our chiefs, and flays our haplefs bands.
Firft Hezron flept ; then virtuous Uzal fell,   485
And brave Shelumiel bade the world farewel,
Next lovely Irad found a haplefs doom ;
And now fweet Mina feeks an early tomb:
Should ftill new courfes unadvis'd be tried,
Frefh wrath may kindle, and frefh ills betide.   490

Let then this chief in peace with thee retire,
'Till Heaven his counsels, and our course, inspire.

  He spoke.   Hareshah with the sage withdrew,
While the sun lingering slowly left the view;
The mourning Hero sought a slight repose,   495
And broken slumbers o'er his eye-lids rose.

  Now Night, in vestments rob'd, of cloudy die,
With sable grandeur cloth'd the orient sky,
Impell'd the sun, obsequious to her reign,
Down the far mountains to the western main;   500
With magic hand, becalm'd the solemn even,
And drew day's curtain from the spangled heaven.
At once the planets sail'd around the throne;
At once ten thousand worlds in splendor shone:
Behind her car, the moon's expanded eye   505
Rose from a cloud, and look'd around the sky:
Far up th' immense her train sublimely roll,
And dance, and triumph, round the lucid pole.
Faint shine the fields, beneath the shadowy ray;
Slow fades the glimmering of the west away;   510
To sleep the tribes retire; and not a sound
Flows through the air, or murmurs on the ground.

  The Chief, arising, o'er the darksome green
Turn'd his slow steps, and view'd the splendid scene;
With wondering gaze, survey'd the vaulted even,   515
The half-seen world, and all the pomp of Heaven.
Wide arch'd the palace of th' Almighty hand,
Its walls far-bending o'er the sea, and land:
Round the vast roof, from antient darkness sprung,
In living pride, immortal tapers hung: 520
The lamp on high an endless lustre shed,
And earth's broad pavement all beneath was spread.
From distant hills, red flames began to rise,
Topp'd the talls towers, and climb'd the kindling skies:
Thick stream'd the transient stars; and all around   525
A still, mild glory rob'd the twilight ground.

Now tow'rd the north he bent his wandering way,
Each scene revolving of the busy day,
When lo! soft sounds his startled ear assail,
Soft as the whisper of the flowing gale.   530
Now mournful murmurs slowly-pensive rise ;
Now languid harmony in silence dies :
Now nobler strains, with animating fire,
Warm the bold raptures of the living lyre.

Whither, O whither is thy beauty gone ?   535
To what far region ? to what world unknown ?
No lone, drear shades of everlasting gloom,
Verg'd on the confines of the icy tomb,
No frozen climes, extend impervious bounds,
Confine thy walks, and bar thy active rounds,   540
Forbid thy upward flight at large to rove,
And climb the mountains of eternal love.

Far other scenes thy lovely spirit claim ;
Far other mansions own thy lasting fame.
Borne on light wings, I see thy guardian come,   545
Unchain thy mind, and point the starry home :
With joy, he clasps thee in immortal arms,
Waves his young plumes, and smiles etherial charms ;
Through fields of air, he wins his purple way,
And rosy choirs, delighted, round him play.   550

There, o'er bright realms, and pure, unchanging skies,
Suns gayly walk, and lucid morns arise ;
Crown'd with new flowers, the streams perpetual roll,
And living beauty blooms around the pole.
Will there, alas! the soft enchantment end ?   555
And can no love to those fair climes ascend ?
It can ; it will ; for there the bless'd improve
Their minds in joy, and where 's the joy, but love ?

Canst thou forget, when, call'd from southern bowers,
Love tun'd the groves, and spring awak'd the flowers,
How, loos'd from slumbers by the morning ray,   561
O'er balmy plains we bent our frequent way ?

On thy fond arm, with pleasing gaze, I hung,
And heard sweet music murmur o'er thy tongue;
Hand lock'd in hand, with gentle ardour press'd,   565
Pour'd soft emotions through the heaving breast,
In magic transport heart with heart entwin'd,
And in sweet languors lost the melting mind.

'Twas then, thy voice, attun'd to wisdom's lay,
Shew'd fairer worlds, and trac'd th' immortal way;   570
In virtue's pleasing paths my footsteps tried,
My sweet companion, and my skillful guide;
Through varied knowledge taught my mind to soar,
Search hidden truths, and new-found walks explore:
While still the tale, by nature learn'd to rove,   575
Slid, unperceiv'd to scenes of happy love.
'Till weak, and lost, the faltering converse fell,
And eyes disclos'd what eyes alone could tell;
In rapturous tumult bade the passions roll,
And spoke the living language of the soul.   580

With what fond hope, through many a blissful hour,
We gave the soul to fancy's pleasing power;
Lost in the magic of that sweet employ
To build gay scenes, and fashion future joy!
We saw mild Peace o'er fair Canäan rise,   585
And shower her pleasures from benignant skies.
On airy hills our happy mansion rose,
Built but for joy, nor room reserv'd for woes.
Round the calm solitude, with ceaseless song,
Soft roll'd domestic ecstasy along: 590
Sweet as the sleep of Innocence, the day,
By raptures number'd, lightly danc'd away:
To love, to bliss, the union'd soul was given,
And each, too happy! ask'd no brighter heaven.
Yet then, even then, my trembling thoughts would rove,
And steal on hour from Irad, and from love,   596
Through dread futurity all-anxious roam,
And cast a mournful glance on ills to come.

Hope not, fond maid, some voice prophetic cried---
A life, thus wasted down th' unruffled tide :   600
Trust no gay, golden doom, from anguish free,
Nor with the laws of Heaven revers'd for thee.
Survey the peopled world ; thy soul shall find
Woes, ceaseless woes, ordain'd for poor mankind.
Life 's a long solitude, an unknown gloom,   605
Clos'd by the silence of the dreary tomb.

    For soon, ah soon shall fleet thy pleasing dreams ;
Soon close the eye, that, bright as angels, beams
Grace irresistible.   To mouldering clay
Shall change the face, that smiles thy griefs away :   610
Soon the sweet music of that voice be o'er,
Hope cease to charm, and beauty bloom no more :
Strange, darksome wilds, and devious ways be trod,
Nor love, nor Irad, steal thy heart from God.
And must the hours in ceaseless anguish roll ?   615
Must no soft sunshine cheer my clouded soul ?
Spring charm around me brightest scenes, in vain ?
And Youth's angelick visions wake to pain ?
Oh come once more, with fond endearments come ;
Burst the cold prison of the sullen tomb ;   920
Thro' favourite walks, thy chosen maid attend ;
Where well-known shades for thee their branches bend :
Shed the sweet poison from thy speaking eye ;
And look those raptures, lifeless words deny !
Still be the tale rehears'd, that ne'er could tire ;   625
But, told each eve, fresh pleasure could inspire :
Still hop'd those scenes, which love and fancy drew ;
But, drawn a thousand times, were ever new !

    Yet cease, fond maid ; 'tis thine alone to mourn :
Yield the bright scenes, that never can return.   630
Thy joys are fled, thy smiling morn is o'er ;
Too bless'd in youth, thou must be bless'd no more.
The hope, that brighten'd, with all-pleasing ray,
Shone, but to charm, and flatter'd, to betray.

No more fair Irad heeds my tender strain ; 635
Dull is the voice, that never call'd in vain ;
Vain the cold languish of these once lov'd eyes ;
And vain the fond desire, that bids him rise.
In life's gay scenes, their highest grace before,
Thy mind, O Youth divine ! must share no more ; 640
Alike unnotic'd, joys and tumults roll,
Nor these disturb, nor those delight, thy soul.

 Again all bright shall glow the morning beam ;
Again soft suns dissolve the frozen stream :
Spring call young breezes from the southern skies, 645
And, cloath'd in splendor, flowery millions rise.
In vain to thee--No morn's indulgent ray
Warms the cold mansion of the slumbering clay.
No mild etherial gale, with tepid wing,
Shall fan thy locks, or waft approaching spring : 650
Unfelt, unknown, shall breathe the rich perfume,
And unhear'd music wave around thy tomb.

 A cold, dumb, dead repose invests thee round ;
Still as the void, ere nature form'd a sound.
In thy dark region, pierc'd by no kind ray, 655
To roll the long, oblivious hours away.
In these wild walks, this solitary round,
Where the pale moon-beam lights the glimmering ground
At each sad turn, I view'd thy spirit come,
And glide, half-seen, behind a neighbouring tomb ; 660
With visionary hand, forbid my stay,
Look o'er the grave, and beckon me away.

 But vain the wish ; for still, around thy tomb,
This faithful hand shall bid the wild rose bloom ;
Each lonely eve, Selima hither rove, 665
And pay the tribute of unalter'd love ;
Till, O fond, lovely youth ! these eyes shall close,
Seal'd in the silence of a long repose ;
Beneath one turf our kindred bodies lie,
And lose, unpain'd, this melancholy sky. 670

With thee, well-pleas'd, the final pang I'll brave;
With thee Death smile, and lightsome be the grave;
O'er earth's broad fields, till heaven forget to reign,
And suns benighted vanish in the main;
This dark recess the cherub then shall find,   675
And wake a form, angelic as thy mind.

Distress'd, kind Joshua heard her moving strain,
But still walk'd onward o'er the shady plain;
Why should his face her mournful thoughts molest,
Tho' soft compassion warm'd his feeling breast;   680
No comfort could he lend, nor joy impart,
While slumbering Irad own'd her tender heart.

And now his footsteps slow and softly rove,
Thro' the black silence of th' extended grove;
Alternate moon-beams feebly pierce the shade,   685
And o'er his path a glimmering horror spread;
Strange, awful objects dimly rise around,
And forms unfinish'd cloath the gloomy ground.
With mournful thoughts the prospect well combin'd,
And sooth'd the wanderings of a drooping mind.   690
Around he cast his melancholy eyes,
And pleas'd, beheld the solemn scenes arise;
Scenes tun'd in concert with his sadden'd soul,
To grief resign'd, and pity's soft controul;
The gloom, the silence, gave a kind relief;   695
Peace sprung from trouble, and delight from grief?
His heart impassion'd mourn'd his daughter's doom,
Her charms, her virtues, banish'd to the tomb.
Then hapless Irad all his woes renew'd,
And copious tears afresh his cheeks bedew'd: 700
At length, the tumults of his struggling breast
Unwish'd, unbidden accents thus express'd.

Oh, when shall Israel's countless sorrow's cease?
And war once more resign to lasting peace?
Each rising morn, more dreadful woes appear,   705
And each sad evening prompts a larger tear.

Why did pale terror Judah's race appal ?
Why princes, chiefs, and generous thousands fall ?
Ah ! why did Heaven to me commit the sway,
And bid his sons this feeble arm obey ?   710
Oh had the Power divine for me ordain'd
Some humble mansion, in a lonely land ;
Where the trump's voice was never never heard :
Nor falchion drawn, nor savage slaughter fear'd !
In quiet then my life had pass'd away,   715
Bless'd without pride, and without splendor gay ;
In death, my soul serenely met her doom,
And my own children built my humble tomb.

At once a wild, and visionary sound,
With sudden murmurs, fill'd the grove around ;   720
The strange alarm now loud and louder grew,
And through the forest bursting splendor flew ;
A Form, the brightest of the morning choir,
Drew near, in all the pomp of heavenly fire ;
Twelve stars of glory crown'd his awful head ;   725
His sun-bright eyes the forky lightening shed ;
Serene, but dreadfully serene, he stood,
And a dire trembling seiz'd the conscious wood.
As when a storm the dark horizon fills,
Long, solemn thunders roll o'er distant hills ;   730
So, from the Vision's voice, a fearful sound
Appall'd his ear, and shook the startled ground.
Chief of thy race ! from heaven's eternal King,
At his command, this sacred charge I bring.
I AM THE LORD. I form'd the earth, and sky,   735
Illum'd the sun, and hung his flames on high ;
Bade worlds, in millions, star th' etherial plain,
And built the secret chambers of the main.
My voice, the heaven, and heaven of heavens obey ;
And Ocean, Earth, and Hell, confess my sway.   740
Through worlds, on worlds, in Being's mighty bounds,
That roll through space' illimitable rounds ;

H h

Where skies, o'er skies, unmeasur'd arches bend,
And stars, o'er stars, in endless pride ascend ;
Where the sun's searching beam hath never ray'd,   745
Nor scarce an angel's pinion'd fancy stray'd ;
My power, my wisdom, with divine controul,
Surveys, preserves, directs and moves, the whole.
All these, with all their scenes, th' eternal Mind,
Ere angels sung, or heaven began, design'd.   750
Whate'er my voice ordain'd to being came,
Touch'd by th' immortal, all-inspiring flame.
In all, though man, with vain, benighted eye,
Of insect ken, unnumber'd blots descry,
From hell's deep caves, to heaven's sublimest bound,   755
No stain, no fault, no error, can be found.

    Whose thoughts shall then my boundless wisdom blame?
Whose wishes rise against my holy Name ?
My spirit form'd thee in the silent womb,
And wrote, with Mercy's hand, thy favourite doom ;   760
Thy soul awak'd, thy infant limbs inspir'd,
With truth illum'd thee, and with virtue fir'd ;
Bade all my sons thy sceptred rule obey,
And stretch'd thy glory with the solar ray.
And shall thy heart my bounteous hand distrust,   765
And mourn that warriors mingle with the dust ?
What though brave Irad from the world retir'd,
Tho' numerous bands around his steps expir'd ;
Without a fear, without a pang, resign ;
That virtuous Youth, and all those bands, were mine.   770
With songs the grace adore, that rais'd thy mind,
From the low confines of the bestial kind,
Where countless throngs plod on their base pursuits,
Above, and just above, their kindred brutes,
To that sublimest honour, man can know,   775
To bless my sons, and shew my praise, below.

    Forgive, O Heaven ! forgive---the Hero cried ;
And milder thus the Vision's voice replied.

O Chief of Ifrael! let no rebel thought   779
Accufe the wonders, God's right hand hath wrought,
While his almighty arm thy courfe fuftains,
Afk not what numbers crowd embattled plains.
From the broad circuit of her various lands,
He call'd to fight Canäan's countlefs bands :
He bids thee fearlefs tempt the martial field,   785
And truft the covert of his guardian fhield.
For there, in virtue's caufe, thy God fhall arm,
And pour the vengeance of the baleful ftorm ;
The fun ftand ftill ; the moon thy voice obey ;
And the bright angel fweep thy foes away.   790

    But now to nobler fcenes thy views extend !
See long futurity in pomp afcend !
The varying doom of Ifrael's wayward race ;
How truth exalts them, and how crimes debafe ;
Their arts, their arms, their towns, and towers, behold,
Fields of fair flocks, and domes inchaf'd with gold !   796
High Heaven around them fpreads his bleffings far
Or proves, and fcourges, with vindictive war !
There too, fucceffive, fee the wonders rife,
That guard, and blefs, the Children of the fkies ;   800
Thy own bright Ifrael ; Heaven's immortal race,
Sav'd by his Son, and fainted by his grace ;
To Jacob's chofen feed at firft confin'd,
Then wide, and wider, fpread to all mankind !
With more than mortal ken, thy raptur'd foul   805
Shall fee far diftant times in vifion roll ;
When Abraham's fons, from earth's remoteft end,
To Salem's heaven-topp'd mountains fhall afcend ;
When round the poles, where frozen fplendors play,
In noontide realms, that bafk in brighter day,   810
On fpicy fhores, where beauteous morning reigns,
Or Evening lingers o'er her favourite plains,
From guilt, from death, reviving nations rife,
And one vaft hymn of tranfport fills the fkies.

Beyond thefe fcenes, fhall nobler wonders fhine,   815
Climes of fweet peace, and years of joy divine,
Where truth's fair fons extend the golden wing
Thro' morn e'er-rifing, ever changing fpring ;
Where unborn Beauty, round whofe awful throne,
All fplendors fade, and funs are dark at noon,   820
Smiles o'er broad regions ever-brightening day,
Fair nature quickening in th' ecftatic ray :
The foul, pure effluence of th' all-beaming Mind,
With virtue diadem'd, with truth refin'd,
With blifs fupreme, with radiance yet unknown,   825
Begins, a ftar, and brightens to a fun ;
Life, Love, and Rapture, bloffom in her fight,
And Glory triumphs o'er the world of light.

THE

CONQUEST OF CANÄAN:

BOOK X.

ARGUMENT.

Vision of futurity. Prospect of the land of Canäan. Prosperous events after the war is finished. Apostacy after the death of Joshua, and consequent judgements. Troubles by Cushan-rishathaim, Hazor, Midian, Ammon, and the Philistines. Samson. Civil War. Philistines' Kings. David's combat with Goliath. War with Ammon, and Syria. Joab. David's glory. Jerusalem. Temple. Dedication. Solomon. Division of the kingdom. Destruction of Israel by Shalmaneser, and of Judah by Nebuchadnezzar. Restoration. Messiah. his Birth Baptism, Miracles, Trial, Death, Resurrection, and Ascension. Destruction of Jerusalem by the Romans. Preaching of the Gospel by the Apostles, and succeeding Ministers. Prospect of America. Slavery of the eastern Continent. Glory of the Western Millennium. Calling of the Jews. Signs which forebode the end of the World. Resurrection, Conflagration, General Judgement, and consummation of all things. Prospect of heaven, and a happy immortality. Angel departs, and Joshua returns to the camp.

THE CONQUEST of CANÄAN.

BOOK X.

THE Vision ceas'd. At once the foreft fled,
  At once an unknown region round them fpread,
Like the ftill fabbath's dawning light ferene,
And fair as blifsful Eden's living green.
High on a hill they ftood, whofe cloudy brow   5
Look'd o'er th' illimitable world below.
In fhining verdure eaftern realms withdrew,
And hills and plains, immingling, fill'd the view :
From fouthern forefts rofe melodious founds ;
Tall northern mountains ftretch'd cerulean bounds ;   10
Weft, all was fea ; blue fkies, with peaceful reign,
Serene roll'd round th' interminable plain.
Then thus the Power. To thee, blefs'd man, 'tis given,
To know the thoughts of all-confidering Heaven :
Scenes form'd eternal in th' unmeafur'd Mind,   15
In yon bright realms, for Abraham's race defign'd,
While the great promife ftands in heaven fecure,
Or earth, or feas, or fkies or ftars endure.

He *spoke*.   At once a *spacious land is *seen,
Bright with young cornfields, and with pa*tures green ; 20
Fair *hine the rivers ; fair the plains extend ;
The tall woods wave, and towering hills a*cend ;
Ten thou*and thou*and flooks around them *pread,
Sport o'er the lawns, and crop the verdant blade ;
Ble*s'd *wains with mu*ic charm their u*eful toil,   25
The cheerful plowmen turn the *able *oil ;
The vine, glad off*pring of the *un, a*pires,
And *miles, and purples, in th' indulgent fires ;
The vales, with humble pride, gay coats adorn,
And plea*ure dances in the beams of morn ;   30
Spring, hand in hand with golden Autumn join'd
Lives in the flowers, and wantons in the wind.

     Then *pacious towns exalt their *tately *pires,
Bend their long walls, and light unnumber'd fires ;
Here all the pomp of haughty *tructures *hines,   35
Youth crowds the dance, and Age in council joins ;
There, built by virtue, *moking altars ri*e,
And clouds of incen*e fill the morning *kies.
When thus the Hero---Say, O Power divine !
What bright and happy *cenes before me *hine,   40
Tell, if tho*e regions I*rael's bli*s di*play,
And flocks, and fields, and cities own their *way.

     Ju*t are thy thoughts---the Seraph's voice return'd,
While ro*y beauty round his a*pect burn'd,
In the*e fair climes *hall I*rael fix her *eat,   45
End her long toils, and find a calm retreat,
Then all the ble*ings, mortals here can know,
From GOD's good hand, in plenteous *treams, *hall flow.
In pure*t beams *hall genial *uns de*cend ;
And moons, and *tars, their *ofte*t radiance lend :   50
The gales waft health; kind flowers the plains renew ;
Morn yield her fragrance ; eve her balmy dew ;
With autumn's prime the wintery fro*t con*pire ;
With *prings mild influence *ummer's *corching fire ;

To nurfe the land of virtue's lov'd recefs,   55
And blefs the nation, Heaven delights to blefs.

  Thefe fcenes of blifsful peace fhalt thou enjoy,
Nor grief difturbs, nor circling foes annoy.
But when death calls thee to divine abodes,
They fly from Heaven, and feek Canäan's gods;   60
To ftocks, to ftones, with ftupid reverence, bow,
Burft every tie, and perjure every vow.
Then war fhall thunder from the realms around;
Then funs malignant parch the fterile ground;
The fields fhall wafte; the flocks to duft decay, 65
And fierce difeafes fweep their tribes away.
Yet fhall his bounty fainted guardians raife,
And fhed rich bleffings on their peaceful days;
Wak'd to new life, the land forget to mourn,
And fruitful feafons to the plains return.   70

  Behold thefe fcenes expanding to thy foul!
From orient realms what blackening armies roll!
See their proud Monarch, in yon glimmering car,
Leads his ftrong hoft, and points the wafte of war.
Till, rais'd by Heaven, the youth, whofe early bloom, 75
Gives a fair promife of his worth to come,
That fecond Irad, Othniel, lifts his hand,
And fweeps the heathens from his wafted land.

  In awful pomp, fee Hazor's bands arife,
Shade the far plains, and lower along the fkies!   80
An unborn Jabin fways thofe fpacious fhores,
And on thefe climes that raging deluge pours.
The little band, thou feeft thy nation fends;
Lo, how the hoft innumerable bends!
Before Jehovah's wrath the millions fly,   85
Drop their weak arms, and lift a leffening cry.

  Behold, in fouthern fkies, what clouds appear!
There Midian's fons the bloody ftandard rear:

242 BOOK X.

Before them, Ruin marks her ravag'd way;
Fire sweeps the plains, and smoke involves the day!   90
Behold yon Angel, rapt on wings of light,
Flames, like a meteor, down the face of night!
His fearful hand accelerates their doom,
And their own weapons plunge them to the tomb.

Beyond fair Jordan, that broad, azure stream,   95
What moony shields, what throngs of lances, gleam!
In long, dark lines, see Jephthah's spreading host
Benight the heavens, and dusk the shady coast!
Lo, wing'd with fear, the ranks of Ammon yield,
Mount their bright cars, and fly the sanguine field!   100

From those dread scenes, now southward turn thine eyes;
Behold, what clouds of Philistines arise!
Ordain'd the terror of Canäan's climes,
The sting of guilt, the scourge of daring crimes;
Illum'd with spears, the gloomy squadrons roll,   105
Dust shades their path, and darkness hides the pole.

See Gaza's thousands, rang'd in black array,
Spread their wide volumes on the setting day!
Behold brave Samson sweep the dreadful plain!
Their falchions flame, their spears are hurl'd, in vain;
Swift from his fateful arm their squadrons fly,   110
And shields behind them glimmer on the sky.

Now, where yon haughty pile in pomp ascends,
His strong-wrought nerves the eyeless hero bends;
The columns shake, the cloudy temple falls,   115
And dusty ruin veils the smoking walls,

See, where proud Gibeah's turrets strike the skies,
On every side embattled armies rise!
There Civil Discord calls her sons to war,
And waves her banner through the troubled air;   120
Against one tribe the swords of all unite,
Destruction hovering o'er the crimson fight.

Line 95) Jud. 11. L. 101) Jud. 13. &c L. 107) Jud. 15, 16.
L. 117) Jud. 20.

See, like a storm, the Philiſtines again
Roll o'er yon hills, and crowd the darkening plain !
Lo Iſrael flees ! the haughty heathens dare,   125
Pollute the ark ; nor know th' Almighty 's there.
The ſacred Prophet lifts his ſuppliant hands,
And calls down vengeance on the impious bands ;
Aghaſt they hear tremendous thunders riſe,
And from the lightenings turn their trembling eyes ; 130
The fields are redden'd with a ſanguine die,
The vanquiſh'd triumph, and the victors fly.

Thus ſcenes of varied life thy nation prove,
Reſtrain their crimes, and fix their wandering love.
At length, impatient of their Maker's hand,   135
Their tribes, with union'd voice ; a king demand.
Firſt choſen to the throne, of truth forlorn,
Blaſting the promiſe of his opening morn,
Saul, impious tyrant, holds the ſacred ſway,
And Iſrael's hapleſs ſons his rod obey.   140
But now the ſcenes a longer view demand ;
Behold what wonders to thine eyes expand !

The hero gaz'd ; at once two mountains roſe,
O'erſpread by ſquadrons of embattled foes.
Proud, from the ſouthern hill a giant ſtrode,   145
Dar'd his pale foes, and brav'd the arm of God.
Vaſt were his limbs, for war and ruin made ;
His towering ſtature caſt a long, dark ſhade ;
His eye glar'd fury, and his buckler's gleam,
Flam'd, like a cloud before the ſetting beam.   150
A youth, in nature's prime, oppos'd his arm,
To the dire threatenings of the lowering ſtorm :
Soft round his aſpect roſy beauty ſmil'd,
Bold but not raſh, and without terror mild.
By his ſtrong hand, like rapid lightening, flung,   155
Full on the giant's front a pebble ſung ;

Line 123) 1 Sam. 7.   L, 143) 1 Sam. 17.

Like some tall oak, the mighty warrior feil,
And with shrill thunders rang his clashing steel.
At once the heathens fled ; their foes pursued,
And boundless death the crimson fields bestrew'd.   160

Then   us the Guide---Here David's skilful hand,
Sinks vast Goliath in the bloody sand.
Call'd, from the peace of sylvan shades unknown,
To rule an empire, and to mount a throne,
This beauteous youth shall stretch a prosperous sway,   165
And bid rude realms, and conquer'd kings, obey ;
Where fertile shores the proud Euphrates laves,
Where yon broad ocean rolls its lucid waves,
Beyond the limits of the Syrian reign,
Or where far southward spreads the crimson main.   170

Behold, in dreadful pomp, from northern skies,
What gloomy clouds, what thronging squadrons rise !
Kings in the flaming van exalt their forms,
Borne in swift cars, and wrapp'd in dazzling arms ;
Here Ammon's sons unnumber'd crowd the fields ;   175
There Syria's millions wave their glimmering shields.

See Israel moves in glory to the fight !
See Joab, circled with a blaze of light !
His lofty port, his firm, undaunted eye,
Shoot terror round, and bid the millions fly.   180

Again what crowds the distant plains invade !
How the world darkens in the sable shade !
Aloft in air the dancing banners fly,
And throngs of lances tremble in the sky.
High in the front majestic David stands,   185
Leads on the conquest, and the fight commands,
Bids death before him sweep the dreadful plain,
And rolls his chariot o'er th' unnumber'd slain.

Nor less shall peace adorn his righteous sway ;
The proud shall tremble, and the rich obey ;   190
With equal hand, great Justice hold the scale ;
In every council Wisdom's voice prevail ;

Line 171) 2 Sam. 10.

The fields grow fat, beneath the culturing hand,
And smiling plenty wanton round the land.
Then spacious towns, with wealth and pomp supplied, 195
Shall bend long walls and lift their spiry pride ;
O'er all imperial Salem's splendors rise,
The boast of earth, and emblem of the skies.

  He spoke : tall mountains rear their summits high,
Crown'd with fair spires, that vanish in the sky ;   200
Upheave huge walls : imperial arches bend,
And golden turrets to the clouds ascend.
So, when dun night begins in heaven to rise,
A long, dark cloud surrounds the northern skies ;
Forth from its spacious womb effulgent stream   205
Tall spires of glory, columns bright of flame ;
There shine gay walls illumin'd towers ascend,
Wave round th' immense, and o'er the concave bend ;
Expanding, reddening, the proud pomp aspires,
And stars faint-tremble through the wonderous fires. 210
Thus wide, thus bright, the splendid scene expands,
Rich with the treasures of surrounding lands:
The long streets wind ; the lofty domes ascend ;
Fair gardens bloom, and crystal fountains bend ;
From flowery millions rich perfumes arise.   215
Load the sweet gales, and breathe upon the skies.

    There, crown'd with towers, and wrapp'd in golden
A bursting dome the wondering Chief descried,   [pride,
On eastern hills its front aerial stood.
Look'd o'er the walls, and distant regions view'd ;   220
There glow'd the beauty of the artists' minds ;
There gates, there spires, there columns, he design'd ;
There, with strong light, etherial wisdom shone,
There blended glories mock'd the noonday sun,
A bright, celestial grandeur towers display'd;   225
And verdant courts, expansive, round them spread.

Line 217) See 2 Chron. 6, 7.

There call'd from circling realms, a gladsome train,
In gayest robes, unnumber'd, hid the plain.
Soft rose their songs ; the harp's bewildering sound,
Breath'd mild inchantment through the domes around,
On shining altars gifts of virtue lay,   231
Rich incense fum'd, and smoke embrown'd the day.
High o'er the rest, a prince majestic stood,
And robes of splendor loosely round him flow'd ;
Spread were his hands ; his face, to earth declin'd, 235
Spoke the calm raptures of a pious mind ;
His voice, on balmy winds, like incense, driven,
Rose, sweetly fragrant, to approving heaven :
At once, as earthquakes, rumbling, rock the ground,
Slow roll'd a long, deep roar the dome around ; 240
O'er the tall towers a cloud convolving spread,
Bedimm'd the skies, and wrapp'd the world in shade ;
Fierce from its womb terrific lightenings came,
The gifts exhaling in the rapid flame ;
The train fell prostrate ; shook the bright abode, 245
And trembling earth confess'd the present GOD.

   Then thus the Guide---This prince, to David born,
With solemn pomp shall Salem's towers adorn ;
To GOD's great name, this glorious pile shall raise,
Fair type of Heaven, and seat of lasting praise. 250

   In his bless'd reign, shall peace extend her sway ;
The poor dwell safely, and the proud obey ;
Israel, secure, in happy fields recline,
Pluck their own figs, and taste their plenteous wine ;
The swain sole monarch of his lands shall reign, 255
And own the products of the grateful plain.
On fame's light wings, his glory shall be borne,
Where smiles fair eve, or blooms etherial morn ;
From distant regions kings enraptur'd throng,
Drink sacred truth, and catch the heavenly song : 260
To him, her boundless wealth shall Egypt yield ;
To him, Sabea ope the spicy field ;

In morn's fair islands, sweets celestial blow;
Wide ocean's realms with pearly splendors glow;
The loom its purple, earth its gems, unfold,   265
And teeming sulphur kindle into gold.

  Long shall bright wisdom gild his prosperous day,
Till magic beauty charm his heart astray;
Wisdom, beyond the narrow thoughts of man,
In clouds involv'd, and bounded by a span;   270
Wisdom, that nature's mysteries shall controul,
And rule the nobler kingdom of the soul.

  At length, when death his spirit shall demand,
Two guilty kings shall sway Canäan's land,
Both to the fatal love of idols given,   275
And both rejected by an angry Heaven:
While their mad kingdoms oft in fight contend,
And flames lay waste their fields, and wars their cities rend.

  Then shall th' Eternal's awful vengeance rise,
His wheels descend, his chariot shake the skies   280
Before his breath the son's of Israel fly,
Like chaff when whirlwinds sweep th' autumnal sky,
To realms, whose beauty endless frosts deform,
To heavens that thunder with eternal storm:
Where o'er yon fiery cliffs, that bound the skies,   285
Dejected suns with feeble influence rise,
At distance hovering round the unbless'd shore,
Where glimmering ice forbids the waves to roar.

  Yet still, while Judah owns his awful sway,
And pious kings their sacred homage pay,   290
Safe in the covert of his guardian hand,
Shall happy subjects share a peaceful land;
Till rous'd to wrath by insolence of crimes,
He rolls deep horror o'er Canäan's climes.

  On that dread morn, shall Salem hear from far   295
The trump's shrill clamour, and the sounding car;
Hosts train'd to blood her shining seats surround,
And all her glories totter to the ground.

Adieu! adieu! thou darling of the skies;
Thy towers begin to shake; thy flames begin to rise. 300
, Where once the palace raptur'd eyes descried,
And the tall temple rear'd its splendid pride,
Round mouldering walls the nightly wolf shall howl;
Sad ruins murmur to the wailing owl;
In domes, once golden, creeping moss be found; 305
The long, rank weed o'erspread the garden's bound;
The wild Idumean cast a mournful eye
On the brown towers, and pass in silence by.

Nor let deep sorrow pain thy pitying eyes;
Lo fairer scenes in quick succession rise! 310
Soon shall the temple crown the sacred hill;
Bright domes ascend; and fields around them smile;
Thy nation gather; great Messiah shine,
And earth be honour'd with a King divine.

From Edom's realms, what mighty form ascends! 315
How the vale blossoms! how the mountain bends!
How shine his limbs, in heaven's immortal pride!
How beams his vesture, in the rainbow died!
'Tis he! 'tis he! who saves a world undone;
The Prince of glory & God's eternal Son! 320
O'er conscious hills he wins his beauteous way;
The plains are transport, and all nature gay.

O sons of men!---th' indulgent Saviour cries---
My raptur'd voice invites you to the skies.
No more to Jacob's narrow race confin'd; 325
A bliss unmeasur'd flows for all mankind;
The life, the youth, of climes forever bless'd;
Increasing glory, and seraphic rest.

Say, what the gain in pleasure's paths to stray,
Where poison blossoms, and where serpents play. 330
Ambition's lofty steep with pain to climb,
Where guilt, and anguish, swell with every crime;

Line 313) Isaiah 63.

To waſte, in weary toils, man's little doom,
For treaſures, raviſh'd by the neighbouring tomb.
Should earth's broad realms beneath your ſceptre roll,
Can worlds exchang'd redeem the deathleſs ſoul ?   336
Riſe then, oh riſe, from ſin's oblivious ſleep !
Lo, wide beneath you gapes th' unfathom'd deep !
Explore, with me, the undeceiving road,
That blooms with virtue, and that leads to God.   340
     What though dire pain, and grief, and ſad diſmay,
And all earth's fury hedge the arduous way ;
Thoſe griefs, thoſe pains, my feet before you brave,
The world's fell hatred, and the gloomy grave ;
I feel ſuperior wiſdom's peace refin'd,   345
And the fair morning of a guiltleſs mind ;
The toils of faith, rewarding as they riſe ;
Befriending ſeraphs, and complacent Skies.
     And O the end ! the bright, immortal end !
Heaven's gates unbar, and angel hoſts attend.   350
Each hour more ſweet, for you her rivers roll ;
A ſky, ſtill brightening, arches round her pole ;
Fair, and more fair, her ſunny manſions glow ;
Pure, and more pure, her airs etherial blow ;
Her hoſt, in growing youth, ſerenely ſhines ;   355
Her glory quickens, and her world refines.
In that fair world, to e'er-beginning joy,
Each hour increaſing, ting'd with no alloy,
Reſt from each toil, relief from every care,
Conqueſt of death, and triumph o'er deſpair,   360
To your own peers, your laſting home, aſcend,
To bliſs' fair fountain, virtue's faithful friend,
Thoſe peers heaven's ſons, that home the bright abode,
That fount an ocean, and that friend a God.
To theſe fair realms to lift the contrite mind,   365
To give bleſs'd faith, and purchaſe peace refin'd,
To man's loſt ſoul the ſtamp of heaven recall,
And build again the ruins of the fall,

From GOD's high throne he comes to every woe,
The world his dungeon, and mankind his foe, 370
Heaven's wrath for thankless wretches dares assume,
Ascends the cross, and tries the darksome tomb.

Lo these dread scenes expanding to thine eye !
Behold yon cloudy pomp invest the sky !
What hosts of angels wave their flamy wings ! 375
The world is silent---hark, what music rings !---
All hail, ye happy swains ! this sacred morn,
Of David's race, the promis'd Saviour 's born ;
In Bethlehem's inn, behold the parent maid,
Her heavenly offspring in a manger laid ! 380
See, see, in yon blue track, his star ascend !
Adore ye angels ! heaven in homage bend !
From earth one cloud of mingling incense rise !
Peace to the world, and glory to the skies !

Before the harbinger behold him stand, 385
And take the sacred sprinkling from his hand ;
On wings of flame the etherial dove descend,
And the glad train with reverent homage bend !
Far round th' immense approving thunders roll, 389
And GOD's own son belov'd resounds from pole to pole.

See, at his touch, the fainting form respires ;
The pale-eyed leper glows with purple fires ;
Light as the hart, th' exulting cripple springs,
And the dumb suppliant new-born praises sings ;
Unusual sounds the cleaving ear surprise, 395
And light, and prospect, charm expanding eyes ;
The dungeon bursts ; the prisoner leaps to day,
And life recall'd reanimates the clay !

At his commands, what throngs of demons flee,
To yon far gulf, that blackens o'er the sea ! 400
Lo, in the skirt of yonder fading storm,
Obscurely sailing, many a dreadful form !

Line 373) Luke 2. L. 385) Mat. 3.

From its deep womb, what sullen murmurs rise!
And what pale lightenings feebly sweep the skies!

But O! what love the harden'd soul can gain!   405
Fair truth compels, Messiah charms, in vain.
Untaught, unmov'd, by hate and fury driven,
His nation rise against the heir of heaven,
Before a heathen's bar tumultuous hale;
Nor worth can move, nor innocence avail.   410
Behold the milder glories round him shine!
What peace serene! what constancy divine!
How silently sublime! how meekly great!
How virtue's splendor shades the glare of state!

By friends denied, by poor vile worms contemn'd,   415
Judg'd without law, and without guilt condemn'd,
While men, while demons, in fond triumph rise,
The Prince of life, the Lord of angels, dies.
At once dire earthquakes heave the shuddering ground,
Rend the hard rocks; the mountains quake around;   420
Far o'er the world blank midnight casts her shade,
And trembling rise the nations of the dead:
Pain'd, from the scene the conscious sun retires,
And nature's voice proclaims--- A God expires.

But not the earth his sacred form confines;   425
The bands dissolve; the grave its trust resigns;
His fair, transforming limbs new life inspires;
Heaven's youth informs, and Godlike beauty fires;
From the dark tomb he wings his lucid way,
Ascends the sky, and glads the climes of day.   430
As thy bold arm, to Israel's chosen band,
Thy foes extinguish'd, gives the promis'd land;
Call'd by thy name, shall he to realms of gloom
Drive vanquish'd Death, and triumph o'er the tomb,
To that bless'd land, the true Canäan, rise,   435
And guide his chosen children to the skies.

Then o'er his foes shall fearful vengeance break;
Heaven shine in arms; earth's listening regions quake;

The fond, vain triumph unknown woes deſtroy,
And clouds of ruin blaſt the tranſient joy.   440
 Behold, in weſtern ſkies, the ſtorm aſcend,
Its terrors blacken, and its flames extend!
There hide the whirlwinds, ſoon ordain'd to roll;
There ſleep fierce thunders, ſoon to rock the pole.
But firſt dread ſigns the guilty world alarm;   445
A ſanguine horror ſhades the ſun's bright form;
In fields of air, unreal hoſts contend;
Shrill arms reſound, and cars the concave rend:
From hell's black ſhores the Peſtilence aſpires,
Roams the wide earth, and breathes her baleful fires: 450
Whole regions wither in her ſickening flight,
And hoſts, and nations, periſh in a night:
Far round the ſhuddering ſky pale meteors glare,
And raging Diſcord ſounds the trump of war.
 Then countleſs millions ſeize the bloody ſhield, 455
And Death's black enſign glooms the fading field.
Lo, Zion's domes what grimly hoſts incloſe!
See ſun-bright eagles lead her gathering foes!
High o'er her walls, what threatening engines riſe!
And hark, what clamours murmuring mount the ſkies;
With clouds, purſuing clouds, the terrors grow;   461
More fierce the blaze, more dark th' invading woe.
But why ſhould diſmal ſcenes diſtreſs thy ſight,
Or grief unnerve thee for th' impending fight?
 Meantime, from land to land with ſpeed convey'd, 465
Meſſiah's ſons his truth and bleſſings ſpread.
On countleſs realms, to guilt and darkneſs given,
Aliens from life, and reprobate of Heaven,
The ſacred Spirit ſheds his healing power,
And ſkies indulgent heavenly bounty ſhower.   470
Low at his name the raptur'd nations bend;
By him perfum'd, unnumber'd prayers aſcend;

Line 441) Mat. 24. L. 455) Taking of Jeruſalem by the Romans.
L. 465) Preaching of the Goſpel by the Apoſtles. &c.

To heaven his name from earth's great houſhold flies,
And one vaſt cloud of incenſe cheers the ſkies.

From Salem's favour'd hills, the bliſs ſhall ſtray,   475
Glad every land, and ſtretch to every ſea ;
But chief far onward ſpeed its weſtern flight,
And bleſs the regions of deſcending light.

Far o'er yon azure main thy view extend,
Where ſeas, and ſkies, in blue confuſion blend,   480
Lo, there a mighty realm, by heaven deſign'd
The laſt retreat for poor, oppreſs'd mankind !
Form'd with that pomp, which marks the hand divine,
And clothes yon vault, where worlds unnumber'd ſhine,
Here ſpacious plains in ſolemn grandeur ſpread ;   485
Here cloudy foreſts caſt eternal ſhade :
Rich vallies wind ; the ſky tall mountains brave,
And inland ſeas for commerce ſpread the wave ;
With nobler floods, the ſea-like rivers roll,
And fairer luſtre purples round the pole.   490
Here, warm'd by happy ſuns, gay mines unfold
The uſeful iron, and the laſting gold ;
Pure, changing gems in ſilence learn to glow,
And mock the ſplendors of the covenant bow :
On countleſs hills, by ſavage footſteps trod,   495
That ſmile to ſee the future harveſt nod,
In glad ſucceſſion, plants unnumber'd bloom,
And flowers unnumber'd breathe a rich perfume ;
Hence life once more a length of days ſhall claim,
And health, reviving, light her purple flame.   500
Far from all realms this world imperial lies ;
Seas roll between, and threatening ſtorms ariſe ;
Alike unmov'd beyond Ambition's pale,
And the bold pinions of the venturous ſail :
Till circling years the deſtin'd period bring,   505
And a new Moſes lifts the daring wing,

Line 479) Viſion of America.

Through trackless feas, an unknown flight explores,
And hails a new Canäan's promis'd shores.

On yon far strand, behold that little train
Ascending, venturous, o'er th' unmeasur'd main.　　　510
No dangers fright ; no ills the course delay ;
'Tis virtue prompts, and God directs the way.
Speed, speed, ye sons of truth ! let Heaven befriend,
Let angels waft you, and let peace attend !
O smile thou sky serene ! ye storms retire !　　　515
And airs of Eden every sail inspire !
Swift o'er the main, behold the canvas fly,
And fade, and fade, beneath the farthest sky ;
See verdant fields the changing waste unfold ;
See sudden harvests dress the plains in gold :　　　520
In lofty walls the moving rocks ascend,
And dancing woods to spires and temples bend !

Meantime, expanding o'er earth's distant ends,
Lo, Slavery's gloom in sable pomp descends ;
Far round each eastern clime her volumes roll,　　　525
And pour, deep-shading, to the sadden'd pole.
How the world droops beneath the fearful blast ;
The plains all wither'd, and the skies o'ercast !
From realm to realm extends the general groan ;
The fainting body stupifies to stone ;　　　530
Benumb'd, and fix'd, the palsied soul expires,
Blank'd all its views, and quench'd its living fires ;
In clouds of boundless shade, the scenes decay ;
Land after land departs, and nature fades away.

In that dread hour, beneath auspicious skies,　　　535
To nobler bliss yon western world shall rise.
Unlike all former realms, by war that stood,
And saw the guilty throne ascend in blood,
Here union'd Choice shall form a rule divine ;
Here countless lands in one great system join ;　　　540

Line. 509] Settlement of North America, by the English, for the
enjoyment of Religion.　L. 525) Slavery of the eastern Continent.
L. 535) Freedom and glory of the North American States.

The sway of Law unbroke, unrivall'd grow,
And bid her bleffings every land o'erflow.

In fertile plains, behold the tree afcend,
Fair leaves unfold, and fpreading branches bend !
The fierce, invading ftorm fecure they brave,   545
And the ftrong influence of the creeping wave,
In heavenly gales with endlefs verdure rife,
Wave o'er broad fields, and fade in friendly fkies.
There fafe from driving rains, and battering hail,
And the keen fury of the wintry gale,   550
Frefh fpring the plants ; the flowery millions bloom,
All ether gladdening with a choice perfume ;
Their haftening pinions birds unnumber'd fpread,
And dance, and wanton, in th' aerial fhade.   554

Here Empire's laft, and brighteft throne fhall rife ;
And Peace, and Right, and Freedom, greet the fkies :
To morn's far realms her fhips commercing fail,
Or lift their canvas to the evening gale ;
In wifdom's walks, her fons ambitious foar,
Tread ftarry fields, and untried fcenes explore.   560
And hark what ftrange, what folemn-breathing ftrain
Swells, wildly murmuring, o'er the far, far main !
Down time's long, leffening vale, the notes decay,
And, loft in diftant ages, roll away.

When earth commenc'd, fix morns of labour rofe,   565
Ere the calm Sabbath fhed her foft repofe.
Thus fhall the world's great week direct its way,
And thoufand circling funs complete the day.
Faft were two days, ere beam'd the law divine ;
Two days muft roll, ere great Meffiah fhine ;   570
Two changeful days, the Gofpel's light fhall rife ;
Then facred quiet hufh the ftormy fkies.
O'er orient regions funs of toil fhall roll,
Faint luftre dawn, and clouds obfcure the pole :

Line 565) The Jews have an ancient tradition of this nature.

But o'er yon favourite world, the Sabbath's morn,   575
Shall pour unbounded day, and with clear splendor burn.

    Hence, o'er all lands shall sacred influence spread,
Warm frozen climes, and cheer the death-like shade ;
To nature's bounds, reviving Freedom reign,
And Truth, and Virtue, light the world again.   58●

    No more in arms shall battling nations rise ;
Nor war's hoarse thunders heave the earth and skies ;
No hungry vulture, from the rock's tall brow,
Eye the red field, and slaughtering host, below ;
No famine waste ; no tender infant fear ;   585
The meek-eyed virgin drop no painful tear ;
Soft to the lyre the trumpet sink refin'd,
And peace' mild music still the stormy mind.
The savage, nurs'd in blood, with wondering eye,
Sees all the horrors of the desert fly :   590
Dread war, once rapturous, now his soul affrights ;
Sweet peace allures, and angel love delights ;
His melting thoughts with softer passion glow ;
His tears steal gently o'er the plaint of woe ;
To virtuous toils his feet instinctive turn ;   595
Or seek the temple in the smiles of morn ;
Each stormy purpose truth's mild rays serene,
And spring celestial clothes the waste within.

    See, round the lonely wild, with glad surprise,
Strange verdure blooms, and flowery wonders rise !   60●
Hark how the sounds of gushing waters roll !
What new Arabias breathe upon the soul !
On russet plains returning Sharon blows ;
Her fragrance charms ; her living beauty glows ;
Each mount a Lebanon in pomp ascends ,   605
And, topp'd with cloudy pride, the cedar bends ;
To meads, to sports, with lambs the wolf retires,
Sooth'd his wild rage, and quench'd his gloomy fires,

Line 577) Beginning of the millennium. See Isaiah and the other
prophets.

The viper fierce, the hissing asp, grow mild,.
Refuse their prey, and wanton with the child :   610
New hymns the plumy tribes inraptur'd raise,
And howling forests harmonize to praise.

Shine soft, O sun ! ye skies around them smile !
Your showers propitious balmy heavens distil !
In every waste what cheerful domes arise !   615
What golden temples meet the bending skies ;
To yon bright world what clouds of incense roll ;
How Virtue's songs breathe sweet from pole to pole !

Through earth's wide realms let solemn silence flow !
Be hush'd thou main ! ye winds forget to blow !   620
JEHOVAH speaks---Beneath the farthest skies,
My trump shall sound, my sacred standard rise ;
From morn to eve the lucid banner shine,
And saints, ecstatic, hail th' illustrious sign.
Wak'd from the slumbers of the world unknown,   625
See raptur'd Sion mount the starry throne,
Round her fair gates, her thronging sons behold,
Dress'd in white garments, and adorn'd with gold !

Arise, O child of fostering heaven, arise ;
Queen of the world, and favourite of the skies ;   630
In sunny robes, with living splendor, shine ;
Be all thy vestments as thyself divine !

Seize the loud harp, arouse the breathing string ;
Exalt thine eyes, and hymns of transport sing ;
Behold thy ruin'd walls again ascend ;   635
Thy towers shoot up ; thy spacious arches bend ;
Thy gardens brighten ; streams reviving roll,
And gales of paradise intrance the soul.

Where long, long howl'd the solitary blast,
O'er the brown mountain, and the dreary waste ;   640
Where famish'd wolves proclaim'd their nightly roam,
And raging lions found a bloody home ;

Line 619) Calling of the Jews.

Again glad funs command thy towers to burn,
And o'er thy fplendors burfts the raptur'd morn ;
In vales of fragrance hymns of angels ring ;   645
The mountains leap ; the confcious forefts fing ;
To thy fair realms the bloom of Eden given
Tranfcends the morn, and rivals opening heaven.

Lo, from the weft, and eaft, and fouth, and north,
In countlefs millions, Gentile throngs break forth !   650
Their garlands bloom ; their golden offerings blaze ;
Their harps inftinctive tremble to thy praife.
For thee, what prayers from gathering lands afcend !
What fuppliant nations at thine altars bend ! :
With what foft mufic founds th' etherial fong !   655
What love, what ecftacy, attunes the tongue !
How gay the heavens ! how fair the earth ferene !
How joy illumes, how incenfe charms the fcene !
Lo, in each face primæval beauty glows !
In every vein primæval vigour flows ;   660
In every bofom brightens peace refin'd,
And endlefs funfhine lights th' unclouded mind !
Without one terror, fhuts the willing eye
And the foul wafts in flumber to the fky.
See mighty Juftice lifts his awful reign !   665
Behold new Jofhuas fway thy realms again !
Again the Prophet lights the earthly gloom ;
Heaven's gates difclofe, and climes beyond the tomb ;
To earth glad angels fpeed their beauteous flight,
And call their fellows to the domes of light !   670

In eaftern climes, where funs begin to roll,
Or where clear fplendors gild the fparkling pole,
Or where, illum'd by nature's faireft ray,
Smile the blefs'd regions of defcending day,
Unnumber'd fhips, like mift the morn exhales,   675
Stretch their dim canvas to the rufhing gales.
Behold, afcending, cloud-like, in the fkies,
How their fails whiten ! how their mafts arife !

The world all moves! the far-extended main
Is loft beneath th' immeasurable train!   680
Here earth impatient all her treasures yields,
Fruits of gay mines, and sweets of spicy fields;
Fair robes of silken splendor mock the morn,
And sun-bright gems with changing lustre burn.

Exult, O earth! ye heavens with joy survey   685
Her charms, her glories, hold the lingering day!
Lo, wrapp'd in sparkling gold, thy wide walls burn;
Thy stones to pearls, thy gates to diamonds, turn,
Thy domes to palaces, thy seats to thrones,
To queens thy daughters, and to kings thy sons.   690
      Awake, awake, ye tenants of the tomb!
Burst your cold chains, and hail your destin'd home!
Lo, the night fades; the sky begins to burn,
And ruddy splendor opes the living morn!
See tombs, instinctive, break the sleepy charm,   695
And gales divine the dust imprison'd warm;
From finish'd slumbers changing patriarchs rise;
Life crowns their heads, and transport fires their eyes;
Dress'd in the youth of heaven, again are join'd
The form angelic and the sainted mind.   700
      From bliss to bliss the circling hours shall flow;
With my own smiles the pure expansion glow;
Bright as the moon, the stars invest the pole;
Bright as the sun, the moon sublimely roll;
Unmeasur'd glories round the sun arise,   705
And every morn light nations to the skies.
      Long, long shall these fair scenes the bosom charm,
And light, and love, refining nature warm;
Till earth slow-mouldering hear the great decree,
And time's last waves approach th' unfathom'd sea,   710
There o'er wild regions, round the distant pole,
Shall war's tremendous voice begin to roll,

Line 707] Signs which forbode the end of the world. See Mat.
24, and Rev. 19.

From hell's dark caverns Difcord fierce afcend,
Refound her trump, and ftartled nature rend ;
All heaven re-echo to the deep alarms,   715
And maddening nations fwiftly rufh to arms.
See, high in air, her banner, wide unfurl'd,
Streams in black terror o'er the trembling world ;
From pole to pole the rage of combat flies,
And realms 'gainft realms with ardent vengeance rife !720
To fcenes of flaughtering Fight the millions pour ;
Loud thunders roll, and flafhing fwords devour ;
On delug'd plains unnumber'd corfes lie,
And fhouts, and groans, immingled, cleave the fky.
To Cities then fhe fteers her dufky way ;   725
The turrets fhake, the walls in fmoke decay :
O'er the tall domes, and fpires in gold array'd,
Where Pomp fate thron'd, and Joy and Friendfhip play'd,
Fierce drives the nimble flame ; the whirlwinds throng,
Howl through the walls, and drive the ftorm along. 730
Now to the Fields fhe wings her rapid force,
The world involving in her wafting courfe ;
Before her car, a fiery tempeft flies ;
Behind, long hofts interminably rife ;
From her pale face th' etherial orbs retire ;   735
Deep heaves the ground ; the blackening groves expire ;
Horror, and wild difmay the earth appall,
And one unbounded ruin buries all.
    Mid thefe dire fcenes, more awful fcenes fhall rife ;
Sad nations quake, and trembling feize the fkies. 740
From the dark tomb fhall fearful lights afcend ;
And fullen founds the fleeping manfion rend ;
Pale ghofts with terror break the dreamer's charm,
And death-like cries the liftening world alarm.
Then midnight pangs fhall tofs the cleaving plains ; 745
Fell Famine wanton o'er unburied trains ;
From crumbling mountains baleful flames afpire ;
Realms fink in floods, and towns diffolve in fire ;

In every blaft, the fpotted plague be driven,
A . angry meteors blaze athwart the heaven.   750
Clouds of dark blood fhall blot the fun's broad light,
Spread round th' immenfe,and fhroud the world in night,
With pale, and dreadful ray, the cold moon gleam ;
The dim, lone ftars diffufe an anguifh'd beam ;
Storms rock the fkies ; afflicted ocean roar,   755
And fanguine billows die the fhuddering fhore :
And round earth thunder, from the almighty throne,
The voice irrevocable--- IT IS DONE.

  Rous'd on the fearful morn, fhall nature hear
The trump's deep terrors rend the troubled air ;   760
From realm to realm the found tremendous roll,
Cleave the broad main, and fhake th' aftonifh'd pole ;
The flumbering bones th' Archangel's call infpire ;
Rocks fink in duft, and earth be wrapp'd in fire ;
From realms far-diftant orbs unnumber'd come,   765
Sail thro' immenfitv, and learn their doom :
And all yon changelefs ftars, that, thron'd on high,
Reign in immortal luftre round the fkv,
In folemn filence fhroud their living light,
And leave the world to undiftinguifh'd night.   770

   Hark, what dread founds, defcending from the pole,
Wave following wave, in fwelling thunders roll !
How the tombs cleave ! What awful forms arife !
What crowding nations pain the failing eyes !
From land to land behold the mountains rend ;   775
From fhore to fhore the final flames afcend,
Round the dark poles with boundlefs terror reign,
With bend immeafurable fweep the main,
From morn's far kingdoms ftretch to realms ofeven,
And climb, and climb, with folemn roar to heaven.   780
What fmoky ruins wrap the leffening ground !
What firey fheets fail through the vaulted round !

Line 759) Refurrection and Conflagration.   787] Laft Judgement.

Pour'd in one mass, the lands, and seas, decay;
Inroll'd, the heavens, dissolving, fleet away;
The moon departs; the sun's last beams expire,   785
And nature's buried in the boundless fire.

Lo, from the radiance of the bless'd abode,
Messiah comes, in all the pomp of God!
Borne on swift winds, a storm before him flies;
Stars crown his head, and rainbows round him rise; 790
Beneath his feet, a sun's broad terrors burn,
And cleaving darkness opes a dreadful morn:
Through boundless space careering flames are driven;
Truth's sacred hosts descend, and all the thrones of heaven.
See crowding millions, call'd from earth's far ends, 795
See hell's dark world, with fearful gloom, ascends,
In throngs incomprehensible! Around
Worlds after worlds, from nature's farthest bound,
Call'd by th' Archangel's voice, from either pole,
Self-mov'd, with all created nations, roll   800
From this great train, his eyes the   vide,
Price of his life, and being's fair   pride;
Rob'd by his mighty hand, the starry throngs
From harps of transport call exstatic songs.

Hail, heirs of endless peace! ordain'd to rove   805
Round the pure climes of everlasting love.
For you the sun first led the lucid morn;
The world was fashion'd, and Messiah born;
For you high heaven with fond impatience waits,
Pours her fair streams, and opes her golden gates;   810
Each hour, with purer glory, gayly shines,
Her courts enlarges, and her air refines.

But O unhappy race! to woes consign'd,
Lur'd by fond pleasure, and to wisdom blind.
What new Messiah shall the spirit save,   815
Stay the pent flames, and shut th' eternal grave?
Where sleeps the music of his voice divine?
Where hides the face, that could so sweetly shine?

Now hear that flighted voice to thunder turn !
See that mild face with flames of vengeance burn !   820
High o'er your heads the storm of ruin roars,
And, round th' immense no friend your fate deplores.

Lo, there to endless woe in throngs are driven,
What once were angels, and bright ftars of heaven !
The world's gay pride ! the king with splendor crown'd !
The chief refiftlefs, and the fage renown'd !   826
Down, down, the millions fink ; where yon broad main
Heaves her dark waves, and fpreads the feats of pain :
Where long, black clouds, emblaz'd with awful fire, 829
Pour fullen round their heads, and in dread gloom retire.

Then, tumult's hideous din forever o'er,
All foes fubdued, and doom'd to rife no more,
Sin forc'd from each fair clime to final flight,
And hell's dark prifon lock'd in endlefs night ;
To heaven's extremes diviner peace fhall roll,   835
And fpread through countlefs worlds, beyond each diftant
Crown'd with glad triumph, from the toils of war, [pole.
On angel's wings, fhall fail Meffiah's car ;
To the great Sire his conquering hand reftore
Th' etherial enfigns of unmeafur'd power ;   840
Prefent his fons, before the palace bright,
And feek the bofom of unborrow'd light.

Then fcenes, in heaven before unknown, fhall rife,
And a new æra blefs th' angelic fkies ;
Through boundlefs tracts, a nobler kingdom fhine,   845
Nor Seraphs' minds conceive the pomp divine.
All realms, all worlds above, combin'd in one ;
The heaven of heavens the bright, eternal throne ;
The fubjects faints ; the period endlefs fpring ;
The realm immenfity, and God the king.   850

As fix'd, unchang'd, yon central world of fire
Leads on fublime the planetary choir,

Line 831) Confummation of all things.

Lights all the living lamps, and round the sky;
In midnight splendor calls the moon to fly ;
Creates their smiles, instructs their orbs to roll,   855
Fair eye of nature, and the world's great soul :
So, in the beams of clear perfections shrin'd,
Shall his great Source, the Uncreated Mind,
Through all the Morning Stars that round him glow,
Rove in his smiles, and at his altar bow,   860
Through countless trains, where worlds unnumber'd rise,
And cloth'd in starry pomp superior skies,
Pure rays of endless peace indulgent shine,
And warm immensity with love divine.

   Love's mighty chain shall boundless beings bind,   865
Join world to world, and mind unite with mind ;
O'er the great houshold heaven's eternal pride,
From age to age, th' Almighty Sire preside ;
Around his awful throne, with searching eyes,
See fairer sons, and priests, and kings, arise ;   870
Bid his own essence in their hearts revive,
His beauty brighten, and his glory live :
From harps etherial living raptures fall,
Heaven fill th' immense, and GOD BE ALL IN ALL.

   In glory wafted down the lucid pole,   875
See Salem's walls their solemn scenes unroll !
Less beauteous charms the lovely spouse array,
When beams of rapture light the bridal day.
Behold, new skies serenely round her glow ;
Pure fragrance breathes, and purple splendors flow :   880
In pomp ascends the ever-rising morn,
And starry rainbows round her chariot burn !

    There, from the distant wave, no suns arise ;
No moon's pale radiance gleams in evening skies ;
Round the broad region, with unfading ray,   885
JEHOVAH smiles immeasurable day :

    Line 875) Prospect of heaven, and a happy immortality.

With living luftre, fruits celeftial glow,
And ftreams of life in endlefs beauty flow.

 In robes of angels, fee the chofen fhine;   890
Waft on the floods; or walk in light divine;
Or tafte the changing tree, whofe fruit fupplies
The youth of heaven, and beauty of the fkies !

 There, drefs'd in bloom, and young in rofy years,
Th' immortal Father of mankind appears: 895
In clear effulgence, Ifrael's Prophet fhines,
And no dark veil his eager wifh confines:
With fmiles of joy ferene, the Friend of God
Counts his glad fons, and opes the blefs'd abode.

 To thefe fair realms thy footfteps fhall afcend;   900
Here crowns await thee, and bright robes attend:
At nature's call, thy guardian feraph come,
And guide his chofen to th' eternal home;
Before the facred throne, thy thoughts appear,
Thy virtuous toils; thy truth, and love, fincere: 905
His witnefs'd favourite, God with fmiles approve,
And join to nations of immortal love.

 O blifsful hour ! when, freed from bonds of clay,
Thy path commences to the climes of day;
When from the fun thy wing begins to rife   910
Through the broad regions of unmeafur'd fkies;
When time's dark years behind thy flight fhall roll,
And all eternity invade thy foul.

 In that blefs'd hour, the fons of light fhall come,
And fhout thee welcome to thy deftin'd home;   915
With heightening beauty bloom each angel mind,
Glow with pure joy, and yearn with love refin'd;
In ftrains divine, impaffion'd feraphs tell
How with dire treafon heavenly nations fell;
What deeds renown'd have grac'd the fair abode;   920
Truth that endur'd, and zeal that rais'd to God;
How round th' expanfion worlds unnumber'd fprung,
And hofts etherial fky-born praifes fung;
The peace, the charms, to vernal Eden given,
Converfing angels, and approving Heaven.

 In that blefs'd hour, fhall faints of antient days,   925
Lights of mankind, and heirs of deathlefs praife,

Disclose how Adam's sons the world o'erspread,
Borne to far isles, and o'er wide seas convey'd ;
How the lone ark the seeds of nations bore,
And boundless ocean toss'd without a shore ;   930
Embattled hosts the patriarch's faith o'ercame,
Nor votive Isaac quench'd the living flame ;
Through the long devious desert Israel rov'd ;
The angel wrestled, and the brother lov'd.
Rapt in thy bless'd arrival, there shall glow   935
The faithful partners of thine every woe ;
Their hopes, their fears, their toils, with thee run o'er,
Pains far retir'd, and griefs that haunt no more :
His long-lov'd friend unspotted Hezron join,
Add song to song, and mingle bliss with thine ;   940
Irad, divinest flower ! to meet thee rise,
And cast rich fragrance round delighted skies.

     With this great concourse lost in joys serene,
No tongue can utter, and no fancy feign,
Dissolv'd in friendship, chain'd to friends, divine,   945
Whose thoughts, whose converse, every power refine,
Thy unknown ages swift shall glide away,
Lost in th' immense of never-ending day.
Thro' heaven's expanded field thy feet shall rove,
Th' all-beauteous region of ecstatic love ;   950
Her gates of pearl, her towers of gems, behold,
Her streets, her mansions, of pellucid gold :
Where each fair gate cherubic watchmen guard,
And GOD, approving, showers the vast reward.
     There shalt thou feel, when, freed from sin's alloy, 955
Souls lift their pinions to the climes of joy,
Around all heaven what speechless transports roll,
Blend smile with smile, and mingle soul with soul ;
There hail, ecstatic, to the bright abode,
The crowns, the trophies, of Messiah's blood.   960
     There GOD's own hand shall lift the curtain high,
And all earth's wonders open to thine eye :
In time's mysterious reign, thy soul pursue
Power ever glorious, wisdom ever new ;
See boundless good, Creation's single end,   965
And GOD his own, and being's, faithful friend ;

In all, the present God refulgent shine,
And boundless glory fill the work divine.

Fed with perennial springs of bliss refin'd,
Divine effusions of th' All-lovely Mind,   970
With endless ardour shall thy spirit glow,
And love immense from heaven's great fountain flow ;
Unbounded grace fill unconfin'd desire,
Warm thy rapt bosom, and thy songs inspire.

Each hour, thy spreading thoughts shall swift improve ;
Each hour increase the transports of thy love ;   975
With morning beauty, Youth around thee shine,
Implant new senses, and the old refine ;
From height to height thy rising wishes grow,
And, at their birth, the full enjoyment flow ;   980
No care, no want, th' expanding bliss destroy,
But every thought, and sense, and wish, be joy.

From these bless'd scenes thy flight shall oft descend,
And, with thy kindred angels, man attend.
What sweet complacence shall thy bosom warm,   985
To spread fair truth, and every woe to charm ;
Guard the lone cot, where faith delights to dwell ;
Or wake pure fervors in the secret cell ;
Or watch that house, where strong devotions rise ;
And prayers as incense cheer the morning skies ;   990
Where sons to saints, to angels daughters, grow,
And peace, and virtue, build a heaven below.
When fear alarms, shalt thou that fear allay ;
When grief distresses, smile the pangs away ;
When pain torments, the pious eyelids close,   995
Make soft the bed, and breathe serene repose ;
Guide the departing soul to yonder skies,
And teach the young immortal how to rise.
Through scorching sands shalt thou the wanderer bring,
Waft balmy gales, and point the cooling spring ;   1000
Or lure declining feet from flowery ways,
Seal the charm'd ear, and turn the fatal gaze ;
Or with rude whirlwinds the rough main deform ;
Or roll the thunders of the mountain storm ;
Or on the sanguine plain sublimely stand,   1005
Direct the triumph, and the flight command ;

Or o'er some realm in glorious pomp preside,
To saints a guardian, and to kings a guide.

Nor shall one world thy bounded view confine ;
But round all being stretch thy flight divine,   1010
To worlds dispers'd o'er worlds, ambitious rise,
The golden planets of sublimer skies.

Far o'er thy little earth, to man's weak eye,
Encircling roll the glories of the sky.
Yet know, bless'd prince though thus apparent all,   1015
The moon moves singly round this darksome ball,
The earth, with those fair fires of wandering light,
That shed soft lustre o'er the darksome night,
All worlds alike, with countless nations crown'd,
In circling course, the sun's bright orb surround.   1020
Still their glad faces to his splendor turn,
Imbibe his beams, and meet the grateful morn.

This mighty scene thy mind with awe inspires,
With beauty raptures, and with wonder fires.
But O thou man belov'd ! yon vault survey,   1025
Where stars in millions blind the midnight ray ;
In space' broad fields so far the pomp retires,
Yon sapphire concave scarce their twinkling fires :
Hence vainly deem'd the gems of inborn light,
Ordain'd to tremble through the gloom of night :   1030
In near approach, those stars, with constant rays,
Shoot round th' expansion, noon's excessive blaze,
Confine the empire of surrounding night,
And reign, and glory, in immortal light.   1034
For know, bless'd favourite, suns are those fair flames ;
Worlds round them roll, and day perpetual beams :
Those worlds unnumber'd circling moons adorn,
And with long splendors comets mid them burn.
As in the world of minds, with golden chain,
Attractive Love extends her blissful reign,   1040
In one pure realm all sainted beings joins,
God with his sons, his sons with God combines :
The bond to all of pure perfection given,
The life, the beauty, peace, and joy of heaven :
So this stupendous frame, by him alone   1045
Who calls their names, supported, number'd, known,

These countless systems in one system join'd,
Their size, their distance, with nice art design'd,
A great, attracting power, on all impress'd,
Connects, moves, governs, and forbids to rest.   1050

By this great power, impelling and impell'd,
All worlds move on through space' unmeasur'd field.
Around their planets moons refulgent stray ;
Around their suns those planets trace their way ;
Around your central heaven all systems roll ;   1055
And one great circling motion rules the whole.
O scene divine, on those bright towers to stand,
And mark the wonders of th' Eternal hand ;
To see thro' space unnumber'd systems driven,
Worlds round their suns, and suns around the heaven ; 1060
To see one ordinance worlds and suns obey ;
Their order, peace, and fair, harmonious way ;
Their solemn silence : varying pomp divine ;
Their fair proportions, and their endless shine !
Some nearer rolling in celestial light ;   1065
Some distant glimmering tow'rd the bordering night ;
'Till far remov'd from thought the regions lie,
Where angels never wing'd the lonely, verging sky,

On the clear glass as smiles the beauteous form,
And youth's fair light, and eyes of glory, charm ;   1070
As lucid streams, with face serene, unfold
Spring's gayest prime, and flowers that bloom in gold ;
As boundless ocean's smooth, resplendent plain
Rebeams the skies, and all their wonderous train,
No part, no wave, but feels the sun's broad ray,   1075
And glows, reflective, with surrounding day :
So round th' immense, on fair creation's breast,
In endless pomp the GODHEAD shines impress'd ;
His love, his beauty, o'er all nature burns ;
Each sun unfolds it, and each world returns ;   1080
Each day, each hour, the glory bright improves,
And GOD, with ceaseless smile, th' immortal image loves.

Wing'd with pure flame thro' space' unmeasur'd rounds,
Thy soul shall visit being's farthest bounds ;
When orbs begin, instruct their mass to roll ;   1085
For changing seasons fix a steady pole ;

Teach eve to purple, golden morn to rife,
And light new funs in folitary fkies.

   Upborne from world to world, fhalt thou behold
How ever-varying wonders God unfold ;   1090
In each new realm, with growing blifs purfue
Scenes unimagin'd, nations ever new ;
See fome through highborn virtues fwiftly foar,
Some humbler duties, humbler thoughts explore ;
To every race, new thoughts new fenfes bring ;   1095
On every plain, new vegetations fpring ;
O'er virtue's fons eternal morning bloom ;
O'er guilt's vile throngs afcend eternal gloom ;
O'er mingled nations mingling feafons roll,
And peace, and tumult, wrap the changing pole.   1100

   To endlefs years, thy mind, infpir'd, fhall rife
Thro' knowledge, love, and beauty, of the fkies ;
To heights angelic, archangelic, foar,
'Till man's faint language paint the heights no more :
When borne to glory, wing'd to flights fupreme,   1105
Thy foul fhall reach creation's firft extreme,
Beyond all thought affume her laft abode,
And feek the bofom of th' involving God.

   The Vifion ceas'd.   At once the fcenes decay'd,
His bright form vanifh'd and his glories fled :   1110
Swift to the camp th' exulting Chief return'd,
While the glad day-ftar in the orient burn'd.

THE

CONQUEST OF CANÄAN:

BOOK XI.

ARGUMENT.

Morning. Hareshab returns to Gibeon. Army assembles. Speech of Caleb. Hanniel. Joshua's advice to him; his reply. Joshua's prayer. Cloud rolls before the army toward Gibeon. Prospect of the Heathen host beyond the city. Speech of Joshua on that occasion. Israelites descend from the mountain. Jabin prepares for battle, and arranges the heathen army on the bank of a small river. Gibeonites ascend the walls to view the battle. Aradon marches his troops out to meet Joshua, who gives the command of them to Almiran. Arrangement of the combatants. Joshua by a stratagem draws the Heathens from their advantageous post. General engagement. Joshua's exploits. He kills Medan and Talmon. Zedeck rallies the heathens; but is forced down the bank, and killed. Egon. Joshua, seeing Hazor strongly posted on the bank, moves down the river, and rescues Almiran, kills Piram, and routs Jarmuth. Japhia. Exploits of Zimri. He kills Hoham, and puts Hebron into confusion. Jabin rallies them, and kills Hanniel. Asher retires. Joshua leaves his division to engage Hazor; and rallies Asher. Combat between him and Jabin. Heathens routed. Storm of Hail. Israelites return to their camp and are met by their wives and children singing praise to the Creator. Conclusion.

THE CONQUEST OF CANAAN.

BOOK XI.

NOW rofe in heaven the great, the final day,
　　Where fates of chiefs, and kings, and kingdoms lay
Morn drefs'd in golden pride the cliffs on high,
Stream'd o'er the groves, and brighten'd round the fky:
No cloud, no mift, obfcur'd the blue ferene;　　　5
And peace, and filence, hufh'd the folemn fcene.

　To Caleb's tent alert the Hero ftrode,
And rous'd Harefhah to the field of blood.---
With active hafte to Gibeon's prince repair;
To range his thoufands be his inftant care:　　　10
Ere the glad fun climb half th' etherial main,
Shall Heaven's broad ftandard tremble on the plain.---
Far o'er the weftern field, with keen delight,
He wing'd his courfe, and vanifh'd from the fight.

　And now once more the clarion's dreadful found　15
Infpires to arms, and fhakes the banner'd ground:
To arms the martial thoufands raptur'd fpring;
Their fongs refound, their clafhing bucklers ring:
Roll'd on the winds, imperial enfigns play,
And wav'd their fplendors to the burfting day.　　20
　Now join'd in marfhall'd ranks the generous train,
And gloomy columns darken'd o'er the plain;
When, rob'd in white, their hoary fathers came,
Great in paft fields, and heirs of deathlefs fame.

One was their voice, and from their reverend eyes,   25
The bold heroic flame began to rife;
The foul stood struggling in the heaving breast,
And every limb their vigorous thoughts exprest.
When Caleb thus---The great concluding day
Now calls to arms, and Heaven directs the way: 30
What tho' unnumber'd hosts against us rife,
And with proud madness brave insulted Skies;
Shall cumbrous throngs the meanest arm dismay?
Or one base thought disdain the glorious day?
Think how bold Abraham swept the midnight plain,   35
While realms oppos'd, and millions fought, in vain;
How two brave patriarchs, in one friendly gloom,
Sunn'd Shechem's towers and op'd a nation's tomb;
Think how these fires for you unbroken toil'd,
Dar'd the rough main, and prov'd the hideous wild;   40
Made spiry towns, and haughty kings a prey,
And forc'd o'er countless lands resistless way.
See your fond partners in sad grief array'd,
Behold your children claim parental aid!
Your hands their freedom and their fate suspend;   45
Your swords must conquer, or your race must end.
Nor let these narrow scenes your thoughts confine;
Claim nobler views and pass the selfish line.
Ages unborn from you shall trace their doom,
Heaven's future Seers, and heroes yet to come;   50
If slaves, or men, this day your hands decide,
The scorn of nations, or the world's great pride:
Empire and bondage in your bosoms lie;
'Tis yours to triumph, or tis ours to die.

He spoke, and silent to th' all-bounteous Skies   55
Stretch'd wide his hands, and rais'd his kindling eyes:
Each glowing visage flash'd disdain around
And hoarse applauses shook the neighbouring ground.

Bright from the lucid main, the sun's broad eye
Look'd in imperial splendor from the sky;   60

With war's gay pomp then shone th' embattled plains;
In proud battalions rose the martial trains;
A broken radiance burst from trembling shields,
And haughty heroes stalk'd along the fields.

   Bold Hanniel there in shining armour stood,   65
And hop'd a deathless name in scenes of blood.
He saw the host to final combat rise,
The champions nations, and a realm the prize.
Now wealth allur'd; the rival now alarm'd;
Strong pride impell'd, and splendid conquest charm'd; 70
His wounds, his pains, in quick oblivion gone,
The wish of glory prompts the warrior on;
Pleas'd, his fond fancy flies from silent shame
To plains of triumph, and to wreaths of fame.

   Him Joshua view'd with pity in his breast,   75
And kindly thus the haughty chief addres'd---
If, when dread war resounds her hoarse alarm,
Health flush the cheek, and vigor brace the arm,
To fight, the warrior virtue fame command,
And knaves alone refuse the needed hand.   80
But thou, brave Hanniel, seek'st the field in vain,
Pale with lost blood, and weak with ceaseless pain,
Unstrung to fight, and impotent to fly,
Useless, alive; nor glorious, should'st thou die.
In fields of frequent strife thy garlands bloom;   85
Let not their verdure wither on thy tomb:
No feeble aid such numerous honours claim,
Nor can base envy crop the growing fame.

   He spoke, impatient Hanniel quick return'd,
And keen resentment in his visage burn'd---   90
While yon bright orb rolls on the mighty doom
Of millions born, and millions yet to come,
What chief, what man, who boasts a reasoning mind,
Will hide in shame, or sleep in tents confin'd?
Let these, if Jacob's race such culprits knows,   95
Shirnk from great scenes, and die in vile repose,

Not such is Hanniel : when my country calls,
I smile at fields of blood, and blazing walls ;
Where clarions roar my ready footsteps hie,
Glue to the fight, and ask no strength to fly.   100
Unbroke by wounds, my voice shall now inspire
The coward's languor, and the warrior's fire ;
This shield, or these frail limbs, well pleas'd, arrest
The lance, that flies to wound a worthier breast.
But Hanniel's glory why should Joshua fear ?   105
Do rival names alarm thy tender ear ?
On yon broad plain unnumber'd stars arise,
Move in gay ranks, and triumph round the skies ;
Each lends his beam to swell the pomp divine,
Nor grieves that neighbouring spangles brighter shine.
How beauteous thus in Honour's Angel-race,   111
When some blest æra numerous heroes grace,
Mean self disdain'd, if virtuous all engage
To fill with light the constellated age.
Some shining deed should this right hand atchieve,   115
Unstain'd, unrivall'd, Joshua's name would live ;
Then wish no more my days consum'd in shame ;
Nor grudge the glory, generous actions claim.

The Leader heard, and wish'd that Heaven had join'd
A heart more honest with so bright a mind :   120
Through his great bosom thrill'd a sudden pain,
Where sweet compassion mix'd with brave disdain.
Sighing he said---How blind is reason's eye,
When Heaven ordains o'er-weening man to die !

Now through the host he cast a piercing view,   125
And every rank, and every station, knew ;
Then, while mute silence hush'd th' adoring bands,
From a tall rock, he rear'd his suppliant hands.----

O thou, whose throne, uprais'd beyond all height,
Glows in th' effulgence of unutter'd light,   130
O'er earth, o'er hell, o'er heaven, extends thy sway ;
Angels, Archangels, Thrones, and Powers obey ;

All scenes, all worlds, confess thy hand divine,
And seas, and skies, and stars, and suns, are thine.
  At thy command, to glory nations rise ;   135
At thy command, each guilty kingdom dies ;
At thy command, awakes the trumpet's roar :
Death walks the plain, and earth is drench'd in gore :
Hush'd by thy sovereign nod, the tempests cease ;
Peace is thy choice, and all the world is peace.   140
  This day, O Power supreme ! against the skies,
Sheath'd in dread arms, unnumber'd thousands rise:
As raging flames the shaggy mountains burn,
The groves to dust, and fields to deserts turn ;
So let thy vengeance sweep th' embattled plain,   145
And teach proud monarchs GOD's eternal reign.
  From endless years thy all-encircling mind
To Abraham's race this beauteous land assign'd :
The land, where Truth shall fix her lasting seat ;
Where sky-born Virtue seeks a calm retreat ;   150
Where blest Redemption opes her living morn ;
Where heaven commences, and where GOD is born.
For this thy voice the sacred promise gave ;
For this thy thunders cleft th' Egyptian wave ;
Rich manna shower'd ; with streams the desart smil'd, 155
And the whole heaven descended on the wild.
Still, O unchanging Mind ! thy bounty shower ;
Draw thy red sword, and stretch thine arm of power.
To gain these realms, the crown of long desire,
Let Heaven protect us, and let Heaven inspire !   160
  He spoke : a rushing voice began to roar,
Like caverns, echoing on the sea-beat shore ;
Deep rang the hollow sound : and o'er the train,
The cloud stupendous sail'd along the plain ;
Broad flames, in fierce effusion, round it play'd,   165
Scorch'd the green fields, and brighten'd all the shade ·
Tow'rd western hills the fearful gloom retir'd,
And all the splendor in one flash expir'd.

Loud rofe the trump ; and rang'd in dread array,
Behind the cloud the fquadrons trac'd their way ;   170
The burnifh'd helm, blue mail, and upright fpear,
Gleam'd o'er the plain, and ftarr'd the kindled air :
High ftrode the Leader in the glorious van,
And round his arms an awful glory ran :
For GOD enrob'd him with a pomp divine,   175
And bade an angel in his countenance fhine.
Thus, when no cloud obfcures th' autumnal even,
And night's dark hand unveils the vault of heaven,
Crown'd with pure beams, her fons in beauty rife,
And glow, and fparkle, o'er unmeafur'd fkies ;   180
The moon, bright regent, leads th' immortal train,
And walks in pride imperial round the plain.

    Now climb'd the bands the mountain's towering height,
And o'er the fubject region caft their fight ;
There glifter'd Gibeon's domes in trembling fires,   185
And all the grandeur of a thoufand fpires.
Beyond her walls, a far-extended plain
Spread, like the furface of the fleeping main :
A mighty hoft there left the bounded eye,
And loft its diftant terrors in the fky.   190
Full in th' effulgence of the morn's broad beam,
Stretch'd the tremendous front, a ridge of flame,
Of length immeafurable.   Ether wide
Wav'd with a thoufand nations' banner'd pride ;
Tofs'd in gay triumph, lucid enfigns fhone,   195
And caft their various fplendor on the fun :
Swift round the region dim-feen chariots roll'd ;
The far fteeds bounded wrapp'd in twinkling gold ,
With fpears and helms adorn'd of countlefs trains,
Rofe the full pomp of conftellated plains ;   200
And proud with wanton beams, the fun-bright fhields
Join'd like unnumber'd moons, and dazzled all the fields.
    Unmov'd, great Jofhua round him caft his eyes,
And faw th' interminable legions rife :

Then thus, while Israel hush'd in silence stood, 205
Rang'd in just ranks, and fac'd the field of blood.
Behold, on yon bright plain, embodied stands
The gather'd force of all Canaan's lands !
Gather'd by Heaven's right hand, and sad despair,
To crown our arms, and sink in one dread war ! 210
Hail my brave sons, with me, th' immortal day,
That opes to blissful peace the glorious way,
The hour, long number'd in impatient skies,
The morn, ordain'd with every pomp to rise,
By angels watch'd, by Heaven's dread signs led on, 215
Sinai's fierce flames, and Jordan's walls of stone.

 Each boundless hope let yon fair field inspire :
Each warrior kindle with a leader's fire :
The spoils of kingdoms each rapt eye behold ;
Ensigns of fame, and shields of moony gold ; 220
The herds, that wanton round a thousand rills ;
The flocks, that whiten on a thousand hills ;
The corn, all verdant o'er unmeasur'd plains ;
The world, where spring with smiling plenty reigns ;
Where olives swell ; where beauteous figs refine ; 225
And warm, and purpling, glows the cluster'd vine.
This day ordains them ours : this mighty day
Through realms unknown shall stretch our potent sway ;
Far as the hills, where suns begin to rise ;
Far as the seas, that limit evening skies ; 230
Till fading years unloose the sleeping grave,
And time's last current joins th' eternal wave.

 There too, my sons, shall boundless glory rise,
And yon bright field of conquest fill the skies.
Through Israel's future tribes the tale shall ring ; 235
The sage record it, and the prophet sing ;
Our deeds, our honours, wake the slumbering lyre ;
Warm the saint's praise, and wake the hero's fire ;
Rous'd by the theme, new arts of virtue grow ;
New chiefs break forth, and rival wonders flow ; 240

Truth's happy fons rehearfe in raptur'd ftrains,
Far through all climes, and ages, Gibeon's plains;
To morn's etherial hoft new blifs be given,
And human triumphs tune the harps of heaven.

    For know, when darknefs laft involv'd the fkies,   245
I faw the promis'd land in vifion rife.
I faw fweet peace exalted joys unfold;
Fair towers afcend, and temples beam in gold;
Kings, fprung from Jacob's lineage, mount the throne,
And ftretch their fway to years and realms unknown;250
Art raife her fceptre; wifdom's light revive,
And angel Virtue bid our glory live.
I faw Meffiah bright from heaven defcend,
And fpread his fway to earth's remoteft end;
Deep Gentile darknefs yield to light refin'd;   255
And truth, and virtue, flow to all mankind.
I faw the world, where Powers and Seraphs bright
Shine in pure robes, and rove in endlefs light;
Where, in new youth, the patriarchs, from their thrones
Hail a long ftarry train of heavenly fons;   260
Where Abraham's fteps his native fkies fuftain,
And Mofes raptur'd meets his God again.

    On you, my fons, thefe mighty fcenes fufpend;
From you fhall Ifrael's fame and blifs defcend;
From you fhall princes, heroes, prophets fpring;   265
From you be born the heaven-appointed king;
On this great day his earthly kingdom ftand,
Reach thro' all times, and flow to every land;
To blifs, in diftant ages, nations rife,
The world ennoble, and expand the fkies: 270
Rufh then to glory; God's tremendous arm
Moves in the flaming front, and guides us to the ftorm.

    He fpoke: a fhout convuls'd the mountain's brow,
And burft fonorous o'er the world below:
Each warrior on the plain in fancy ftood,   275
Drove back whole hofts, and rul'd the fcenes of blood;

Each on his falchion caſt a frequent eye,
And thought it bliſs, in Iſrael's cauſe to die.
As ſullen clouds, when blaſts in ſilence reſt,
Hang black and heavy on the mountain's breaſt;   280
Slow ſink the volumes down its hoary ſide,
Shroud all the cliffs, and roll in gloomy pride :
At once the winds ariſe ; and ſounding rain
Pours with impetuous fury o'er the plain :
So the dark hoſts deſcend in deep array,   285
And o'er the champaign drive their dreadful way.

   From the far plains, great Jabin's eye beheld
The ſquadrons, thickening on the diſtant field.
For when from Joſhua's arm his hoſt retir'd,
Stung by diſgrace, with fierce reſentment fir'd;   290
Some future fight his angry thoughts deſign'd,
To glut the vengeance of his haughty mind.
To Gibeon's fields he ſteers his ſullen courſe,
Where circling kings combin'd their gather'd force ;
Chiefs ruſh'd to conqueſt from a thouſand lands,   295
Whirl'd all their cars, and led their countleſs bands,
To guide their ſtrength againſt their dreaded foes
All with one voice the mighty hero choſe.
He, pleas'd once more to rule the dreadful plain,
Survey'd the terrors of th' unnumber'd train ;   300
Survey'd a hoſt, beyond his wiſhes great,
And aſk'd the gods to give no happier fate.
In ſplendid arms confeſs'd to dreadful views
To final fight, to final fame, he drew,
Full on his ſhield, with various forms inroll'd,   305
OR DEATH, OR CONQUEST---blaz'd in words of gold.

   In fields far weſt, a torrent, with rough waves,
The rocky ſhore with endleſs fury laves.
Here, o'er the ſtream high banks majeſtic hung,
And with ſad murmurs hollow caverns rung ;   310
There, for the ſquadrons, ruſhing to th' affray,
Smooth, ſloping ſhores prepar'd an eaſy way.

O o

High on the western margin of the flood,
A wall of fire, Canäan's millions stood.
Here Jabin's will ordain'd his host to stay,   315
Shields join'd with shields, and wedg'd in firm array.
For well he knew, when Israel's rushing force
Up the rough bank should urge their toilsome course,
Their broken ranks would fall an easy prey,
And fame, and triumph, close th' important day.   320

   Now Israel's host, slow-moving o'er the plain,
Successive roll'd, as waves disturb the main ;
In every face a fix'd, calm bravery shin'd ;
And not a hero cast a look behind.

   High on her ramparts Gibeon's children rose,   325
Survey'd the fields, and eyed th' impending foes.
Here in fond arms, the tender Mother bare
The babe, sweet offspring of her anxious care,
Hung o'er its infant charms, and joy'd to trace
The sire's lov'd image in its blooming face :   330
Then on the combat turn'd a bleeding view,
Wrung her white hands, and shed the glistening dew.
Here the gay Child, with pleas'd, and wondering eye,
Catch'd the broad standard, streaming in the sky ;
On the red armour cast a raptur'd gaze,   335
And rais'd his artless hands, and mark'd the splendid blaze.
Here, bath'd in tears, and whelm'd with timorous care,
In woe more lovely, mourn'd the melting Fair :
O'er Gibeon's host their eyes incessant rov'd,
And each, mid thousands, trac'd the youth she lov'd : 340
Fond hope, ere eve gave champions to his steel,
And at her feet his shining garlands fell.
Then fear presents him weltering on the plain,
Soft, healing, female aid implor'd in vain ;
Clos'd were those eyes, that beam'd etherial fire,   345
Glow'd with young joy, or languish'd sweet desire,
Dumb was the voice, that every wish could move,
And cold the form, that wak'd unutter'd love.

Here hoary Age in new-born pleasure stood,
And war's dread glories fir'd his languid blood ;   350
Long-buried years rush'd forward to the view ;
What hosts they battled, and what chiefs they slew :
Each on his brethren gaz'd with glad surprize,
And the great soul stood kindling in their eyes.

From northern gates her dark battalions pour'd,   355
And many a hero fierce to combat tower'd :
His warlike thousands wise Aradon led,
The white locks trembling o'er his ancient head.
Hail, mighty Chief !---the hoary prince began---
Favourite of God, and virtuous friend of man !   360
Blest be thy steps, that bring this kind relief
To feeble age, and solitary grief.
In fields of conflict once rejoic'd I stood,
With death familiar, and with scenes of blood.
But now sad age my head has whiten'd o'er ;   365
This palsied arm must wield the sword no more.
To mourn, to weep is all my future doom,
Drawn near to death, and bending o'er the tomb.
These bands thy voice obey ; in danger's field
Their manly bosoms never knew to yield :   370
Nor will their feet, long tried in honour's race,
Now learn to flee, and first commence disgrace.
But, fix'd to death, their king, their land to save,
All force will hazard, and all terrors brave.

When round the host I turn my weeping eyes,   375
And gaze, and gaze, my soul, with anguish, cries
Where, where is Elam ? Oh, may no sad doom
Compel thee to a son's untimely tomb !
A happier life, a brighter lot be thine ;
Taste all the rapturing joys that once were mine.   380
From childless age may Heaven his chosen save,
Nor bring thy hoary hairs in sorrow to the grave !

Great prince ! the Chief, with cheering voice, replied--
Thy nation's father, and thy country's pride !

Not singly thou the pangs of grief haft known ;   385
I mourn a daughter, as thou weep'st a son.
From hearts too fond, Heaven call'd the pair away
To fields of blifs, and climes of lasting day.
May every virtue in thy breast refine,
Till those fair climes, and all that blifs be thine.   390

 But now retire, where yon bright chariot stands ;
Let youth and vigour lead thy warlike bands,
For see, to fight Canäan's millions rife !
And hark, what clamors rend the boundless skies !

 The king obey'd. In arms, the ardent throng,   395
Behind Almiran, darkly rush'd along ;
Almiran, Gibeon's noblest, bravest son,
Led the bold heroes, and like lightning shone.

In three vast squadrons stood the heathens strength,
And rose a mighty front of dreadful length.   400
O'er northern banks, where chariots hoarfely rung,
Like clouds of thunder, haughty Hebron hung :
There too fierce Eglon rush'd with dreadful roar,
Like the long murmurs of the sounding shore.

Nor feebler legions fill the southern plain ;   415
There Lachish, Jarmuth there, the fight sustain ;
To the dire centre numerous nations throng,
And Jabin guides the storm, and swiftly flames along.

 With piercing eyes the Chief his foes descried,
And bade his host in three vast squares divide.   410
'Gainst Lachish Gibeon rolls in proud array ;
'Gainst Hebron Asher bends a dreadful way :
As fires pursue a comet's sanguine form,
Behind great Joshua drives the central storm.

 Now o'er the plain, as ocean pours his tide,   415
Their streaming ensigns rear'd in purple pride,
Far north, and southward stretch'd the chosen train,
And cross'd in gloomy pomp the dreadful plain.
Near, and more near, th' undaunted warriors drew ;
For well the Chief, by sure experience knew   420

That nations, taught in sudden fight to rise,
To war by stealth, and triumph by surprise,
To wiles, vain-glorious, fall an easy prey,
And, throng'd in tumult wild, are swept away,
Thence, near the foe he bade the squadrons move, 425
Tempt with keen taunts, and with proud threatnings prove,
That chiefs and men, with childish rage o'ercome,
Might quit the shore, and haste to certain doom.
Now near the stream the sacred thousands stood, 1A
Their breasts all panting for the scenes of blood. 430
At once, as some black storm begins to rise,
A cloud of arrows fill'd the western skies;
The long, ascending gloom all heaven o'erspread,
And the fields darken'd with a transient shade.
Then stones on stones tempestuous ether pour'd ; 435
And darts on darts in quick succession shower'd :
Now here, now there, expiring warriors fell,
And shrill beneath them rung the clashing steel.
At once, as mov'd by fear, the Chief withdrew,
And bade his host the distant walls pursue. 440
With joy, the heathens eyed their backward way,
Rais'd a long shout, and sprang to seize the prey,
Swift rush'd th' exulting thousands down the shore ;
For ranks behind, urg'd on the ranks before ;
Loud ring the chariots, swift the coursers bound, 445
And a deep thunder waves along the ground.
Around, great Jabin cast a mournful view,
And saw his foes retreat, his friends pursue,
His laws contemn'd, that bade the thousands stay,
Till o'er the torrent Israel urg'd their way ; 450
Kenn'd the deep snare, by Joshua wisely laid,
And to himself with sighs thus fiercely said.—
I see, proud chief, I see thy prosperous wiles ;
On me fate frowns ; on thee propitious smiles :
But not alone I prove the general doom ; 455
Ten thousand ghosts shall meet me at the tomb :

Aveng'd, and happy to the shades I'll go,
To bid thy princes quake in realms below.
Thus spoke the king, and deem'd his ruin nigh,
A fearful vengeance reddening in his eye ;   460
Strong, fell despair inflam'd his eager look ;
His bands gaz'd trembling, and his princes shook
    Meantime with smiles the sacred Chief beheld
His foes rush headlong o'er th' embattled field :
At once his piercing voice restrain'd the flight,   465
Wheel'd his long ranks, and marshall'd to the fight.
At once the trump's tremendous blast ascends
The plains all shudder, and the concave rends ;
Loud as the storm's ten thousand thunders rise,
A shout unmeasur'd rocks the lands and skies ;   470
Again high heaven is gloom'd with stony showers ;
Again all ether darts unnumber'd pours ;
With deep convulsion roars the closing war ;
Fierce bounds the steed ; sonorous rolls the car ;
With one broad ruin heaves the earth amain,   475
And Night, and Death, and Horror, shroud the plain.
So pours a storm on Greenland's frozen shore ;
The hoarse winds rage ; the maddening billows roar ;
When boundless darkness wraps the realms on high,
And flaming meteors stream across the sky :   480
Huge isles of raging ice, together driven,
With bursting thunder rend air, sea, and heaven :
Rocks rise o'er rocks ; o'er mountains mountains roll,
And the world trembles to the distant pole.
Thus o'er the field the dreadful tumult grows ;   485
Alike impetuous, foes encounter foes ;
Where Asher's sons proud Hebron's host engage ;
Or where bold Gibeon pours her torrent rage ;
Or where, around the Chief, immingled rise
Triumphant clamours, and expiring cries.   490
    Long roar'd the tumult of the dubious fight,
And no base coward wish'd inglorious flight :

All fierce to combat rush'd th' undaunted train ;
Nor these the palm would lose, nor those could gain ;
Till cloth'd in terror, Joshua's dreadful arm   495
Began the triumph, and led on the storm.

Two chiefs, whose silver arms confess'd their sway,
Rais'd their broad buklers in his fateful way.
By their fair wives a common fire they claim'd ;
And Medan this, and Talmon that, was nam'd ;   500
Of royal race, from Salem's wall they came,
Their deeds just budding in the field of fame.
Cleft through the side brave Medan gasping fell ;
And Talmon trembling fled the lifted steel.
By his own friends a javelin swiftly hurl'd   505
Plung'd his freed spirit to the nether world ;
Far round the field a shout of joy ascends,
And groans re-murmur from his sadden'd friends.

Then swift the Hero wheel'd his flaming sword ;
Like mountain streams his host behind him pour'd ;   510
Loud roar'd the thunders of the dreadful plain,
Rock'd the tall groves, and fill'd th' etherial main :
Increasing horror rent the world around,
And steeds, and cars, and warriors mingled on the ground.

Now near the stream approach'd the sounding war,   515
When fierce to combat roll'd a splendid car ;
There giant Zedeck rose in dreadful view ;
Two furious steeds the mighty monarch drew ;
With wild impetuous rage, they foam'd along,
And, pale before them, fled the parting throng.   520
From Joshua's course he saw his bands retire ;
His reddening aspect flash'd a gloomy fire ;
With huge, hoarse voice the furious hero cried,
While the plains murmur'd, and the groves replied,
Whatever wretch from this bright combat flies,   525
By the just gods, the impious dastard dies.
Nor hope to 'scape the keen, avenging blade
In the still cot, or in the lonely shade.

Soon shall this sword, with victory crown'd, return ;
And wrath, and vengeance, all your dwellings burn ; 530
Your bodies, limb from limb, this arm shall tear,
Nor sons, nor wives, nor sires, nor infants, spare ;
But bid the hungry hawks your race devour,
And call grim wolves to feast in floods of gore.

He spoke, astonish'd, some more nimbly flew ; 535
And some to conflict with fresh ardour drew :
Despair once more the growing flight repell'd,
And gave new horrors to the gloomy field.

Meantime on Joshua drove the sounding car,
And burst impetuous through the thickest war ; 540
Rough, heavy, dreadful, by the giant thrown
Flew the vast fragment of a craggy stone ;
Scarce 'scap'd the wary Chief, with sudden bound,
While the broad ruin plow'd the crumbling ground.
A javelin then the monarch's hand impell'd, 545
That sung and trembled, 'gainst the Hero's shield ;
Swift o'er his head a second hissing flies,
And a pierc'd warrior groans, and falls, and dies.
At once great Joshua rais'd his reeking sword,
And with deep wounds the maddening coursers gor'd ;
Through cleaving ranks the coursers backward flew, 551
And swift from fight the helpless monarch drew.
To the high shore, impendent o'er the flood,
They rush'd, as whirlwinds sweep the rending wood ;
To turn they tried, with short and sudden wheel ; 555
But tried in vain ; the sounding chariot fell.
Prone down the lofty bank the steeds pursued,
Where sharp, and ragged rocks beneath were strew'd ;
All shrill the giant's striking mail resounds :
With clattering crash, the cracking car rebounds ; 560
White o'er his lifeless head the waters roar ---
Lost in the stream, and doom'd to rise no more. ---
As, when the south's fierce blasts the main deform,
And roll the pealful onset of the storm ;

Hung are the heavens with night ; the world around,
Deep-murmuring, trembles to the solemn sound ;   566
Full on dread Longa's wild-resounding shore
Hills, wav'd o'er hills, ascend, and burst, and roar :
Safe in his cot, the hoary sailor hears,
Or drops, for fancied wrecks, unbidden tears.   570
A boundless shout, from Israel's raptur'd train,
Rent the broad skies, and shook the dreadful plain.
For now, their champion, trust, and glory lost,
From Joshua's vengeance flew sad Salem's host ;
Before him nought avail'd the shields, and spears;   575
But chiefs, and foaming steeds, and rattling cars,
Ranks urging ranks, squadrons o'er squadrons borne,
Down the bank plung'd ; the bank behind them torne,
Sunk with a rushing sound : great Joshua's arm
Uplifted, imminent impell'd the storm: 580
Alert, he bounded on the yielding sand,
And scatter'd ruin from his red right hand.
The white waves foam'd around his midway side,
As fierce he thunder'd thro' the rushing tide.
Two blooming youths, he dash'd against the rock,   585
Where Zedeck's chariot felt the fatal shock ;
Their gushing blood ran purple thro' the wave,
And thousands with them found a watery grave.
     There, mid vile throngs, t' untimely fate a prey,
Young, generous Egon breath'd his soul away.   590
Him Salem's nymphs resounded thro' the vales,
Or sung melodious, to responsive gales.
He, from the mountain wilds, and cliffs sublime,
Untrod, uncultur'd, from the first of time,
Drove the fierce beasts, by arms and arts compell'd,   595
To seek their safety in the lowland field.
By flames unclos'd, by hounds and swains pursued,
They fled each fastness of th' impervious wood ;
Ambush'd, in vales beneath the savage prey
Rush'd on the spear, and yell'd their lives away.   600
P p

Then howling wilds the traveller ceas'd t' appall;
Then night spread harmless round th' unguarded stall
His flocks, the rising swain with joy survey'd,
And slaughter'd lambs defil'd no more the glade.
Egon, each pipe, each voice of music sung;   605
And Egon's glory courts and caverns rung:
But pass'd was all his fame; by Joshua's hand
Plung'd in the stream, and choak'd with surging sand,
While from the bank the warriors leap'd amain,
Crush'd, drown'd, he mingled with the numerous slain. 610
  On the steep, western bank all Hazor stood:
A cloud of fire, high-towering o'er the flood:
Their darts unnumber'd Israel's host invade,
And many an eye is clos'd in death's dark shade.
Swift down the shore a rock with fury fell,   615
And crush'd two warriors, wrapp'd in shining steel:
Near Joshua's steps the craggy ruin pour'd;
The Hero sprang; the foaming torrent roar'd.
Then stones on stones, with sounding tempest driven,
Fill'd the wide concave of the troubled heaven: 620
Beneath their shields the prudent warriors stood;
All ether rang and foam'd the reddening flood;
'Till mighty Joshua, breathing wide dismay,
Swift down the raging torrent drove his way.
Where southward waves, expanding ceas'd to roar,   625
The stream was bounded by a sloping shore.
Hither the hero bent his awful course;
His host behind him pour'd their mighty force;
Fierce up the shore he rush'd; a dreadful band
Throng'd round their chief, and darken'd all the strand.
  Here brave Almiran, like a sweeping fire,   631
Urg'd his dread path, and bade his foes expire.
Tall in the gloomy van, the hero sped,
And Lachish pale before him fell or fled:
Such fiery terrors round his visage glow'd;   635
Such streams of slaughter from his falchion flow'd.

'Till, generous youth, an arrow found thy fide,
And down thy armour gufh'd the living tide.
Thy fire had grafp'd his long-neglected fhield,
And follow'd, trembling, to the deathful field :   640
There on thy deeds he caft an anxious view ;
There touch'd with tranfport, felt his youth renew ;
Then faw thee falling, pale, depriv'd of breath,
Plung'd on the foe, and funk in whelming death

   The youth, great Joshua caught in friendly arms,   645
His fhield averting war's impendent harms ;
Chaf'd by his hand, again he op'd his eyes ;
His lips refpir'd ; his bloom began to rife.
Then Gibeon's fons the mighty Leader fir'd,
And forrow prompted, and revenge infpir'd.   650

   Now drefs'd in golden pride, to crimfon war,
Tall, beauteous Piram drove his fhining car.
Born in the ftillnefs of a court ferene,
Where peace, and pleafure led the jocund fcene,
He loath'd dire fight, to gentler thoughts inclin'd ;   655
And love, and mufic, charm'd his feeling mind.
Soft pity touch'd his heart ; and oft a tear
He dropp'd, and mourn'd the human doom fevere ;
Th' unnumber'd ills of wafting pride would rue,
And wifh that kings the fweets of friendfhip knew.   660
Yet, not of fervile kind, his thoughts had foar'd,
In brighter days, and Art's fair realms explor'd.
Such was his foul, as grace from heaven refin'd
Can warm, and ripen, to an angel's mind.

   To combat now the prince reluctant rode,   665
When full before him Ifrael's Leader ftood.
Pleas'd, he beheld the graceful form afcend,
And wifh'd the gods had made the Chief his friend.
But vain his wifhes ; by the Hero thrown,
Full on his forehead burfts a founding ftone,   670
He fell ; his courfers backward rufh'd amain
And fnatch'd the monarch o'er the cloudy plain.

    With dreadful found, he rais'd his voice on high, 381
Froze the pale bands, and thunder'd thro' the sky.--
Hafte, warriors, hafte ; your conquering arms difplay;
Here gafps their leader, to the dogs a prey.
See the flaves fly ; ere evening's dufky hour,   385
The beafts fhall rend them, and the hawks devour.
Receive, illuftrious Oran ! here receive
The poor, the fole reward, thy prince can give.
This victim firft ; a nation foon fhall come
To pay due honours at thy facred tomb,   390
Wide ftreams of gore in rich libations flow,
And fhades unnumber'd wait thy call below.
Here, daftards, here the worthlefs carcafe yield,
Nor wait the vengeance of a future field.
To day this raptur'd hand your camp fhall burn,   395
And fires, and wives, and fons to mingled afhes turn.

    Thus fpoke the haughty Chief : with flafhing eyes,
To fiercer fight infpir'd the warriors rife ;
Clouds after clouds in gloomy pomp afcend,
And ftormy clamours troubled ether rend.   400
The thickening tempeft Judah's hoft furvey'd,
And wedg'd their volumes in the dufty fhade ;
Man lock'd with man, and helm with helm combin'd,
And fword with fword in glimmering order join'd,
A long dread front, impervious, hides the fields,   405
Cloth'd with the grandeur of a thoufand fhields.

    Firft, in the flaming van to vengeance rofe
Bold Irad's train, and dar'd their ardent foes.
Their young, brave minds immortal fame infpires ;
Each glowing thought the patriot's virtue fires ;   410
Serene they fmil'd to fee the ruin nigh ;
In death they triumph'd, but they fear'd to fly.

    O'er the dark deep, as fome tall wave impends,
Its white foam hiffes, and its point afcends ;
'Gainft hoary rocks the burfting ruins roar,   415
Shake all the main, and echo round the fhore,

Swift through his bosom drove the deadly spear,
And all his beauteous dreams dissolv'd in air.   510

Meantime far north the sons of Asher pour'd,
And fierce to combat chiefs and heroes tower'd:
There, like a whirlwind, rapid Zimri flew,
And, like a tempest, countless bands pursue :
Clouds after clouds behind him darkly roll,   715
And shouts of glory heave the murmuring pole.

As when two seas, by winds together hurl'd,
With bursting fury shake the solid world ;
Waves pil'd o'er waves, the watery mountains rise,
And foam, and roar, and rage, against the skies :   720
So join'd the combat ; ranks, o'er ranks impell'd,
Swell'd the hoarse tumult of the hideous field ;
Black drifts of dust becloud the gloomy ground ;
Hoarse groans ascend, and clashing arms resound.

And now, where Zimri broke th' embodied war,   725
Imperious Hoham drove his sounding car ;
Like flames, his rapid courses rush'd along,
Forc'd a red path, and crush'd the thickening throng :
His hissing lances shower'd destruction round,
And streaming bodies strew'd the crimson ground.   730

With joy, bold Zimri kenn'd the prince afar
And wing'd his javelin thro' the flashing air ;
Deep in his throat was lodg'd th' avenging steel ;
With groans, the monarch panting, struggling, fell :
The sword indignant gash'd his cleaving side,   735
Freed the pale ghost, and pour'd the vital tide.

With shouts of triumph swell'd th' etherial main,
And new convulsions shook the stormy plain.
The cars rush'd backward ; foaming coursers bound ;
The shrill swords clash, and hollow groans resound.   740
'Twixt the long banks remurmuring clamors roar,
And eyes unnumber'd wish the farthest shore.
As, swell'd with rains, th' autumnal stream ascends,
Foams o'er the rocks, and all the mountain rends,

Heav'd deep, with groans th' uprooted foreſt yields,　745
And huge, unwieldy oaks, plunge cumbrous to the fields ;
So furious Aſher, with reſiſtleſs ſway,
On Hebron burſting broke a dreadful way ;
Swift o'er the floods the warriors eager fly,
And ſteeds, and men, on earth immingled lie.　　750

　　On theſe dire ſcenes great Jabin caſt his view,
And ſaw his friends retire, his foes purſue,
Then, while the ſtorm of war brave Zedeck bore,
He whirl'd his chariot down the weſtern ſhore.
As, ſtain'd with blood, a meteor's midnight beam　755
Cleaves the dun clouds, and trails a length of flame ;
At once, with dreadful burſt, its terrors fly,
And a deep thunder rocks the ſhuddering ſky :
So, thron'd tremendous in his ſun-bright car,
Ruſh'd the impetuous Hero to the war ;　　760
Loud to their ears his voice terrific came,
And his fierce eyeballs flaſh'd a withering flame---
Rouſe, rouſe to fight, to triumph bend your way ;
Nor yield theſe ſlaves the wiſh'd immortal day.
Shall Hebron's ſons, that never knew to fly,　　765
Now turn inglorious, and like daſtards die ?
Let all your antient deeds each ſoul inſpire,
And each bold warrior emulate his ſire.
This hour propitious brings the glorious doom,
And ſweeps theſe wretches to the coward's tomb.　　770

　　He ſpoke, and furious, with reſiſtleſs force
Burſt on his foes and ſtopp'd their eager courſe :
All Hebron round him ſwift to conflict turn'd,
New life inform'd them, and new bravery burn'd ;
Squadrons on ſquadrons wedg'd their deep array,　775
And darker horrors gloom'd the dreadful day.

　　Him Hanniel ſaw ; for here in fierceſt fight
With joy he mingled, and diſdain'd baſe flight.
No griding anguiſh now his limb diſtreſs'd ;
No thought, but glory, triumph'd in his breaſt ;　　780

Chiefs to his arm had given the parting breath,
And vulgar warriors ftain'd his fword with death.
Alive, impetuous, burn'd the martial flame,
And every hope beat high for endlefs fame.

On Jabin's car th' undaunted warrior flew :   785
The car, like whirlwinds near him fwiftly drew.
This the blefs'd hour the hero deem'd to gain
The garland, wifh'd fo long, but wifh'd in vain.
The Chief of foes his raptur'd eye furvey'd,
The deftin'd victim of his conquering blade.   790
No fear difturb'd, left combat's fickle doom
Should change the lot, and ope another's tomb :
He fmil'd, from Joshua fure the palm to win,
And felt frefh honours round his temples twine.

At once, by Jabin's hand like lightening driven,   795
A fpear flew nimbly through the dufty heaven ;
Deep in his forehead funk th' unerring fteel ;
Without a groan the haughty warrior fell :
No foul more reftlefs e'er from earth retir'd,
Nor pride more boundlefs e'er in duft expir'd.   800

As, when bold youths, the mount's dim fummit gain'd,
Upheave the huge, hoar crag, with toilfome hand ;
From point to point th' unwieldy ruin tofs'd,
Smokes down the fteep, and grinds the cliffs to duft ;
High bounding, finking headlong, feeks the plain,   805
Cleaves the torne ground, and plows the foaming main ;
Far plunge the crafhing pines ; the wild rocks roar,
Hurl'd with tumultuous fury to the fhore ;
Wide-rolling duft the neighbouring concave fills,
And a long, fwelling roar runs murmuring round the hills.
So down the bank, tremendous Jabin's car   811
Urg'd the pale throng, and drove the founding war :
His foes plung'd headlong in the crimfon wave,
And chiefs, and warriors, found a liquid grave.

While thus in dreadful fight the hofts engag'd,   815
The tumults thicken'd, and the clamours rag'd ;

From Joshua's terrors Hazor's sons withdrew,
And diftant from the fhore their front renew.
With hideous ftrength, their ridgy lines afcend ;
Red flame the fhields ; fwords tremble ; fpears protend :
Pleas'd, the Chief views ; too generous not to know, 821
And own, with praife, the merit of a foe.

From a tall rock he caft his flafhing eyes,
And faw the varied fcenes of combat rife.
While every foe bold Gibeon fiercely drove ;   825
The tribes of Zimri backward flowly move :
Tow'rd the high walls afcending volumes roll,
And clouds on clouds fucceffive wrap the pole.
Greatly ferene, he view'd the threatening doom,
Nor veil'd his vifage with a tranfient gloom ;   830
But bade his chiefs, their bands for fight array'd,
Lead on the war, and Hazor's hoft invade.

Then, where the fields difplay'd an eafy courfe,
Along the fhore he wing'd his rapid force ;
Swift as a tempeft down the bank he flies,   835
Cuts the red ftream, and lifts tremendous cries---
Heavens ! what difhonour pains this bleeding eye ?
See, loft to fhame, my friends, my heroes fly !
Turn, turn to triumph ; fwift to glory turn ;
With generous fhame let every bofom burn !   840
Shall your brave fires, that never knew to flee,
With pangs your flight, and tarnifh'd honour, fee ;
And wifh high Heaven had lent a milder doom,
And fwept them childlefs to an earlier tomb ?
Shall Dan, fhall Afher, names of long renown,   845
Now lofe the fplendors of a deathlefs crown !
Forbid it Heaven ! now wipe the hateful ftain ;
One bold exertion wins th' immortal plain.

He fpoke : at once, unfurl'd in glorious pride,
The facred ftandard caft the view afide ;   850
There Dan's bright eagle, high in pomp difplay'd,
Stretch'd his long wings, and rear'd his golden head ;

Of gold his form in lucid triumph turn'd,
And streamy lightnings round him fiercely burn'd.
At once all Asher furious rush'd to fight,   855
Each ardent warrior spurn'd inglorious flight.
With wider ruin heave the trembling fields ;
Cars burst ; cries roar ; groans murmur ; sound the shields.
As in some forest two red flames aspire,
And whelm huge pines in floods of surging fire,   860
Then swift through falling groves together driven
Roll o'er the mountain tops, and kindle heaven :
So, fierce and dreadful, front to front oppos'd,
Mid clouds of dust, the thundering squadrons clos'd : 864
Earth shakes ; air rends ; the trembling skies resound,
And night, and sad dismay, invade th' embattled ground.

For war undaunted Hebron fiercely burn'd,
Nor even in Joshua's path to flight were turn'd.
Full on his sword they rush'd, and bravely fell ;
New bands with transport fac'd the slaughtering steel.
Incessant cries o'er all the combat rung ;   871
Incessant spears through darken'd ether sung ;
Swift flew the courser ; swift the raging car :
Hoarse rose the tumult of the maddening war :
Less loud through forests winds impetuous roll,   875
The huge pines sink, and tempest rends the pole :
Less loud 'gainst Zembla mountain billows roar,
When the storm thunders on the frozen shore.
For Hebron's thousands Jabin's voice inspir'd,
And Joshua's deeds the sons of Israel fir'd.   880

Now where the Chief terrific swept the field,
And, cloth'd in terror, ranks on ranks repell'd ;
Whilst a red deluge o'er his footsteps spread,
And countless torrents spouted from the dead ;
Swift to his path a chief of Asher ran,   885
Wild with dismay, and quivering thus began---
Wing, wing, thou best of men, thy friendly path---
Oh save the hero, or avenge his death !---

Now Zimri dies; from yon ascending ground,
I saw fierce Jabin point the fatal wound---   890
He spoke; at once, from all the Heathen train,
A voice of thunder heav'd th' affrighted plain:
Loud as hoarse whirlwinds torrent flames inspire,
When up the mountains rolls tempestuous fire;
Loud as th' Almighty's voice, through ether driven, 895
Pales the wide world, and shakes the walls of heaven;
Long shouts tremendous from the fields arise,
Burst o'er the hosts, and rend the clouded skies.
Through Israel's thousands thrills a dire alarm,
When thus great Joshua nerves each fainting arm--- 900
Urge, my brave warriors, urge the glorious strife;
Wheel your red swords, and save the leader's life---
Shall Zimri die, whilst each astonish'd stands,
Nor sees these falchions useless in our hands?
Alive the fainting hero meets my sight,   905
And yet maintains the solitary fight---
¹He spoke, and furious wheel'd his dreadful sword;
Back roll'd the heathens; streams of slaughter pour'd:
Behind him Asher's host in deep array
Throng'd darkening; clouds and death involv'd their way:
The bounding steeds bedew'd their hoofs in blood, 911
And chiefs and monarchs swell'd the purple flood.

Now, where bold Zimri brav'd the deathful ground,
O'erhung with foes, and pierc'd with many a wound,
Whilst labouring, panting, heav'd his frequent breath,
And o'er his helmet flash'd descending death;   916
Great Joshua, flaming, drove th' embattled train;
Their lances flew, their falchions rag'd in vain.
Dire as a peal of thunder sweeps the skies,
He rush'd, and Death sate frowning in his eyes: 920
For now brave Zimri scarce sustain'd the strife;
Sunk on one knee, and wish'd to sell his life.
Thro' the thick tumults of the broken war
Impetuous Jabin wing'd his rapid car;

With ruddy beams his lance uplifted fhone ;   925
His waving buckler mock'd the fanguine fun ;
'Twixt the bold chiefs, undaunted at the ftorm,
Sublime great Joshua rear'd his mighty form.
   Now front to front the frowning heroes ftood ;
Their eyes red flames ; their faces dropp'd with blood ; 930
Their fwords the lightning ; two broad moons, their fhields
Shot a fierce glory through the dreadful fields.
Then Jabin's heart, though form'd of ftubborn fteel,
Firft fhook with terror, and firft learn'd to feel.
But rous'd by keen difdain, and vengeful ire,   935
Quick from his eye-balls blaz'd infernal fire ;
To earth, impatient, from the car he fprang ;
His breaft beat high ; his rattling armour rang ;
To die refolv'd, but as a king to die,
Like fudden thunder rofe his burfting cry---   940
From this right hand receive, thou bafe-born flave,
A death too noble, but a daftard's grave ;
Torne by the dogs, thy carcafe here fhall lie,
Or glut the fowls, that fweep th' avenging fky.
The Chief difdain'd return. The Heathen's fteel   945
Full on his helm with rapid fury fell,
Glanc'd by his fword, it clave the bloody ground ;
Elfe had the Hero known no future wound.
Then with fwift wheel, through Jabin's yielding fide
Rufh'd his keen blade, and pour'd the fable tide ;   950
Aghaft, their monarch's fall his hoft beheld,
And fullen groans rung murmuring round the field.
   Like Heaven's dread thunder Joshua rais'd his voice ;
Hofts backward roll'd ; earth trembled at the noife---
On Gibeon's turrets ftand thou ftill, O Sun !   955
Look down, thou Moon, on dreary Ajalon !
Fix'd in high heaven the awful fplendors ftood,
And flam'd tremendous on the field of blood ;
From each dread orb enfanguin'd ftreams afpire,
The fkies all mantling in fierce-waving fire ;   960

Amaz'd, Canaan's realms the pomp defcried ;
The world grew pale ; the hearts of nations died :
The bounding Hero feiz'd the fhining car,
Snatch'd the long reins, and fhouted to the war :
Behind, fierce Afher fwift to vengeance flew ;   965
All dropp'd their fpears, and all their falchions drew ;
A fudden blaze gleam'd round the dufty gloom,
And plung'd ten thoufand warriors to the tomb.
For now, o'er all the fight, the heathens yield,
And Ifrael triumphs round the dreadful field.   970
High in the van, fublime great Jofhua rode,
Wing'd the dire flight, and fwell'd the tide of blood ;
Aghaft, they fee the lightning of his eyes,
And hear the thunders of his voice arife.
The plains are tumult all, convuls'd affright,   975
Fierce ruin, wild amaze, and raging flight ;
The Chariots ftream ; the fteeds all eager bound,
Stretch o'er the plains, and fweep the rifing ground ;
O'er rocks, o'er floods the thoufands headlong fly,
And fwords, and fpears, and fhields, behind them lie ;
No ftop, nor backward look, nor liftening ear,   981
From plains to forefts pants the full career ;
Behind, the Hero wings his rapid way,
And duft and darknefs fhroud the beams of day.
So, borne in clouds of fire, an Angel's form   985
On impious Sodom drove the dreadful ftorm.
From heaven, in dreadful pomp, the Vifion came ;
Far, far behind him, ftream'd the angry flame ;
The dark-red thunder, from his right hand hurl'd,
Upheav'd the fky, and fir'd the rocking world ;   990
High o'er the ftorm, on wings of light, he rode,
And fail'd, in lucid triumph, to th' approving God.
    Long rufh'd the victors o'er the fanguine field,
And fcarce were Gibeon's loftieft fpires beheld ;
When up the weft dark clouds began to rife,   995
Sail'd o'er the hills, and lengthen'd round the fkies.

A ridge of folding fire their summits shone ;
But fearful blackness all beneath was thrown.
Swift round the sun the spreading gloom was hurl'd,
And night, and solitude, amaz'd the world.   1000
    At once the voice of deep-resounding gales
Rung slow, and solemn, in the distant vales ;
Then through the groves, and o'er th' extended plain,
With stormy rage the rapid whirlwinds ran :
Red o'er the glimmering hills, with pomp divine,   1005
The lightning's flaming path began to shine ;
Far round th' immense unusual thunders driven,
Proclaim'd the onset of approaching Heaven ;
Astonish'd Nature own'd the strange alarm,
And the world trembled at th' impendent storm.   1010
O'er the dark fields aghast Canäan stream'd ;
Thick in their course the scatter'd bucklers gleam'd :
Behind them, Joshua urg'd the furious car,
And tenfold horrors hover'd round the war.
    But when the Chief the spreading storm survey'd,   1015
And trac'd almighty arms in heaven display'd ;
With piercing voice, he gave the great command---
Stand still, ye chosen sons, admiring stand !
Behold, what awful scenes in heaven arise !
Adore the power that brightens in the skies !   1020
Now God's tremendous arm asserts his laws ;
Now bids his thunder aid the righteous cause ;
Unfolds how Virtue saves her chosen bands,
And points the vengeance doom'd for guilty lands.   1024
Behold, what flames shoot forth ! what gloom ascends !
How nature trembles ! how the concave rends !
How the clouds darken ! see, in yonder sky,
Their opening skirts proclaim th' Almighty nigh !
    He spoke, and from the north a rushing sound   1029
Roll'd through the heavens, and shook th' embattled
At once a rapid path of dreadful flame   [ground :
Burst from the skies, and pour'd a sanguine stream :

Thron'd on a dark red cloud, an Angel's form
Sail'd awfully sublime, above the storm.
Half veil'd in mist, his countenance, like a sun,   1035
Inflam'd the clouds, and through all æther shone ;
Long robes of crimson light behind him flow'd ;
His wings were flames ; his looks were died in blood ;
Ten thousand fiery shapes were round him driven,
And all the dazzling pomp of opening heaven.   1040
   Now, save Canäan's cries, that feebly rung,
Round the dark plain a horrid silence hung.
Stretch'd in dire terror o'er her quivering band,
Th' etherial Vision wav'd his sun-bright hand ;
At once from opening skies red flames were hurl'd, 1045
And thunders, roll'd on thunders, rock'd the world,
In one broad deluge sunk th' avenging hail,
And, fill'd with tempest, roar'd the hoary vale ;
The headlong whirlwinds boundless nature blend ;
The streams rush backward ; tottering mountains bend ;
Down the tall steep their bursting summits roll,   1051
And cliffs on cliffs, hoarse-crashing, rend the pole :
Far round the earth a wild drear horror reigns ;
The high heavens heave, and sink the gloomy plains :
One sea of lightnings all the region fills :   1055
Long waves of fire ride surging o'er the hills ;
The nodding forests plunge in flame around,
And with huge caverns gapes the shuddering ground
Swifter than rapid winds Canäan driven,
Refuse the conflict of embattled Heaven.   1060
But the dire hail in vain the victims fly,
And death unbounded shook from all the sky ;
The thunder's dark career ; the Seraph's arm,
Fierce vengeance blazing down th' immense of storm.
From falling groves to burning plains they flew ; 1065
Hail roars around, and angry blasts pursue ;
From shaking heavens almighty arms are hurl'd,
And all the gloomy concave bursts upon the world.

No day like this the guilty earth had known ;
Not Egypt's storm with equal terror shone ;   1070
No day like this o'er eastern hills shall rife,
Till Gabriel's trump inrolls the sinking skies.
For Heaven's dread stores, reserv'd for death, and war,
Fierce hail, and lightning, fill'd the rending air.
In vain the host attempted still to fly ;   1075
They fell, they rose again ; but rose to die.
Mid thousand corfes, there, beneath his shield,
Stalk'd a lone trembler through the founding field :
Here, scatter'd wretches roam'd along the plain,
And sheltering bucklers hid their heads in vain.   1080
On every side resistless foes engag'd ;
The lightning's livid blast around them rag'd ;
While the shrill torrents of th' avenging hail
Rush'd on the pinions of the sweeping gale.
Rare, and more rare, were seen the sinking host,   1085
'Till, whelm'd beneath the deluge, all were lost.
   Thus, when black midnight's terrors earth deform,
From the tall Andes bursts a blazing storm ;
From steep to steep the ridgy flames aspire,
Bend o'er wide realms, and wrap the heavens in fire ; 1090
All nature trembles ; tottering mountains rend ;
Down the cliffs thunder ; showers of fire descend ;
Huge hills of ice, dissolv'd, and wastes of snow
Plunge in one deluge on the world below ;
O'er half Peru the floods tempestuous sweep,   1095
And rocks, and groves, and towns, roll mingled to the deep.
The form began to move ; the clouds gave way,
Their skirts all brightening with the crimson ray ;
Far south, on wings of fire, the Angel flew,
And his clear splendors lessening left the view,   1100
Down the broad regions of the mid-day skies,
Where glittering domes were seen, and scarcely seen to rise.
   Through the long day, Canäan's widows stood,
And look'd, all-anxious, toward the plain of blood ;

Look'd for the hoſt, with victory's garlands crown'd, 1105
Enrich'd with ſpoils, and with fair fame renown'd.
Their hands, to glad their friends with choice repaſt,
Cull'd every ſweet, and wines of daintieſt taſte ;
Oft as a duſty cloud the whirlwinds rear'd,
In diſtant fields they thought their lords appear'd ; 1110
Then, with new terrors, gaz'd, and gaz'd again,
'Till night, and ſorrow darken'd every plain.

The ſtorm retir'd ; the enſigns gave command,
And round their Leader throng'd the conquering band.
Here ſparkling eyes with joy and triumph burn'd ; 1115
Here pity ſilent from the ſlaughter turn'd ;
Here for fallen friends the tear was ſeen to flow,
And ſighs oft ſpoke unutterable woe :
While Joſhua's thoughts mount upward to the ſkies,
And fear, and wonder, in his boſom riſe.   1120
The ſtream, the walls they paſs'd ſerenely ſlow,
Climb'd the tall hills, and ſought the plain below ;
There crown'd with flowers, their wives and children came
And ſongs roſe grateful to th' Eternal Name---
Bleſs'd be the Power divine-- rejoic'd they ſung,--- 1125
The green vales echoed, and the foreſt rung---
Bleſs'd be the hand, that clave the conſcious ſea,
And, rob'd in thunder, ſwept our foes away !
Let endleſs bleſſings round our nation riſe,
Cheer all our lives, and waft us to the ſkies !   1130
Thus ſtrains of rapture charm'd the liſtening gales,
While the low ſun-beam glimmer'd on the vales :
To reſt the camp retir'd : ten-thouſand fires
Thro' the calm ſilence rais'd their bending ſpires :
The bright moon roſe ; winds cool'd the chearful even,
And wide magnificence enkindled heaven.   1136

T H E   E N D.